ISBN 978-1-330-28237-3
PIBN 10012405

1 MONTH OF
FREE
READING

at
www.ForgottenBooks.com

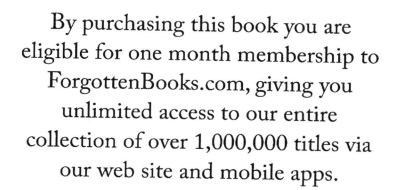

By purchasing this book you are eligible for one month membership to ForgottenBooks.com, giving you unlimited access to our entire collection of over 1,000,000 titles via our web site and mobile apps.

To claim your free month visit:
www.forgottenbooks.com/free12405

English
Français
Deutsche
Italiano
Español
Português

www.forgottenbooks.com

Mythology Photography **Fiction**
Fishing Christianity **Art** Cooking
Essays Buddhism Freemasonry
Medicine **Biology** Music **Ancient
Egypt** Evolution Carpentry Physics
Dance Geology **Mathematics** Fitness
Shakespeare **Folklore** Yoga Marketing
Confidence Immortality Biographies
Poetry **Psychology** Witchcraft
Electronics Chemistry History **Law**
Accounting **Philosophy** Anthropology
Alchemy Drama Quantum Mechanics
Atheism Sexual Health **Ancient History**
Entrepreneurship Languages Sport
Paleontology Needlework Islam
Metaphysics Investment Archaeology
Parenting Statistics Criminology
Motivational

Teutonic Mythology

The style here shown, as used for "Teutonic Mythology," is a hand-tooled copy of one made for Diane of Poictiers, Duchess de Valentinois, mistress of Henri II. Indeed, it is maintained that no less a personage than the beautiful Duchess herself, famous for her taste in bindings, actually made the design, into which she artistically worked the monogram D. H. C., which are the initials respectively of Henri, the King, Diane, his mistress, and Catherine de Medici, the Queen. The oval center encloses two quivers crossed by arrows, and on the sides are stringless bows. Surrounding the oval are beautiful examples of foliated arabesque lines, borrowed from Moorish patterns. The original was used on "Architecture," by Vitruvius, and is now in the Musée Louvre, Paris.

T. H. SMART
1905

Teutonic Mythology

Gods and Goddesses
of the Northland

IN

THREE VOLUMES

By VIKTOR RYDBERG, Ph.D.,

MEMBER OF THE SWEDISH ACADEMY; AUTHOR OF "THE LAST ATHENIAN"
AND OTHER WORKS.

AUTHORISED TRANSLATION FROM THE SWEDISH

BY

RASMUS B. ANDERSON, LL.D.,

EX-UNITED STATES MINISTER TO DENMARK; AUTHOR OF "NORSE
MYTHOLOGY," "VIKING TALES," ETC.

HON. RASMUS B. ANDERSON, LL.D., Ph.D.,
EDITOR IN CHIEF.

J. W. BUEL, Ph.D.
MANAGING EDITOR.

VOL. II.

PUBLISHED BY THE
NORRŒNA SOCIETY,
LONDON COPENHAGEN STOCKHOLM BERLIN NEW YORK
1907

TEUTONIC MYTHOLOGY.

TABLE OF CONTENTS.

VOLUME TWO

	Page
Myth in Regard to the Lower World	353
Myth Concerning Mimer's Grove	379
Mimer's Grove and Regeneration of the World	389
Gylfaginning's Cosmography	395
The Word Hel in Linguistic Usage	406
Border Mountain Between Hel and Nifelhel	414
Description of Nifelhel	426
Who the Inhabitants of Hel are	440
The Classes of Beings in Hel	445
The Kingdom of Death	447
Valkyries, Psycho-messengers of Diseases	457
The Way of Those who Fall by the Sword	462
Risting with the Spear-point	472
Loke's Daughter, Hel	476
Way to Hades Common to the Dead	482
The Doom of the Dead	485
The Looks of the Thingstead	505
The Hades Drink	514
The Hades Horn Embellished with Serpents	521

	Page
The Lot of the Blessed	528
Arrival at the Na-gates	531
The Places of Punishment	534
The Hall in Nastrands	540
Loke's Cave of Punishment	552
The Great World-Mill	565
The World-Mill makes the Constellations Revolve	579
Origin of the Sacred Fire	586
Mundilfore's Identity with Lodur	601
Nat, Mother of the Gods	608
Narfi, Nat's Father	611
Giant Clans Descended from Ymer	624
Identity of Mimer and Nidhad	630
Review of Mimer's Names and Epithets	641
The Mead Myth	644
The Moon and the Mead	669
Myths of the Moon-God	680

Frontisp

Wa:

The Pun:

Gefion an.

Page
......528
......531
......534
......540

......565
......579
......586
......601
......608
......611
......624
......630
......641
......644
......669
......680

LIST OF PHOTOGRAVURES.

VOL. II.

Frontispiece—Valkyries Bringing the Body of a Slain
  Warrior to Valhalla.

Page

Thor Destroys the Giant Thrym.....................456
The Punishment of Loke 552
Gefion and King Gylphi 616

THE MYTH IN REGARD TO THE LOWER WORLD.

(*Part IV. Continued from Volume I.*)

53.

AT WHAT TIME DID LIF AND LEIFTHRASER GET THEIR
PLACE OF REFUGE IN MIMER'S GROVE? THE ASMEGIR.
MIMER'S POSITION IN MYTHOLOGY. THE NUMINA OF
THE LOWER WORLD.

It is necessary to begin this investigation by pointing
out the fact that there are two versions of the last line of
strophe 45 in Vafthrudnersmal. The version of this line
quoted above was—*enn thadan af aldir alaz*: "Thence
(from Lif and Leifthraser in Mimer's grove) races are
born." Codex Upsalensis has instead—*ok thar um alldr
alaz*: "And they (Lif and Leifthraser) have there (in
Mimer's grove) their abiding place *through ages.*" Of
course only the one of these versions can, from a text-
historical standpoint, be the original one. But this does
not hinder both from being equally legitimate from a
mythological standpoint, providing both date from a time
when the main features of the myth about Lif and Leifthraser were still remembered. Examples of versions
equally justifiable from a mythological standpoint can be
cited from other literatures than the Norse. If we in
the choice between the two versions pay regard only to

353

the **age** of the manuscripts, then the one in Codéx Up-salensis, which is copied about the year 1300,* has the preference. It would, however, hardly be prudent to put the chief emphasis on this fact. Without drawing any conclusions, I simply point out the fact that the oldest version we possess of the passage says that Lif and Leif-thraser live through ages in Mimer's grove. Nor is the other version much younger, so far as the manuscript in which it is found is concerned, and from a mythological standpoint that, too, is beyond doubt correct.

In two places in the poetic Edda (Vegtamskv., 7, and Fjolsvinnsm., 33) occurs the word *ásmegir*. Both times it is used in such a manner that we perceive that it is a mythological *terminus technicus* having a definite, limited application. What this application was is not known. It is necessary to make a most thorough analysis of the passages in order to find the signification of this word again, since it is of importance to the subject which we are discussing. I shall begin with the passage in Fjols-vinnsmal.

The young Svipdag, the hero in Grogalder and in Fjolsvinnsmal, is in the latter poem represented as stand-ing before the gate of a citadel which he never saw be-fore, but within the walls of which the maid whom fate has destined to be his wife resides. Outside of the gate is a person who is or pretends to be the gate-keeper, and calls himself Fjolsvinn. He and Svipdag enter into con-versation. The conversation turns chiefly upon the re-markable objects which Svipdag has before his eyes.

---

*8· Bugge, Sæmund. Edda, xxvi. Thorl. Jónsson's Edda, Snorra St., viii.

Svipdag asks questions about them, and Fjolsvinn gives him information. But before Svipdag came to the castle, within which his chosen one awaits him, he has made a remarkable journey (alluded to in Grogalder), and he has seen strange things (thus in str. 9, 11, 33) which he compares with those which he now sees, and in regard to which he also desires information from Fjolsvinn. When the questions concern objects which are before him at the time of speaking, he employs, as the logic of language requires, the present tense of the verb (as in strophe 35— *segdu mèr hvat that bjarg heitir, er ek sè brudi á*). When he speaks of what he has seen before and elsewhere, he employs the past tense of the verb. In strophe 33 he says:

> Segdu mér that, Fjölsvidr,
> er ek thik fregna mun
> ok ek vilja vita;
> hverr that gördi,
> er ek fyr gard sák
> innan ásmaga?

"Tell me that which I ask you, and which I wish to know, Fjolsvinn: Who made that which I saw within the castle wall of the *ásmegir?*"*

---

*Looking simply at the form, the strophe may also be translated in the following manner: "Tell me, Fjolsvinn, what I ask of you, and what I wish to know. Who of the *ásmegir* made what I saw within the castle wall?" Against this formal possibility there are, however, several objections of facts. Svipdag would then be asking Fjolsvinn who had made that which he once in the past had seen within a castle wall without informing Fjolsvinn in regard to which particular castle wall he has reference. It also presupposes that Svipdag knew that the *ásmegir* had made the things in question which were within the castle wall, and that he only wished to complete his knowledge by finding out which one or ones of the *ásmegir* it was that had made them. And finally, it would follow from Fjolsvinn's answer that the dwarfs he enumerates are sons of Asas. The formal possibility pointed out has also a formal probability against it. The gen. pl. *ásmaga* has as its nearest neighbour *gard*, not *hverr*, and should therefore be referred to *gard*, not to *hverr*, even though both the translations gave an equally satisfactory meaning so far as the facts related are concerned; but that is not the case.

Fjolsvinn answers (str. 34) :

> Uni ok Iri,
> Bari ok Ori,
> Varr ok Vegdrasil,
> Dori ok Uri;
> Dellingr ok vardar
> lithsci alfr, loki.

"Une and Ire, Bare and Ore, Var and Vegdrasil, Dore and Ure, Delling, the cunning elf, is watchman at the gate."*

Thus Svipdag has seen a place where beings called *ásmegir dwell*. It is well enclosed and guarded by the elf Delling. The myth must have laid great stress on the fact that the citadel was well guarded, since Delling, whose cunning is especially emphasised, has been entrusted with this task. The citadel must also have been distinguised for its magnificence and for other qualities, since what Svipdag has seen within its gates has awakened his astonishment and admiration, and caused him to ask Fjolsvinn about the name of its builder. Fjolsvinn enumerates not less than eight architects. At least three of these are known by name in other sources—namely, the "dwarfs" Var (Sn. Edda, ii. 470, 553), Dore, and Ore. Both the last-named are also found in the list of dwarfs incorporated in Völuspa. Both are said to be dwarfs in Dvalin's group of attendants or servants (*i Dvalins lidi*—Völuspa, 14).

---

*I follow the text in most of the manuscripts, of which Bugge has given various versions. One manuscript has in the text, another in the margin, *Lidscialfr*, written in one word (instead of *lithsci alfr*). Of this Munch made *Lidskjalfr*. The dative loki from *lok*, a gate (cp. *luka loka*, to close, enclose) has been interpreted as Loki, and thus made the confusion complete.

The problem to the solution of which I am struggling on—namely, to find the explanation of what beings those are which are called *ásmegir*—demands first of all that we should find out where the myth located their dwelling seen by Svipdag, a fact which is of mythological importance in other respects. This result can be gained, providing Dvalin's and Delling's real home and the scene of their activity can be determined. This is particularly important in respect to Delling, since his office as gatekeeper at the castle of the *ásmegir* demands that he must have his home where his duties are required. To some extent this is also true of Dvalin, since the field of his operations cannot have been utterly foreign to the citadel on whose wonders his sub-artists laboured.

The author of the dwarf-list in Völuspa makes all holy powers assemble to consult as to who shall create "the dwarfs," the artist-clan of the mythology. The wording of strophe 10 indicates that on a being by name *Modsognir, Motsognir,* was bestowed the dignity of chief* of the proposed artist-clan, and that he, with the assistance of Durin (*Durinn*), carried out the resolution of the gods, and created dwarfs resembling men. The author of the dwarf list must have assumed—

That Modsogner was one of the older beings of the world, for the assembly of gods here in question took place in the morning of time before the creation was completed.

That Modsogner possessed a promethean power of creating.

---

*Thar (in the assembly of the gods) *var Modsognir mæstr um ordinn dverga allra.*

That he either belonged to the circle of holy powers himself, or stood in a close and friendly relation to them, since he carried out the resolve of the gods.

Accordingly, we should take Modsogner to be one of the more remarkable characters of the mythology. But either he is not mentioned anywhere else than in this place—we look in vain for the name Modsogner elsewhere—or this name is merely a skaldic epithet, which has taken the place of a more common name, and which by reference to a familiar *nota characteristica* indicates a mythic person well known and mentioned elsewhere. It cannot be disputed that the word looks like an epithet. Egilsson (Lex. Poet.) defines it as the *mead-drinker*. If the definition is correct, then the epithet were badly chosen if it did not refer to Mimer, who originally was the sole possessor of the mythic mead, and who daily drank of it (Völuspa, 29—*dreckr mióð Mimir morgin hverjan*). Still nothing can be built simply on the definition of a name, even if it is correct beyond a doubt. All the indices which are calculated to shed light on a question should be collected and examined. Only when they all point in the same direction, and give evidence in favour of one and the same solution of the problem, the latter can be regarded as settled.

Several of the "dwarfs" created by Modsogner are named in Völuspa, 11-13. Among them are Dvalin. In the opinion of the author of the list of dwarfs, Dvalin must have occupied a conspicuous place among the beings to whom he belongs, for he is the only one of them all who is mentioned as having a number of his own

kind as subjects (Völuspa, 14). The problem as to
whether Modsogner is identical with Mimer should
therefore be decided by the answers to the following
questions: Is that which is narrated about Modsogner
also narrated of Mimer? Do the statements which we
have about Dvalin show that he was particularly connected with Mimer and with the lower world, the realm
of Mimer?

Of Modsogner it is said (Völuspa, 12) that he was
mæstr ordinn dverga allra: he became the chief of all
dwarfs, or, in other words, the foremost among all artists. Have we any similar report of Mimer?

The German middle-age poem, "Biterolf," relates that
its hero possessed a sword, made by Mimer the Old,
Mime der alte, who was the most excellent smith in the
world. To be compared with him was not even Wieland (Volund, Wayland), still less anyone else, with
the one exception of Hertrich, who was Mimer's co-la-
bourer, and assisted him in making all the treasures he
produced:

> Zuo siner (Mimer's) meisterschefte
> ich nieman kan gelichen
> in allen fürsten richen
> an einen, den ich nenne,
> daz man in dar bi erkenne:
> Der war Hertrich genant.
>
> .   .   .   .
> Durch ir sinne craft
> so hæten sie geselleschaft
> an werke und an allen dingen. (Biterolf, 144.)

Vilkinasaga, which is based on both German and Norse

sources, states that Mimer was an artist, in whose work-shop the sons of princes and the most famous smiths learned the trade of the smith. Among his apprentices are mentioned Velint (Volund), Sigurd-Sven, and Ecki-hard.

These echoes reverberating far down in Christian times of the myth about Mimer, as chief of smiths, we also perceive in Saxo. It should be remembered what he relates about the incomparable treasures which are pre-served in Gudmund-Mimer's domain, among which in addition to those already named occur *arma humanorum corporum habitu grandiora* (i., p. 427), and about Mimin-gus, who possesses the sword of victory, and an arm-ring which produces wealth (i. 113, 114). If we consult the poetic Edda, we find Mimer mentioned as *Hodd-Mimer*, Treasure-Mimer (Vafthr. 45) ; as *naddgöfugr jotunn*, the giant celebrated for his weapons (Grogalder, 14) ; as *Hoddrofnir*, or *Hodd-dropnir*, the treasure-drop-ping one (Sigrdr., 13) ; as *Baugreginn*, the king of the gold-rings (Solarlj., 56). And as shall be shown here-after, the chief smiths are in the poetic Edda put in con-nection with Mimer as the one on whose fields they dwell, or in whose smithy they work.

In the mythology, artistic and creative powers are closely related to each other. The great smiths of the Rigveda hymns, the Ribhus, make horses for Indra, create a cow and her calf, make from a single goblet three equally good, diffuse vegetation over the fields, and make brooks flow in the valleys (Rigveda, iv. 34, 9; iv. 38, 8; i. 20, 6, 110, 3, and elsewhere). This they do although they are "mortals," who by their merits acquire immortality. In the Teutonic mythology Sindre and Brok forge from a pig-skin Frey's steed, which looks like a boar, and the sons of Ivalde forge from gold locks that grow like other hair. The ring *Draupnir,* which the "dwarfs" Sindre and Brok made, possesses itself creative power and produces every ninth night eight gold rings of equal weight with itself (Skaldsk., 37). The "mead-drinker" is the chief and master of all these artists. And on a closer examination it appears that Mimer's mead-well is the source of all these powers, which in the mythology are represented as creating, forming, and ordaining with wisdom.

In Havamál (138-141) Odin relates that there was a time when he had not yet acquired strength and wisdom. But by self-sacrifice he was able to prevail on the celebrated Bolthorn's son, who dwells in the deep and has charge of the mead-fountain there and of the mighty runes, to give him (Odin) a drink from the precious mead, drawn from *Odrærir*:

Tha nam ec frovaz	Then I began to bloom
oc frodr vera	and to be wise,
oc vaxa oc vel nafaz;	and to grow and thrive;
ord mer af ordi	word came to me
orz leitadi,	from word,
verc mer af verki	deed came to me
vercs leitadi.	from deed.

It is evident that Odin here means to say that the first drink which he received from Mimer's fountain was the turning-point in his life; that before that time he had not

blossomed, had made no progress in wisdom, had possessed no eloquence nor ability to do great deeds, but that
he acquired all this from the power of the mead. This
is precisely the same idea as we constantly meet with in
Rigveda, in regard to the soma-mead as the liquid from
which the gods got creative power, wisdom, and desire
to accomplish great deeds. Odin's greatest and most
celebrated achievement was that he, with his brothers,
created Midgard. Would it then be reasonable to suppose that he performed this greatest and wisest of his
works before he began to develop fruit, and before he got
wisdom and the power of activity? It must be evident
to everybody that this would be unreasonable. It is
equally manifest that among the works which he considered himself able to perform after the drink from Mimer's fountain had given him strength, we must place in
the front rank those for which he is most celebrated: the
slaying of the chaos-giant Ymer, the raising of the crust
of the earth, and the creation of Midgard. This could
not be said more clearly than it is stated in the above
strophe of Havamál, unless Odin should have specifically
mentioned the works he performed after receiving the
drink. From Mimer's fountain and from Mimer's hand
Odin has, therefore, received his creative power and his
wisdom. We are thus able to understand why Odin regarded this first drink from Odrœrer so immensely important that he could resolve to subject himself to the
sufferings which are mentioned in strophes 138 and 139.
But when Odin by a single drink from Mimer's fountain is endowed with creative power and wisdom, how

can the conclusion be evaded, that the myth regarded Mimer as endowed with Promethean power, since it makes him the possessor of the precious fountain, makes him drink therefrom every day, and places him nearer to the deepest source and oldest activity of these forces in the universe tian Odin himself? The given and more instantaneous power, thanks to which Odin was made able to form tie upper world, came from the lower world and from Mimer. The world-tree has also grown out of the lower world and is Mimer's tree, and receives from his hands its value. Thus the creative power with which the dwarf-list in Völuspa endowed the "mead-drinker" is rediscovered in Mimer. It is, therefore, perfectly logical when the mythology makes him its first smith and chief artist, and keeper of treasures and the ruler of a group of dwarfs, underground artists, for originally these were and remained creative forces personified, just as Rigveda's Rubhus, who smithied flowers and grass, and animals, and opened the veins of tie earth for fertilising streams, while they at the same time made implements and weapons.

That Mimer was the profound counsellor and faithful friend of the Asas has already been shown. Thus we discover in Mimer Modsogner's governing position among the artists, his creative activity, and his friendly relation to the gods.

Dvalin, created by Modsogner, is in the Norse sagas of the middle ages remembered as an extraordinary artist. He is there said to have assisted in the fashioning of the sword Tyrfing (Fornald. Saga, i. 436), of Freyja's splendid ornament Brisingamen, celebrated also in Anglo-Saxon poetry (Fornald. Saga, i. 391). In the Snofrid song, which is attributed to Harald Fairhair, the drapa is likened unto a work of art, which rings forth from beneath the fingers of Dvalin (*hrynr fram ur Dvalin's greip*—Fornm. Saga, x. 208; Flat., i. 582). This beautiful poetical figure is all the more appropriately applied, since Dvalin was not only the producer of the beautiful works of the smith, but also sage and skald. He was one of the few chosen ones who in time's morning were permitted to taste of Mimer's mead, which therefore is called his drink (*Dvalin's drykkr*—Younger Edda, i. 246).

But in the earliest antiquity no one partook of this drink who did not get it from Mimer himself.

Dvalin is one of the most ancient rune-masters, one of those who brought the knowledge of runes to those beings of creation who were endowed with reason (Havamál, 143). But all knowledge of runes came originally from Mimer. As skald and runic scholar, Dvalin, therefore, stood in the relation of disciple under the ruler of the lower world.

The myth in regard to the runes (cp. No. 26) mentioned three apprentices, who afterwards spread the knowledge of runes each among his own class of beings. Odin, who in the beginning was ignorant of the mighty and beneficent rune-songs (Havamál, 138-143), was by birth Mimer's chief disciple, and taught the knowledge of runes among his kinsmen, the Asas (Havamál, 143), and among men, his protégés (Sigdrifm.,

18). The other disciples were Dain (*Dáinn*) and Dvalin (*Dvalinn*). Dain, like Dvalin, is an artist created by Modsogner (Völuspa, 11, Hauks Codex). He is mentioned side by side with Dvalin, and like him he has tasted the mead of poesy (*munnvigg Dáins*—Fornm. Saga, v. 209). Dain and Dvalin taught the runes to their clans, that is, to elves and dwarfs (Havamál, 143). Nor were the giants neglected. They learned the runes from *Ásvidr*. Since the other teachers of runes belong to the clans, to which they teach the knowledge of runes —"Odin among Asas, Dain among elves, Dvalin among dwarfs"—there can be no danger of making a mistake, if we assume that *Ásvidr* was a giant. And as Mimer himself is a giant, and as the name *Ásvidr* (=*Ásvinr*) means Asa-friend, and as no one—particularly no one among the giants—has so much right as Mimer to this epithet, which has its counterpart in Odin's epithet, *Mims vinr* (Mimer's friend), then caution dictates that we keep open the highly probable possibility that Mimer himself is meant by *Ásvidr*.

All that has here been stated about **Dvalin** shows that the mythology has referred him to a place within the domain of Mimer's activity. We have still to point out two statements in regard to him. Sol is said to have been his *leika* (Fornald., i. 475; Allvism, 17; Younger Edda, i. 472, 593). *Leika,* as a feminine word and referring to a personal object, means a young girl, a maiden, whom one keeps at his side, and in whose amusement one takes part at least as a spectator. The examples which we have of the use of the word indicate that the *leika* herself, and the person whose *leika* she is, are presupposed to have the same home. Sisters are called *lefkur,* since they live together. Parents can call a foster-daughter their *leika.* In the neuter gender *leika* means a plaything, a doll or toy, and even in this sense it can rhetorically be applied to a person.

In the same manner as Sol is called Dvalin's *leika,* so the son of Nat and Delling, Dag, is called *leikr Dvalins,* the lad or youth with whom Dvalin amused himself (Fornspjal., 24).

We have here found two points of contact between the mythic characters Dvalin and Delling. Dag, who is Dvalin's *leikr,* is Delling's son. Delling is the watchman of the castle of the *ásmegir,* which Dvalin's artists decorated.

Thus the whole group of persons among whom Dvalin is placed—Mimer, who is his teacher; Sol, who is his *leika;* Dag, who is his *leikr;* Nat, who is the mother of his *leikr;* Delling, who is the father of his *leikr*—have their dwellings in Mimer's domain, and belong to the subterranean class of the *numina* of Teutonic mythology.

From regions situated below Midgard's horizon, Nat, Sol, and Dag draw their chariots upon the heavens. On the eastern border of the lower world is the point of departure for their regular journeys over the heavens of the upper world ("the upper heavens," *upphiminn*—Völuspa, 3; Vafthr., 20, and elsewhere; *uppheimr*—Alvm., 13). Nat has her home and, as shall be shown hereafter, her birthplace in dales beneath the ash Ygdrasil. There she takes her rest after the circuit of ıer journey has been completed. In the lower world Sol and Nat's son, Dag, also ıave their halls where tıey take their rest. But where Delling's wife and son ıave their dwellings there we should also look for Delling's own abode. As the husband of Nat and the father of Dag, Delling occupies the same place among the divinities of nature as the dawn and tıe glow of sunrise among the phenomena of nature. And outside the doors of Delling, the king of dawn, mythology has also located the dwarf *thjódreyrir* ("he who moves the people"), who sings songs of awakening and blessing upon tıe world: "power to the Asas, success to the elves, wisdom to Hroptatyr" (*afl asom, enn alfum frania, hyggio Hroptaty*—Havam., 160).

Unlike ıis kinsmen, Nat, Dag, and Sol, Delling ıas no duty which requires him to be absent from home a part of the day. The dawn is merely a reflection of Midgard's eastern horizon from Delling's subterranean dwelling. It can be seen only when Nat leaves the upper heaven and before Dag and Sol have come forward, and it makes no journey around the world. From a mythological standpoint it would therefore be possible to entrust the keeping of the castle of the *ásmegir* to the elf of dawn. The sunset-glow has another genius, Billing, and he, too, is a creation of Modsogner, if the dwarf-list is correct (Völuspa, 12). Sol, who on her way is pursued by two giant monsters in wolf-guise, is secure when she comes to her forest of the Varns behind the western horizon (*til varna vidar*—Grimn., 30). There in western halls (Vegtamskv., 11) dwells Billing, the chief of the Varns (*Billing veold Ver-num*—Cod. Exon., 320). There rests his daughter Rind bright as the sun on her bed, and his body-guard keeps watch with kindled lights and burning torches (Havam., 100). Thus Billing is the watchman of the western boundary of Mimer's domain, Delling of the eastern.

From this it follows:

That the citadel of the *ásmegir* is situated in Mimer's lower world, and there in the regions of the elf of dawn.

That Svipdag, who has seen the citadel of the *ásmegir,* has made a journey in the lower world before he found Menglad and secured her as his wife.

The conclusion to which we have arrived in regard to the subterranean situation of the citadel is entirely confirmed by the other passage in the poetic Edda, where the *ásmegir* are mentioned by this name. Here we have an opportunity of taking a look within their castle, and of seeing the hall decorated with lavish splendour for the reception of an expected guest.

Vegtamskvida tells us that Odin, being alarmed in regard to the fate of his son Balder, made a journey to the lower world for the purpose of learning from a vala what foreboded his favourite son. When Odin had rode through Nifelhel and come to green pastures (*foldvegr*), he found there below a hall decorated for festivity, and he asks the prophetess:

> hvæim eru bekkir
> baugum sánir,
> flæt fagrlig
> floti gulli?

"For whom are the benches strewn with rings and the gold beautifully scattered through the rooms?"

And the vala answers:

> Her stændr Balldri
> of' bruggin miodr,
> skirar væigar,
> liggr skiolldr yfir
> æn ásmegir
> i ofvæni.

"Here stands for Balder mead prepared, pure drink; shields are overspread, and the *ásmegir* are waiting impatiently."

Thus there stands in the lower world a hall splendidly decorated awaiting Balder's arrival. As at other great feasts, the benches are strewn (cp. *breida bekki, strá bekki, bua bekki*) with costly things, and the pure wonderful mead of the lower world is already served as an offering to the god. Only the shields which cover the mead-vessel need to be lifted off and all is ready for the feast. Who or what persons have, in so good season, made these preparations? The vala explains when she mentions the *ásmegir* and speaks of their longing for Balder. It is this longing which has found utterance in the preparations already completed for his reception. Thus, when Balder gets to the lower world, he is to enter the citadel of the *ásmegir* and there be welcomed by a sacrifice, consisting of the noblest liquid of creation, tie strength-giving *soma-madhu* of Teutonic mythology. In the old Norse heathen literature there is only one more place where we find the word *ásmegir*, and that is in Olaf

Trygveson's saga, c1. 16 (Heimskringla). For the sake of completeness this passage should also be considered, and when analysed it, too, sheds much and important light on the subject.

We read in this saga that Jarl Hakon proclaimed throughout his kingdom that the inhabitants should look after their temples and sacrifices, and so was done. Jarl Hakon's hird-skald, named Einar Skalaglam, who in the poem "Vellekla" celebrated 1is deeds and exploits, mentions his interest in the heathen worship, and the good results this was supposed to have produced for the jarl himself and for the welfare of his land. Einar says:

> Ok hertharfir hverfa
> hlakkar móts til blóta,
> raudbrikar fremst rækir
> rikr, ásmegir, sliku.
> Nu grær jörd sem adan, &c.

Put in prose: *Ok hertharfir ásmegir hverfa til blóta; hlakkar móts raudbrikar rikr rækir fremst sliku. Nu grær jörd sem ádan.*

Translation: "And the *ásmegir* required in war, turn themselves to the sacrificial feasts. Tie mighty promoter of the meeting of the red target of the goddess of war has honour and advantage thereof. Now grows the earth green as heretofore."

There can be no doubt that "the *ásmegir* required in war" refer to the men in the territory ruled by Hakon, and that "the mighty promoter of the meeting of tie red target of the goddess of war" refers to the warlike Hakon himself, and hence the meaning of the passage in its plain prose form is simply this: "Hakon's men again devote themselves to the divine sacrifices. This is both an honour and an advantage to Hakon, and the earth again yields bountiful harvests."

To these thoughts the skald has given a garb common in poetry of art, by adapting them to a mythological background. The persons in this background are the *ásmegir* and a mythical being called "the promoter of the red target," *raudbríkar rœkir*. The persons in the foreground are the men in Hakon's realm and Hakon himself. The persons in the foreground are permitted to borrow the names of the corresponding persons in the background, but on the condition that the borrowed names are furnished with adjectives which emphasise the specific difference between the original mythic lenders and the real borrowers. Thus Hakon's subjects are allowed to borrow the appellation *ásmegir,* but this is then furnished with the adjective *hertharfir* (required in war), whereby they are specifically distinguished from the *ásmegir* of the mythical background, and Hakon on his part is allowed to borrow the appellation *raudbríkar rœkir* (the promoter of the red target), but this appellation is then furnished with the adjective phrase *hlakkar móts* (of the meeting of the goddess of war), whereby Hakon is specifically distinguished from the *raudbríkar rœkir* of the mythical background.

The rule also requires that, at least on that point of which the skald happens to be treating, the persons in the mythological background should hold a relation to each other which resembles, and can be compared with, the relation between the persons in the foreground. Hakon's men stand in a subordinate relation to Hakon himself; and so must the *ásmegir* stand in a subordinate relation to that being which is called *raudbríkar rækir,* providing the skald in this strophe as in the others has produced a tenable parallel. Hakon is, for his subjects, one who exhorts them to piety and fear of the gods. *Raudbríkar rækir,* his counterpart in the mythological background, must have been the same for his *ásmegir.* Hakon's subjects offer sacrifices, and this is an advantage and an honour to Hakon, and the earth grows green again. In the mythology the *ásmegir* must have held some sacrificial feast, and *raudbríkar rækir* must have had advantage and honour, and the earth must have regained its fertility. Only on these conditions is the figure of comparison to the point, and of such a character that it could be presented unchallenged to heathen ears familiar with the myths. It should be added that Einar's greatness as a skald is not least shown by his ability to carry out logically such figures of comparison. We shall later on give other examples of this.

Who is, then, this *raudbríkar rækir,* "the promoter of the red target?"

In the mythological language *raudbrik* (red target) can mean no other object than the sun. Compare *rödull,* which is frequently used to designate the sun. If this needed confirmation, then we have it immediately at hand in the manner in which the word is applied in the continuation of the paraphrase adapted to Hakon. A common paraphrase for the shield is the sun with suitable adjectives, and thus *raudbrik* is applied here. The adjective phrase is here *hlakkar móts,* "of the meeting of the war-goddess" (that is, qualifying the red target), whereby the red target (= sun), which is an attribute of the mythic *rækir* of the background, is changed to a shield, which becomes an attribute of the historical *rækir* of the foreground, namely Hakon jarl, the mighty warrior. Accordingly, *raudbríkar rækir* of the mythology must be a masculine divinity standing in some relation to the sun.

This sun-god must also have been upon the whole a god of peace. Had he not been so, but like Hakon a war-loving shield-bearer, then the paraphrase *hlakkar móts raudbríkar rækir* would equally well designate him as Hakon, and thus it could not be used to designate Hakon alone, as it then would contain neither a *nota characteristica* for him nor a *differentia specifica* to distinguish him from the mythic person, whose epithet *raudbríkar rækir* he has been allowed to borrow.

This peaceful sun-god must have descended to the lower world and there stood in the most intimate relation with the *ásmegir* referred to the domain of Mimer, for he is here represented as their chief and leader in the path of piety and the fear of the gods. The myth must have mentioned a sacrificial feast or sacrificial feasts celebrated by the *ásmegir*. From this or these sacrificial feasts the peaceful sun-god must have derived advantage and honour, and thereupon the earth must have regained a fertility, which before that had been more or less denied it.

From all this it follows with certainty that *raudbríkar*

rækir of the mytiology is Balder. The fact suggested by the Vellekla strophe above analysed, namely, that Balder, physically interpreted, is a solar divinity, the mythological scholars are almost a unit in assuming to be the case on account of the general character of the Balder myth. Thougi Balder was celebrated for heroic deeds he is substantially a god of peace, and after his descent to tie lower world he is no longer connected with the feuds and dissensions of the upper world. We have already seen that he was received in the lower world with great pomp by the *ásmegir,* who impatiently awaited his arrival, and that tiey sacrifice to him that bright mead of the lower world, whose wonderfully beneficial and bracing influence shall be discussed below. Soon afterwards he is visited by Hermod. Already before Balder's funeral pyre, Hermod upon the fastest of all steeds hastened to find him in the lower world (Gylfag., 51, 52), and Hermod returns from him and Nanna with the ring *Draupnir* for Odin, and with a veil for the goddess of earth, Fjorgyn-Frigg. The ring from which other rings drop, and the veil which is to beautify the goddess of earth, are symbols of fertility. Balder, the sun-god, had for a long time before his death been languishing. Now in tie lower world he is strengthened with the bracing mead of Mimer's domain by the *ásmegir* who gladly give offerings, and the earth regains her green fields.

Hakon's men are designated in the strophe as *hertharfir ásmegir.* When they are permitted to borrow the name of the *ásmegir,* then the adjective *hertharfir,* if chosen with the proper care, is to contain a specific distinction between them and the mythological beings whose name they have borrowed. In other words, if the real *ásmegir* were of such a nature that they could be called *hertharfir*, then that adjective would not serve to distinguish Hakon's men from them. The word *hertharfir* means "those who are needed in war," "those who are to be used in war." Consequently, the *ásmegir* are beings who are *not* to be used in war, beings whose dwelling, environment, and purpose suggest a realm of peace, from which the use of weapons is banished.

Accordingly, the parallel presented in Einar's strophe, which we have now discussed, is as follows:

Mythology.	*History.*
Peaceful beings of the lower world (ásmegir).	Warlike inhabitants of the earth (hertharfir ásmegir).
at the instigation of their chief,	at the instigation of their chief,
the sun-god Balder (raudbríkar rækir).	the shield's Balder. Hakon (hlakkar móts raudbríkar rækir),
go to offer sacrifices.	go to offer sacrifices.
The peaceful Balder is thereby benefited.	The shield's Balder is thereby benefited.
The earth grows green again.	The earth grows green again.
ok ásmegir,	ok hertharfir ásmegir
hverfa til blóta;	hverfa til blóta
raudbrikar rikr rækir	hlakkar móts raudbríkar rikr rækir
fremst sliku.	fremst sliku.
Nú grær jörd sem ádan.	Nu grær jörd sem ádan.

In the background which Einar has given to his poetical paraphrase, we thus have the myth telling how the sun-god Balder, on his descent to the lower world, was strengtiened by tie soma-sacrifice brought iim by tie *ásmcgir*, and how he sent back wit1 Hermod t1e treasures of fertility w1ic1 had gone with him and Nanna to the lower world, and which restored the fertility of the earth.

To what category of beings do the *ásmcgir* then belong? We have seen the word applied as a technical term in a restricted sense. The possibilities of application whic1 the word with reference to its definition supplies are:

(1) The word may be used in the purely physical sense of Asa-sons, Asa-descendants. In this case the subterranean *ásmegir* would be by t1eir very descent members of that god-clan that resides in Asgard, and whose father and clan-patriarc1 is Odin.

(2) T1e word can be applied to men. They are the children of t1e Asa-father in a double sense: the first human pair was created by Odin and his brothers (Völusp., 16, 17; Gylfag., 9), and their offspring are also in a moral sense Odin's children, as they are subject to his guidance and care. He is Alfather, and the father of the succeeding generations (*allfadir, aldafadir*). A word resembling *ásmegir* in character is *ásasynir*, and this is used in Allvismal, 16, in a manner which shows t1at it does not refer to any of those categories of beings that are called gods (see further, No. 62)* The concep-

---

*Sol heitir med monnom,
enn sunna med godum,
kalla dvergar Dvalin's leika
eyglo iotnar,
alfar fagra hvel
alscir asa synir.

376

tion of men as sons of the gods is also implied in the all mankind embracing phrase, *megir Heimdallar* (Völusp., 1), with which the account of Rig-Heimdal's journey on the earth and visit to the patriarchs of the various classes is connected.*

The true meaning of the word in this case is determined by the fact that the *ásmegir* belong to the dwellers in the lower world already before the death of Balder, and that Balder is the first one of the Asas and sons of Odin who becomes a dweller in the lower world. To this must be added, that if *ásmegir* meant Asas, Einar would never have called the inhabitants of Norway, the subjects of jarl Hakon, *hertharfir ásmegir*, for *hertharfir* the Asas are themselves, and that in the highest degree. They constitute a body of more or less warlike persons, who all have been "needed in conflict" in the wars around Asgard and Midgard, and they all, Balder included, are gods of war and victory. It would also have been *malapropos* to compare men with Asas on an occasion when the former were represented as bringing sacrifices to the gods; that is, as persons subordinate to them and in need of their assistance.

The *ásmegir* are, therefore, human beings excluded from the surface of the earth, from the mankind which dwell in Midgard, and are inhabitants of the lower world, where they reside in a splendid castle kept by the elf of dawn, Delling, and enjoy the society of Balder, who descended to Hades. To subterranean human beings re-

---

*Cp. also Gylfag. 9, in regard to Odin: *Ok fyrir thvi má hann heita Allfodr, at hann er fadir alra godanna ok manna ok alls thess, er af honom ok hans krapti var fullgjort.*

fers also Grimnismal, 21, which says that men (*mennzkir
menn*) dwell under tie roots of Ygdrasil; and Allvismal,
16 (to be compared wit1 18, 20, and ot1er passages),
and Skirnersmal, 34, w1ich calls t1em *áslithar,* a word
which Gudbrand Vigfusson has rig1tly assumed to be
identical with *ásmegir.*

Thus it is also demonstrated that the *ásmegir* are identical with t1e subterranean 1uman persons Lif and Leifthraser and their descendants in Mimer's grove. The
care wit1 which t1e mythology represents the citadel of
the *ásmegir* kept, shown by t1e fact t1at t1e elf Delling,
the counterpart of Heimdal in the lower world, has been
entrusted with its keeping, is intelligible and proper when
we know t1at it is of the greatest importance to shield
Lif and Leifthraser's dwelling from all ills, sickness, age,
and moral evil (see above). It is also a beautiful poetic
thought that it is t1e elf of t1e morning dawn—he outside of whose door t1e song of awakening and bliss is
sung to the world—who has been appointed to watch
those who in the dawn of a new world s1all people the
earth with virtuous and happy races. That the *ásmegir*
in the lower world are permitted to enjoy the society of
Balder is explained by t1e fact that Lif and Leifthraser
and their offspring are after Ragnarok to accompany Balder to dwell under his sceptre, and live a blameless life
corresponding to his wishes. They are to be his disciples, knowing their master's commandments and having
them written in their hearts.

We have now seen that the *ásmegir* already before
Balder's death dwell in Mimer's grove. We 1ave also

seen that Svipdag on his journey in the lower world had observed a castle, which he knew belonged to the *ásmegir*. The mythology knows two fimbul-winters: the former raged in time's morning, the other is to precede Ragnarok. The former occurred when Freyja, the goddess of fertility, was treacherously delivered into the power of the frost-giants and all the air was blended with corruption (Völusp., 26); when there came from the Elivogs stinging, ice-cold arrows of frost, which put men to death and destroyed the greenness of the earth (Fornspjallsljod); when King Snow ruled, and there came in the northern lands a famine which compelled the people to emigrate to the South (Saxo, i. 415). Svipdag made his journey in the lower world during the time preceding the first fimbul-winter. This follows from the fact that it was he who liberated Freyja, the sister of the god of the harvests, from the power of the frost-giants (see Nos. 96-102). Lif and Leifthraser were accordingly already at that time transferred to Mimer's grove. This ought to have occurred before the earth and her inhabitants were afflicted by physical and moral evil, while there still could be found undefiled men to be saved for the world to come; and we here find that the mythology, so far as the records make it possible for us to investigate the matter, has logically met this claim of poetic justice.

54.

THE IRANIAN MYTH CONCERNING MIMER'S GROVE.

In connection with the efforts to determine the age of the Teutonic myths, and their kinship with the other

Aryan (Indo-European) mythologies, the fact deserves attention that the myth in regard to a subterranean grove and the human beings there preserved for a future regenerated world is also found among the Iranians, an Asiatic race akin to the Teutons. The similarity between the Teutonic and Iranian traditions is so conspicuous that the question is irresistible—Whether it is not originally, from the standpoint of historical descent, one and the same myth, which, but little affected by time, has been preserved by the Teutonic Aryans around the Baltic, and by the Iranian Aryans in Baktria and Persia? But the answer to the question requires the greatest caution. The psychological similarity of races may, on account of the limitations of the human fancy, and in the midst of similar conditions and environments, create myths which resemble each other, although they were produced spontaneously by different races in different parts of the earth. This may happen in the same manner as primitive implements, tools, and dwellings which resemble each other may have been invented and used by races far separated from each other, not by the one learning from the other how these things were to be made, nor on account of a common descent in antiquity. The similarity is the result of similar circumstances. It was the same want which was to be satisfied; the same human logic found the manner of satisfying the want; the same materials offered themselves for the accomplishment of the end, and the same universal conceptions of form were active in the development of the problems. Comparative mythology will never become a science in the strict sense of this word before it ceases to build hypotheses on a solitary similarity, or even on several or many resemblances between mythological systems geographically separated, unless these resemblances unite themselves and form a whole, a mythical unity, and unless it appears that this mythical unity in turn enters as an element into a greater complexity, which is similar in fundamental structure and similar in its characteristic details. Especially should this rule be strictly observed when we compare the myths of peoples who neither by race nor language can be traced back to a prehistoric unity. But it is best not to relax the severity of the rules even when we compare the myths of peoples who, like the Teutons, the Iranians, and the Rigveda-Aryans, have the same origin and same language; who through centuries, and even long after their separation, have handed down from generation to generation similar mythological conceptions and mythical traditions. I trust that, as this work of mine gradually progresses, a sufficient material of evidence for the solution of the above problem will be placed in the hands of my readers. I now make a beginning of this by presenting the Iranian myth concerning Jima's grove and the subterranean human beings transferred to it.

In the ancient Iranian religious documents Jima is a holy and mighty ancient being, who, however, does not belong to the number of celestial divinities which surround the highest god, Ahuramazda, but must be counted among "the mortals," to the oldest seers and prophets of antiquity. A hymn of sacrifice, dedicated to the sacred mead, the liquid of inspiration (*homa*, the *soma* and *soma-madhu* of the Rigveda-Aryans, the last word being the same as our word *mead*), relates that Jima and his father were the first to prepare the mead of inspiration for the material world; that he, Jima, was the richest in honour of all who had been born, and that he of all mortals most resembled the sun.   In his kingdom there was neither cold nor heat, neither frost nor drought, neither aging nor death.   A father by the side of his son resembled, like the son, a youth of fifteen years.   The evil created by the demons did not cross the boundaries of Jima's world (The Younger *Jasna,* ch. 9).

Jima was the favourite of Ahuramazda, the highest god.   Still he had a will of his own.   The first mortal with whom Ahuramazda talked was Jima, and he taught him the true faith, and desired that Jima should spread it among the mortals.   But Jima answered: "I am not suited to be the bearer and apostle of the faith, nor am I believed to be so" (*Vendidad*).   [In this manner it is explained why the true doctrine did not become known among men before the reformer Zarathustra came, and why Jima the possessor of the mead of inspiration, nevertheless, was in possession of the true wisdom.]

It is mentioned (in *Gosh Jasht* and *Râm Jasht*) that Jima held two beings in honour, which did not belong to Ahuramazda's celestial circle, but were regarded as worthy of worship.   These two were:

1.   The cow (*Gosh*), that lived in the beginning of time, and whose blood, when she was slain, fertilised the earth with the seed of life.

2.   *Vajush,* the heavenly breeze.   He is identical with

the ruler of the air and wind in Rigveda, the mighty god *Vâyu-Vâta.*

In regard to the origin and purpose of the kingdom ruled by Jima, in which neither frost nor drought, nor aging nor death, nor moral evil, can enter *Vendidad* relates the following:*

Avesta.	*Zend.*
21. A meeting was held with the holy angels of Ahuramazda, the creator. To this meeting came, with the best men, Jima, the king rich in flocks.	A meeting was held with the best men of Jima, the king, the one rich in flocks. To this meeting came, with the holy angels, Ahuramazda, the creator.
22. Then said Ahuramazda to Jima: "Happy Jima Vivanghana! In the material world there shall come an evil winter, and consequently a hard, killing frost."	In the material world there shall come an evil winter, consequently much snow shall fall on the highest mountains, on the tops of the rocks.
23. From three places, O Jima, the cows should be driven to well-enclosed shelters; whether they are in the wildernesses, or in the heights of the mountains, or in the depths of the valleys.	From three places, O Jima, the cows should be driven to well-enclosed shelters; whether they are in the wilderness, or on the heights of the mountains, or in the depths of the valleys.
24. Before the winter this land had meadows. Before that time the water (the rain) was wont to flow over it, and the snow to melt; and there was found, O Jima, in the	

*The outlines of the contents are given here from the interpretation found in Haug-West's *Essays on the Sacred Language of the Parsis* (London, 1878).

material world, water-soaked places, in which were visible the footprints of the cattle and their offspring.

25. Now give this enclosure (above, "the well-enclosed shelters") on each of its four sides the length of one . . . and bring thither the seed of your cattle, of oxen, of men, of dogs, and of birds, and red blazing fires.

26. Gather water there in a canal, the length of one hâtira. Place the landmarks there on a gold-coloured spot, furnished with imperishable nourishment. Put up a house there of mats and poles, with roof and walls.

Now give the enclosure the length of one . . . on each of its four sides as a dwelling for men, and give the same length to each of the four sides as a field for the cows.

27. Bring thither seed of all men and women, who are the largest, best, and most fair on this earth. Bring thither seed of all domestic animals that are the largest, best, and fairest on this earth.

28. Bring thither seed of all plants which are the highest and most fragrant on this earth. Bring thither seed of all articles of food which are the best tasting and most fragrant on this earth. And make pairs of them unceasingly, in order that these beings may have their existence in the enclosures.

29. There shall be no pride,
no despondency, no sluggish-
ness, no poverty, no deceit,
no dwarf-growths, no blem-
ish ... nor aught else of those
signs which are Angrô-main-
yush's curses put on men.

30. Make, in the uppermost
part of that territory, nine
bridges; in the middle, six; in
the lowest part, three. To the
bridges of the upper part you
must bring seed of a thousand
men and women, to those of
the middle the seed of six
hundred, to those of the
lower, of three hundred. . . .
And make a door in the enclosure, and a self-luminous
window on the inside.

33. Then Jima made the
enclosure.

39. Which are th
thou just Ahurama
give light in the
made by Jima?

40. Ahuramazda
Once (a year) the
moon and the sun
seen to rise and se

41. And they (
within Jima's
think that one year
Every fortieth yea
sons are born by
sons. These pers
the greatest bliss
closures made by J

42. Just creator! Who preached the pure faith in the enclosures which Jima made? Ahuramazda answered: The bird Karshipta.

Jima's garden has accordingly been formed in connection with a terrible winter, which, in the first period of time, visited the earth, and it was planned to preserve that which is noblest and fairest and most useful within the kingdoms of organic beings. That the garden is situated in the lower world is not expressly stated in the above-quoted passages from Vendidad; though this seems to be presupposed by what is stated; for the stars, sun, and moon do not show themselves in Jima's garden excepting after long, defined intervals—*at their rising and setting;* and as the surface of the earth is devastated by the unparalleled frost, and as the valleys are no more protected therefrom than the mountains, we cannot without grave doubts conceive the garden as situated in the upper world. That it is subterranean is, however, expressly stated in *Bundehesh,* ch. 30, 10, where it is located under the mountain Damkan; and that it, in the oldest period of the myth, was looked upon as subterranean follows from the fact that the Jima of the ancient Iranian records is identical with Rigveda's Jama, whose domain and the scene of whose activities is the lower world, the kingdom of death.

As Jima's enclosed garden was established on account of the fimbul-winter, which occurred in time's morning, it continues to exist after the close of the winter, and preserves through all the historical ages those treasures of uncorrupted men, animals, and plants which in the beginning of time were collected there. The purpose of this is mentioned in Minokhird, a sort of catechism of the legends and morals of the Avesta religion. There it is said that after the conflagration of the world, and in the beginning of the regeneration, the garden which Jima made shall open its gate, and thence men, animals and plants shall once more fill the devastated earth.

The lower world, where Jima, according to the ancient Iranian records, founded this remarkable citadel, is, according to Rigveda, Jama's kingdom, and also the kingdom of death, of which Jama is king (Rigv., x. 16, 9 ; cp. i. 35, 6, and other passages). It is a glorious country, with inexhaustible fountains, and there is the home of the imperishable light (Rigv., ix. 7, 8,; ix. 113, 8). Jama dwells under a tree "with broad leaves." There he gathers around the goblet of mead the fathers of antiquity, and there he drinks with the gods (Rigv., x. 135, 1).

Roth, and after him Abel Bergaigne (Religion Ved., i. 88 ff.), regard Jama and Manu, mentioned in Rigveda, as identical. There are strong reasons for the assumption, so far as certain passages of Rigveda are concerned; while other passages, particularly those which mention Manu by the side of Bhriga, refer to an ancient patriarch of human descent. If the derivation of the word *Mimer, Mimi,* pointed out by several linguists, last by Müllenhoff (*Deutsche Alt.,* vol. v. 105, 106), is correct, then it is originally the same name as *Manu,* and like it is to be referred to the idea of thinking, remembering.

What the Aryan-Asiatic myth here given has in common with the Teutonic one concerning the subterranean persons in Mimer's grove can be summarised in the following words:

The lower world has a ruler, who does not belong to the group of immortal celestial beings, but enjoys the most friendly relations with the godhead, and is the possessor of great wisdom. In his kingdom flow inexhaustible fountains, and a tree grown out of its soil spreads its foliage over his dwelling, where he serves the mead of inspiration, which the gods are fond of and wiich he was the first to prepare. A terrible winter threatened to destroy everything on the surface of the earth. Then the ruler of the lower world built on his domain a well-fortified citadel, within which neither destructive storms, nor physical ills, nor moral evil, nor sickness, nor aging, nor death can come. Thither he transferred the best and fairest human beings to be found on earth, and decorated the enclosed garden with the most beautiful and useful trees and plants. The purpose of this garden is not simply to protect the beings collected there during the great winter; they are to remain there through all historical ages. When these come to an end, there comes a great conflagration and then a regeneration of the world. The renewed earth is to be filled with the beings who have been protected by the subterranean citadel. The people who live there have an instructor in the pure worship of the gods and in the precepts of morality, and in accordance with these precepts they are to live for ever a just and happy life.

It should be added that the two beings whom the Iranian ruler of the lower world is said to have honoured are found or have equivalents in the Teutonic mythlogy. Both are there put in theogonic connection with Mimer. The one is the celestial lord of the wind, Vayush, Rigveda's Vâyu-Vâta. Vâta is thought to be the same name as Wodan, Odinn (Zimmer, Haupt's Zeitschr., 1875; cp. Mannhardt and Kaegi). At all events, Vâta's tasks are the same as Odin's. The other is the primeval cow, whose Norse name or epithet, *Audhumla* is preserved in Gylfag., 6. Andhunla liberates from the frost-stones in Chaos Bure, the progenitor of the Asa race, and his son Bor is married to Mimer's sister Bestla, and with her becomes the father of Odin (Havam., 140; Gylfag., 6).

55.

THE PURPOSE OF MIMER'S GROVE IN THE REGENERATION OF THE WORLD.

We now know the purpose of *Odainsakr*, Mimer's land and Mimer's grove in the world-plan of our mythology. We know who the inhabitants of the grove are, and why they, though dwellers in the lower world, must be *living persons*, who did not come there through the *gate of death*. They must be living persons of flesh and blood, since the human race of the regenerated earth must be the same.

Still the purpose of Mimer's land is not limited to being, through this epoch of the world, a protection for the fathers of the future world against moral and physical corruption, and a seminary where Balder educates them in virtue and piety. The grove protects, as we have seen, the *ásmegir* during Ragnarok, whose flames do not penetrate thither. Thus the grove, and the land in which it is situated, exist after the flames of Ragnarok are extinguished. Was it thought that the grove after the regencration was to continue in the lower world and there stand uninhabited, abandoned, desolate, and without a purpose in the future existence of gods, men and things?

The last moments of the existence of the crust of the old earth are described as a chaotic condition in which all elements are confused with each other. The sea rises, overflows the earth sinking beneath its billows, and the crests of its waves aspire to heaven itself (cp. Völusp., 54, 2—*Sigr fold i mar,* with Hyndlulj., 42, 1-3—*Haf gengr hridum vid himinn sialfann, lidr lond yfir*). The atmosphere, usurped by the sea, disappears, as it were (*loft bilar*—Hyndlulj., 42, 4). Its snow and winds (Hyndlulj., 42, 5-6) are blended with water and fire, and form with them heated vapours, which "play" against the vault of heaven (Völusp., 54, 7-8). One of the reasons why the fancy has made all the forces and elements of nature thus contend and blend was doubtless to furnish a sufficiently good cause for the dissolution and disappearance of the burnt crust of the earth. At all events, the earth is gone when the rage of the elements is subdued, and thus it is no impediment to the act of regeneration which takes its beginning beneath the waves.

This act of regeneration consists in the rising from the depths of the sea ˙ a new earth, which on its very rising possesses living beings and is clothed in green. The fact that it, while yet below the sea, could be a home for beings which need air in order to breathe and exist, is not necessarily to be regarded as a miracle in mythology. Our ancestors only needed to have seen an air-bubble rise to the surface of the water in order to draw the conclusion that air can be found under the water without mixing with it, but with the power of pushing water away while it rises to the surface. The earth rising from the sea has, like the old earth, the necessary atmosphere around it. Under all circumstances, the seeress in Völuspa sees after Ragnarok—

upp koma
audro sinni
iord or ægi
ithia græna (str. 56).

The earth risen from the deep has mountains and cascades, which, from their fountains in the fells, hasten to the sea. The waterfalls contain fishes, and above them soars the eagle seeking its prey (Völusp., 56, 5-8). The eagle cannot be a survivor of the beings of the old earth. It cannot have endured in an atmosphere full of fire and steam, nor is there any reason why the mythology should spare the eagle among all the creatures of the old earth. It is, therefore, of the same origin as the mountains, the cascades, and the imperishable vegetation which suddenly came to the surface.

The earth risen from the sea also contains human beings, namely, Lif and Leifthraser, and their offspring. Mythology did not need to have recourse to any hocus-pocus to get them there. The earth risen from the sea

1ad been t1e lower world before it came out of the deep, and a paradise-region in the lower world had for centuries been the abode of Lif and Leifthraser. It is more than unnecessary to imagine t1at the lower world with this Paradise was duplicated by anot1er with a similar Paradise, and that the living creatures on the former were by some magic manipulation transferred to the latter. Mythology has its miracles, but it also has its logic. As its object is to be trusted, it tries to be as probable and consistent with its premises as possible. It resorts to miracles and magic only when it is necessary, not otherwise.

Among the mountains which rise on the new earth are found those whic1 are called *Nida fjöll* (Völusp., 62), Nide's mountains. The very name Nide suggests the lower world. It means the "lower one." Among t1e abodes of Hades, mentioned in Völuspa, there is also a hall of gold on Nide's plains (*a Nitha vollum*—str. 36), and from *Solarljod* (str. 56) we learn—a statement confirmed by much older records—t1at Nide is identical with Mimer (see No. 87). Thus, Nide's mountains are situated on Mimer's fields. Völuspa's seeress discovers on the rejuvenated earth Nidhog, the corpse-eating demon of the lower world, flying, with dead bodies under his wings, away from the rocks, where he from time immemorial had had his abode, and from which he carried his prey to Nastrands (Völusp., 39). There are no more dead bodies to be had for him, and his task is done. Whether the last line of Völuspa has reference to Nidhog or not, when it speaks of some one "who must sink," can-

not be determined. Müllenhoff (*Deutsche Alt.*) assumes
this to be the case, and he is probably right; but as the text
has *hon* (she) not *han* (he) [*un man hon scyquas*], and
as I, in this work, do not base anything even on the most
probable text emendation, this question is set aside, and
the more so, since Völuspa's description of the regenerated
earth under all circumstances shows that Nidhog has
naught there to do but to fly thence and disappear. The
existence of Nide's mountains on the new earth confirms
the fact that it is identical with Mimer's former lower
world, and that Lif and Leifthraser did not need to move
from one world to another in order to get to the daylight
of their final destination.

Völuspa gives one more proof of this.

In their youth, free from care, the Asas played with
strange tablets. But they had the tablets only *i arla-
daga,* in the earliest time (Völusp., 8, 58). Afterwards,
they must in some way or other have lost them. The
Icelandic sagas of the middle ages have remembered this
game of tablets, and there we learn, partly that its strange
character consisted in the fact that it could itself take
part in the game and move the pieces, and partly that it
was preserved in the lower world, and that Gudmund-
Mimer was in the habit of playing with tablets (Fornalder
Sagas, i. 443; iii. 391-392; iii. 626, &c. In the last passages the game is mentioned in connection with the other
subterranean treasure, the horn.) If, now, the mythology
had no special reason for bringing the tablets from the
lower world before Ragnarok, then they naturally should
be found on the risen earth if the latter was Mimer's

domain before. Völuspa (str. 58) also relates that they were found in its grass:

> Tıar muno eptir
> undrsamligar
> gullnar tavlor
> i grasi finaz.

"There were the wonderful tablets found left in the grass (*finaz eptir*)."

Tıus, the tablet-game was refound in the grass, in the meadows of the renewed earth, having from the earliest time been preserved in Mimer's realm. Lif and Leifthraser are found after Ragnarok on the earth of the regenerated world, having had their abode there for a long time in Mimer's domain. Nide's mountains, and Nidhog with them, have been raised out of the sea, together with the rejuvenated earth, since these mountains are located in Mimer's realm. The earth of the new era —the era of virtue and bliss—have, though concealed, existed through thousands of years below the sin-stained earth, as the kernel within the shell.

Remark—Völuspa (str. 56) calls the earth rising from the sea *idjagræna*:

> Ser hon upp koma
> audro sinni
> iord or ægi
> ithia græna.

The common interpretation is *ithia græna,* "the ever green" or "very green," and this harmonises well with the idea preserved in the sagas mentioned above, where it was stated that the winter was not able to devastate Gudmund-Mimer's domain. Thus the idea contained in the expression *Haddingjalands oskurna ax* (see Nos. 72, 73) recurs in Völuspa's statement that the fields unsown yield harvests in the new earth. Meanwhile the composition *idja-grœna* has a perfectly abnormal appearance, and awakens suspicion. Müllenhoff (*Deutsche Alt.*) reads *idja, grœna,* and translates "the fresh, the green." As a conjecture, and without basing anything on the assumption; I may be permitted to present the possibility that *idja* is an old genitive plural of *ida,* an eddying body of water. *Ida* has originally had a *j* in the stem (it is related to *id* and *idi*), and this *j* must also have been heard in the inflections. From various metaphors in the old skalds we learn that they conceived the fountains of the lower world as roaring and in commotion (*e.g., Odreris alda thytr* in Einar Skalaglam and *Bodnar bára ter vaxa* in the same skald). If the conjecture is as correct as it seems probable, then the new earth is characterised as "the green earth of the eddying fountains," and the fountains are those famous three which water the roots of the world-tree.

56.

THE COSMOGRAPHY. CRITICISM ON GYLFAGINNING'S COSMOGRAPHY.

In regard to the position of Ygdrasil and its roots in the universe, there are statements both in Gylfaginning and in the ancient heathen records. To get a clear idea, freed from conjectures and based in all respects on evidence, of how the mythology conceived the world-tree and its roots, is of interest not only in regard to the cosmograpiy of the mythology, to which Ygdrasil supplies the trunk and the main outlines, but especially in regard to the mythic conception of the lower world and tie whole eschatology; for it appears that each one of the Ygdrasil roots stands not alone above its particular fountain in tie lower world but also over its peculiar lower-world domain, which again has its peculiar cosmological character and its peculiar eschatological end.

Tie first condition, however, for a fruitful investigation is that we consider the heathen or heathen-appearing records by themselves without mixing tieir statements with those of Gylfaginning. We must bear in mind that the autior of Gylfaginning lived and wrote in the 13th century, more than 200 years after the introduction of Christianity in Iceland, and that his statements accordingly are to be made a link in that chain of documents which exist for the scholar, who tries to follow the fate of the myths during a Christian period and to study their gradual corruption and confusion.

This caution is the more important for the reason that an examination of Gylfaginning very soon siows that the whole cosmographical and eschatological structure which it has built out of fragmentary mythic traditions is based on a conception wholly foreign to Teutonic mythology, that is, on the conception framed by the scholars in Frankish cloisters, and then handed down from chronicle to chronicle, that the Teutons were descended from the Trojans, and that their gods were originally Trojan chiefs and magicians. This "learned" conception found its way to the North and finally developed its most luxurious and abundant blossoms in the Younger Edda preface and in certain other parts of that work.

Permit me to present in brief a sketch of how the cosmography and eschatology of Gylfaginning developed themselves out of this assumption:—The Asas were originally men, and dwelt in the Troy which was situated on the centre of the earth, and which was identical with Asgard (*thar næst gerdu their ser borg i midjum heimi, er kallat er Asgardr; that köllum ver Trója; thar bygdu gudin ok ættir theirra ok gjördust thadan af mörg tidindi ok greinir bædi á jord ok á lopti*—ch. 9).

The first mythic tradition which supplies material for the structure which Gylfaginning builds on this foundation is the bridge Bifrost. The myth had said that this bridge united the celestial abodes with a part of the universe situated somewhere below. Gylfaginning, which makes the Asas dwell in Troy, therefore makes the gods undertake an enterprise of the greatest boldness, that of building a bridge from Troy to the heavens. But they are extraordinary architects and succeed (*Gudin gjördu brú til himins af jördu*—ch. 13).

The second mythic tradition employed is Urd's fountain. The myth had stated that the gods daily rode from their celestial abodes on the bridge Bifrost to Urd's (subterranean) fountain. Thence Gylfaginning draws the correct conclusion that Asgard was supposed to be situated at one end of the bridge and Urd's fountain near the other. But from Gylfaginning's premises it follows that

397

if Asgard-Troy is situated on the surface of the earth Urd's fountain must be situated in the heavens, and that the Asas accordingly when they ride to Urd's fountain must ride *upward*, not downward. The conclusion is drawn with absolute consistency (*"Hvern dag rida æsir thangat upp um Bifröst"*—ch. 15).

The third mythic tradition used as material is the world-tree, which went (down in the lower world) to Urd's fountain. According to Völuspa (19), this fountain is situated beneath the ash Ygdrasil. The conclusion drawn by Gylfaginning by the aid of its Trojan premises is that since Urd's fountain is situated in the heavens, and still under one of Ygdrasil's roots, this root must be located still further up in the heavens. The placing of the root is also done with consistency, so that we get the following series of wrong localisations:—Down on the earth, Asgard-Troy; thence up to the heavens the bridge Bifrost; above Bifrost, Urd's fountain; high above Urd's fountain, one of Ygdrasil's three roots (which in the mythology are all in the lower world).

Since one of Ygdrasil's roots thus had received its place far up in the heavens, it became necessary to place a second root on a level with the earth, and the third one was allowed to retain its position in the lower world. Thus was produced a just distribution of the roots among the three regions which in the conception of the middle ages constituted the universe, namely, the heavens, the earth, and hell.

In this manner two myths were made to do service in regard to one of the remaining Ygdrasil roots. The one myth was taken from Völuspa, where it was learned that Mimer's fountain is situated below the sacred world-tree; the other was Grimnismal (31), where we are told that frost-giants dwell under one of the three roots. At the time when Gylfaginning was written, and still later, popular traditions told that Gudmund-Mimer was of giant descent (see the middle-age sagas narrated above). From this Gylfaginning draws the conclusion that Mimer was a frost-giant, and it identifies the root which extends to the frost-giants with the root that extends to Mimer's fountain. Thus this fountain of creative power, of world-preservation, of wisdom, and of poetry receives from Gylfaginning its place in the abode of the powers of frost, hostile to gods and to men, in the land of the frost-giants, which Gylfaginning regards as being Jotunheim, bordering on the earth.

In this way Gylfaginning, with the Trojan hypothesis as its starting-point, has gotten so far that it has separated from the lower world with its three realms and three fountains Urd's realm and fountain, they being transferred to the heavens, and Mimer's realm and fountain, they being transferred to Jotunheim. In the mythology these two realms were the subterranean regions of bliss, and the third, Nifelhel, with the regions subject to it, was the abode of the damned. After these separations were made, Gylfaginning, to be logical, had to assume that the lower world of the heathens was exclusively a realm of misery and torture, a sort of counterpart of the hell of the Church. This conclusion is also drawn with due consistency, and Ygdrasil's third root, which in the mythology descended to the well Hvergelmer and to the lower world of the frost-giants, Nifelhel, Nifelheim, extends over the whole lower world, the latter being regarded as identical with Nifelheim and the places of punishment therewith connected.

This result carries with it another. The goddess of the lower world, and particularly of its domain of bliss, was in the mythology, as shall be shown below, the goddess of fate and death, Urd. also called Hel, when named after the country over which she ruled. In a local sense, the name Hel could be applied partly to the whole lower world, which rarely happened, partly to Urd's and Mimer's realms of bliss, which was more common, and Hel was then the opposite of Nifelhel, which was solely the home of misery and torture. Proofs of this shall be given below. But when the lower world had been changed to a sort of hell, the name Hel, both in its local and in its personal sense, must undergo a similar change, and since Urd (the real Hel) was transferred to the heavens, there was nothing to hinder Gylfaginning from substituting for the queen of the lower world Loke's daughter cast down into Nifelhel and giving her the name Hel and the sceptre over the whole lower world.

This method is also pursued by Gylfaginning's author without hesitation, although he had the best of reasons for suspecting its correctness. A certain hesitancy might here have been in order. According to the mythology, the pure and pious Asa-god Balder comes to Hel, that is to say, to the lower world, and to one of its realms of bliss. But after the transformation to which the lower world had been subjected in Gylfaginning's system, the descent of Balder to Hel must have meant a descent to and a remaining in the world of misery and torture, and a relation of subject to the daughter of Loke. This should have awakened doubts in the mind of the author of Gylfaginning. But even here he had the courage to be true to his premises, and without even thinking of the absurdity in which he involves himself, he goes on and endows the sister of the Midgard-serpent and of the Fenris-wolf with that perfect power which before belonged to Destiny personified, so that the same gods who before had cast the horrible child Loke down into the ninth region of Nifelhel are now compelled to send a minister-plenipotentiary to her majesty to treat with her and pray for Balder's liberation.

But finally, there comes a point where the courage of consistency fails Gylfaginning. The manner in which it has placed the roots of the world-tree makes us first of all conceive Ygdrasil as lying horizontal in space. An attempt to make this matter intelligible can produce no other picture of Ygdrasil, in accord with the statements of Gylfaginning, than the following:

The root over heaven and over Urd's fountain.	
The root over Jotunheim and over Mimer's well.	
The root over the lower world and over Hvergelmer's fountain.	Ygdrasil's trunk.

But Gylfaginning is not disposed to draw this conclusion. On the contrary, it insists that Ygdrasil stands erect on its three roots. How we, then, are to conceive its roots as united one with the other and with the trunk of this it very prudently leaves us in ignorance, for this is beyond the range of human imagination.

The contrast between the mythological doctrine in regard to the three Ygdrasil roots, and Gylfaginning's view of the subject may easily be demonstrated by the following parallels:

The Mythology.

1. Ygdrasil has three roots.
2. All three roots are subterranean.

Gylfaginning.

1. Ygdrasil has three roots.
2. One is in the lower world; a second stands over Jotunheim on a level with the earth; a third stands over the heavens.

3. To each root corresponds a fountain and a realm in the lower world. The lower world consists of three realms, each with its fountain and each with its root.

4. Under one of the subterranean roots dwells the goddess of death and fate, Urd, who is also called Hel, and in her realm is Urd's fountain.

5. Under the other (subterranean) root dwells Mimer. In his realm is Mimer's fountain and Mimer's grove, where a subterranean race of men are preserved for the future world. This root may, therefore, be said to stand over mennskir menn (Grimnersmal).

3. To each root corresponds a fountain and a realm; the realms are the heavens, Jotunheim, and the lower world, which are located each under its root.

4. Under one of the roots, that is the one which stands over heaven, dwells Urd the goddess of fate, and there is Urd's fountain.

It is said that one of the roots stands over mennskir menn (Grimnersmal). By this is meant, according to Gylfaginning, not the root over Mimer's well, but the root over Urd's fountain, near which the Asas hold their assemblies, for the Asas are in reality men who dwelt on earth in the city of Troy.

6. Under the third (subterranean) root dwell frost-giants. Under this root is the well Hvergelmer, and the realm of the frost-giants is

6. Under the third (and only subterranean) root dwell the souls of sinners and those who have died from sickness and age. Under this root is

Nifelhel (Nifelheim). Under Nifelhel are nine regions of torture.

the well Hvergelmer and the whole lower world. The lower world is called Nifelhel or Nifelheim, and contains nine places of torture.

7. The sister of the Midgard-serpent and of the Fenris-wolf was cast by the gods into the regions of torture under Nifelhel, and received the rule over the places where the damned are punished.

7. The sister of the Midgard-serpent and of the Fenris-wolf was cast by the gods into the regions of torture under Nifelhel, and received the rule over the whole lower world, which consists of Nifelhel with the nine regions of torture.

8. The name Hel can be applied to the whole lower world, but means particularly that region of bliss where Urd's fountain is situated, for Urd is the personal Hel. The Loke-daughter in Nifelhel is her slave and must obey her commands.

8. As Hel means the lower world, and as the sister of the Midgard-serpent governs the whole lower world, she is meant by the personal Hel.

Gylfaginning does not stop with the above results. It continues the chain of its conclusions. After Hvergelmer has been selected by Gylfaginning as the only fountain in the lower world, it should, since the lower world has been made into a sort of hell, be a fountain of hell, and in this respect easily recognised by the Christian conception of the middle ages. In this new character Hvergelmer becomes the centre and the worst place in Gylfaginning's description of the heathen Gehenna. No doubt because the old dragon, which is hurled down into the abyss (Revelation, chap. 20), is to be found in the hell-fountain of the middle ages, Gylfaginning throws Nidhog down into Hvergelmer, which it also fills with serpents and dead bodies found in Grimnismal (Str. 34, 35), where they have no connection with Hvergelmer. According to Völuspa it is in Nastrands that Nidhog sucks and the wolf tears the dead bodies (*náir*). Gylfaginning follows Völuspa in speaking of the other terrors in Nastrands, but rejects Völuspa's statements about Nidhog and the wolf, and casts both these beasts down into the Hvergelmer fountain. As shall be shown below, the Hvergelmer of the mythology is the mother-fountain of all waters, and is situated on a high plain in the lower world. Thence its waters flow partly northward to Nifelheim, partly south to the elysian fields of heathendom, and the waves sent in the latter direction are shining, clear, and holy.

It was an old custom, at least in Iceland, that booths for the accommodation of the visitors were built around a remote thing-stead, or place for holding the parliament. Gylfaginning makes its Trojan Asas follow the example of the Icelanders, and put up houses around the thing-stead, which they selected near Urd's fountain, after they had succeeded in securing by Bifrost a connection between Troy and heaven. This done, Gylfaginning distributes as best it can the divine halls and abodes of bliss mentioned in the mythology between Troy on the earth and the thing-stead in heaven.

This may be sufficient to show that Gylfaginning's pretended account of the old mythological cosmography is, on account of its making Troy the starting-point, and doubtless also to some extent as a result of the Christian

methods of thought, with which the author interpreted
the heathen myths accessible to him, is simply a monstrous caricature of the mythology, a caricature which is
continued, not with complacency and assurance, but in
a confused and contradictory manner. in the eschatology
of Gylfaginning.

My chief task will now be to review and examine all
the passages in the Elder Edda's mythological songs,
wherein the words Hel and Nifelhel occur, in order to
find out in this manner in which sense or senses these
words are there employed, and to note at the same time all
the passages which may come in my way and which are
of importance to the myth concerning the lower world.

57.

THE WORD HEL IN LINGUISTIC USAGE.

The Norse Hel is the same word as the Gothic *Halja,*
the Old High German *Hella,* the Anglo-Saxon *Hellia,*
and the English Hell. On account of its occurrence with
similar signification in different Teutonic tongues in their
oldest linguistic monuments, scholars have been able to
draw the conclusion that the word points to a primitive
Teutonic *Halja,* meaning lower world. lower world divinity. It is believed to be related to the Latin *oc-cul-crc,*
cel-are, clam, and to mean the one who "hides," "conceals," "preserves."   .

When the books of the New Testament were for the
first time translated into a Teutonic tongue, into a Gothic
dialect, the translator, Ulfilas, had to find some way of

distinguishing with suitable words between the two realms of the lower world mentioned in the New Testament, Hades and Gehenna (*geen a*).

Hades, the middle condition, and the locality corresponding to this condition, which contains both fields of bliss and regions of torture, he translated with Halja, doubtless because the signification of this word corresponded most faithfully with the meaning of the word Hades. For Gehenna, hell, he used the borrowed word *gaiainna*.

The Old High German translation also reproduces Hades with the word *Hella*. For Gehenna it uses two expressions compounded with Hella. One of these, Hellawisi, belongs to the form which afterwards predominated in Scandinavia. Both the compounds bear testimony that the place of punishment in the lower world could not be expressed with Hella, but it was necessary to add a word, which showed that a subterranean place *of punishment* was meant. The same word for Gehenna is found among the Christian Teutons in England, namely, Hellewite; that is to say, *the* Hellia, that part of the lower world where it is necessary to do penance (*vite*) for one's sins. From England the expression doubtless came to Scandinavia, where we find in the Icelandic *Helvíti,* in the Swedish *Hälvete,* and in the Danish *Helvede.* In the Icelandic literature it is found for the first time in Hallfred, the same skald who with great hesitation permitted himself to be persuaded by Olaf Trygveson to abandon the faith of his fathers.

Many centuries before Scandinavia was converted to

Christianity, the Roman Church had very nearly obliterated t1e boundary line between the subterranean Hades
and Gehenna of the New Testament. The lower world
had, as a whole, become a realm of torture, though with
various gradations. Regions of bliss were no longer to be
found there, and for Hel in the sense in which Ulfilas used
Halja, and the Old High German translation Hella, there
was no longer room in the Christian conception. In the
North, Hel was therefore permitted to remain a heathen
word, and to retain its heat1en signification as long as the
Christian generations were able or cared to preserve it.
It is natural that the memory of this signification should
gradually fade, and that the idea of the Christian hell
should gradually be transferred to the heathen *Hel*. This
change can be pretty accurately traced in the Old Norse
literature. It came slowly, for the doctrine in regard to
the lower world in the Teutonic religion addressed itself
powerfully to the imagination, and, as appears from a
careful examination, far from being indefinite in its outlines, it was, on the contrary, described with the clearest
lines and most vivid colours, even down to the minutest
details. Not until the thirteenth century could such a
description of the heathen Hel as Gylfaginning's be possible and find readers who would accept it. But not even
then were the memories (preserved in fragments from the
heathen days) in regard to the lower world doctrine so
confused, but that it was possible to present a far more
faithful (or rather not so utterly false) description thereof. Gylfaginning's representation of the heathen Hades
is based less on the then existing confusion of the tradi-

tions than on the conclusions drawn from the author's own false premises.

In determining the question, how far Hel among the heathen Scandinavians has had a meaning identical with or similar to that which Halja and Hella had among their Gothic and German kinsmen—that is to say, the signification of a death-kingdom of such a nature that it could not with linguistic propriety be used in translating Gehenna —we must first consult that which really is the oldest source, the usage of the spoken language in expressions where Hel is found. Such expressions show by the very presence of Hel that they have been handed down from heathendom, or have been formed in analogy with old heathen phrases. One of these modes of speech still exists: *i hjäl* (slå ihjäl, svälta ihjäl, frysa ihjäl, &c.), which is the Old Norse *i Hel.* We do not use this expression in the sense that a person killed by a weapon, famine, or frost is relegated to the abyss of torture. Still less could the heathens have used it in that sense. The phrase would never have been created if the word Hel had especially conveyed the notion of a place of punishment. Already in a very remote age *i Hel* had acquired the abstract meaning *to death,* but in such a manner that the phrase easily suggested the concrete idea—the realm of death (an example of this will be given below). What there is to be said about *i Hel* also applies to such phrases as *bida Heljar,* to await Hel (*death*); *buask til Heljar,* to become equipped for the journey to Hel (to be shrouded); *liggja milli heims ok Heljar,* to lie between this world and Hel (between life and death); *liggja á Heljar thremi,* to lie on Hel's threshold. A funeral could be called a *Helför* (a Hel-journey) ; fatal illness *Helsótt* (Hel-sickness) ; the deceased could be called *Helgengnir* (t1ose gone to Hel). Of friends it is said that Hel (death) alone could separate t1em (Fornm., vii. 233).

Thus it is evident that Hel, in the more general local sense of the word, referred to a place common for all t1e dead, and that the word was used wit1out any additional suggestion of damnation and torture in the minds of those employing it.

58.

THE WORD HEL IN VEGTAMSKVIDA AND IN VAFTHRUD-NERSMAL.

When Odin, according to Vegtamskvida, resolved to get reliable information in the lower world in regard to the fate whch threatened Balder, he saddled his Sleipner and rode thither. On the way he took he came first to Nifelhel. While he was still in Nifelhel, he met on his way a dog bloody about the breast, which came from the direction where that division of the lower world is situated, which is called Hel. Thus the rider and the dog came from opposite directions, and the former con-tinned his course in the direction whence the latter came. The dog turned, and long pursued Odin with his barking. Then the rider reached a *foldvegr,* that is to say, a road along grass-grown plains. The way resounded under the hoofs of the steed. Then Odin finally came to a high dwelling which is called *Heljarrann* or *Heljar rann.* The name of the dwelling shows t1at it was situated in Hel, not in Nifelhel. This latter realm of t1e lower world Odin now had had behind 1im ever since 1e reached t1e green fields, and since the dog, evidently a watc1 of the borders between Nifelhel and Hel, had left him in peace. The high dwelling was decorated as for a feast, and mead was served. It was, Odin learned, the abode where the *ásmegir* longingly waited for the arrival of Balder. Thus Vegtamskvida:

> 2. Ræid 1ann (Odin) nidr thathan
> Niflhæljar til,
> mætti 1ann hvælpi
> t1eim ær or hæliu kom.

> 3. Sa var blodugr
> um briost framan
> ok galldrs födur
> gol um længi.

> 4. Framm ræid Odinn,
> foldvægr dundi,
> han kom at 1afu
> Hæliar ranni.

> 7. Her standr Balldri
> of brugginn miödr.
> Ok ásmegir
> i ofvæno.

Vegtamskvida distinguishes distinctly between Nifelhel and Hel. In Hel is the dwelling which awaits the son of the gods, the noblest and most pious of all the Asas. The dwelling, which reveals a lavish splendour, is described as the very antithesis of that awful abode which, according

to Gylfaginning, belongs to the queen of the lower world.
In Vafthrudnersmal (43) the old giant says:

Fra iotna runom	Of the runes of giants
oc allra goda `	and of all the gods
cc kann segia satt,	I can speak truly;
thviat hvern hefi cc	for I have been
1eim um komit:	in every world.
nio kom cc 1eima	In nine worlds I came
fyr Niflhel nedan,	below Nifelhel,
hinig deyja or Helio 1alir.	thither die "1alir" from Hel.

Like Vegtamskvida, so Vafthrudnersmal also distinguishes distinctly between Hel and Nifelhel, particularly
in those most remarkable words that thither, *i.e.,* to Nifel-
1el and the regions subject to it, *die* "halir" from Hel.
Halir means men, human beings; applied to beings in the
lower world *halir* means dead men, the spirits of deceased
human beings (cp. Allvism., 18, 6; 20, 6; 26, 6; 32, 6; 34,
6, with 28, 3). Accordingly, nothing less is here said than
that deceased persons who have come to the realm called
Hel, may there be subject to a second death, and that
through this second death they come to Nifelhel. Thus
the same sharp distinction is here made between life in
Hel and in Nifelhel as between life on earth and that in
Hel. These two subterranean realms must therefore
represent very different conditions. What these different
conditions are, Vafthrudnersmal does not inform us, nor
will I anticipate the investigation on this point; still less
will I appeal to Gylfaginning's assurance that the realms
of torture lie under Nifelhel, and that it is wicked men
(*vândir menn*) who are obliged to cross the border from

Hel to Nifelhel.   So far it must be borne in mind that it
was in Nifelhel Odin met the bloody dog-demon, who
barked at the Asa-majesty, though he could not hinder
the father of the mighty and protecting sorceries from
continuing his journey; while it was in Hel, on the other
hand, that Odin saw the splendid abode where the *ásmegir*
had already served the precious subterranean mead for his
son, the just Balder.   This argues that they who through
a second death get over the border from Hel to Nifelhel,
do not by this transfer get a better fate than that to
which Hel invites those who have died the first death.
Balder in the one realm, the blood-stained kinsman of
Cerberus in the other—this is, for the present, the only,
but not unimportant weight in the balance which is to
determine the question whether that border-line which a
second death draws between Hel and Nifelhel is the boundary between a realm of bliss and a realm of suffering, and
in this case, whether Hel or Nifelhel is the realm of bliss.

This expression in Vafthrudnersmal, *hinig deyja or
Helio halir,* also forces to the front another question,
which as long as it remains unanswered, makes the former
question more complicated.   If Hel is a realm of bliss,
and if Nifelhel with the regions subject thereto is a realm
of unhappiness, then why do not the souls of the damned
go at once to their final destination, but are taken first
to the realm of bliss, then to the realm of anguish and
pain, that is, after they have died the second death on
the boundary-line between the two?   And if, on the contrary, Hel were the realm of unhappiness and Nifelhel
offered a better lot, then why should they who are destined

for a better fate, first be brought to it through the world
of torture, and then be separated from the latter by a
second death before they could gain the more happy goal?
These questions cannot be answered until later on.

59.

THE WORD HEL IN GRIMNERSMAL. HVERGELMER'S FOUN-
TAIN AND ITS DEFENDERS. THE BORDER MOUNTAIN
BETWEEN HEL AND NIFELHEL. THE WORD HEL-
BLOTINN IN THORSDRAPA.

In Grimnersmal the word **Hel** occurs twice (str. 28,
31), and this poem is (together with Gylfaginning) the
only ancient record which gives us any information about
the well Hvergelmer under this name (str. 26, ff.).

From what is related, it appears that the mythology
conceived Hvergelmer as a vast reservoir, the mother-
fountain of all the waters of the world (*thadan eigo votn
aull vega*). In the front rank are mentioned a number
of subterranean rivers which rise in Hvergelmer, and seek
their courses thence in various directions. But the waters
of earth and heaven also come from this immense fountain, and after completing their circuits they return
thither. The liquids or saps which rise in the world-
tree's stem to its branches and leaves around **Herfather's**
hall (Valhal) return in the form of rain to Hvergelmer
(Grimnersmal, 26).

Forty rivers rising there are named. (Whether they
were all found in the original text may be a subject of
doubt. Interpolators may have added from their own

knowledge.) Three of them are mentioned in other records—namely, *Slidr* in Völuspa, 36, *Gjöll* in that account of Hermod's journey to Hel's realm, which in its main outlines was rescued by the author of Gylfaginning (Gylfag., ch. 52), and *Leiptr* in Helge Hund., ii. 31—and all three are referred to in such a way as to prove that they are subterranean rivers. Slid flows to the realms of torture, and whirls weapons in its eddies, presumably to hinder or frighten anybody from attempting to cross. Over *Gjöll* there is a bridge of gold to Balder's subterranean abode. *Leiptr* (which name means "the shining one") has clear waters which are holy, and by which solemn oaths are sworn, as by Styx. Of these last two rivers flowing out of Hvergelmer it is said that they flow down to Hel (*falla til Heljar,* str. 28). Thus these are all subterranean. The next strophe (29) adds four rivers—*Körmt* and *Örmt,* and the two *Kerlögar,* of which it is said that it is over these Thor must wade every day when he has to go to the judgment-seats of the gods near the ash Ygdrasil. For he does not ride like the other gods when they journey down over Bifrost to the thingstead near Urd's fountain. The horses which they use are named in strophe 30, and are ten in number, like the asas, when we subtract Thor who walks, and Balder and *Hödr* who dwell in Hel. Nor must Thor on these journeys, in case he wished to take the route by way of Bifrost, use the thunder-chariot, for the flames issuing from it might set fire to the Asa-bridge and make the holy waters glow (str. 29). That the thunder-chariot also is dangerous for higher regions when it is set in motion, thereof Thjo-

dolf gives us a brilliant description in the poem Haustlaung. Thor being for this reason obliged to wade across
four rivers before he gets to Urd's fountain, the beds of
these rivers must have been conceived as crossing the paths
travelled by the god journeying to the thingstead.
Accordingly they must have their courses somewhere in
Urd's realm, or on the way thither, and consequently they
too belong to the lower world.

Other rivers coming from Hvergelmer are said to turn
their course around a place called *Hodd-goda* (str. 27
ther hverfa um Hodd-goda). This girdle of rivers,
which the mythology unites around a single place, seems
to indicate that this is a realm from which it is important
to shut out everything that does not belong there. The
name itself, *Hodd-goda,* points in the same direction.
The word *Hodd* means that which is concealed (the treasure), and at the same time a protected sacred place. In
the German poem *Heliand* the word *hord,* corresponding
to *hodd,* is used about the holiest of holies in the Jerusa-
lem temple. As we already know, there is in the lower
world a place to which these references apply, namely, the
citadel guarded by Delling, the elf of dawn, and decorated
by the famous artists of the lower world—a citadel in
which the *ásmegir* and Balder—and probably *Hodr* too,
since he is transferred to the lower world, and with Balder
is to return thence—await the end of the historical time
and the regeneration. The word *goda* in Hodd-goda
shows that the place is possessed by, or entrusted to,
beings of divine rank.

From what has here been stated in regard to Hvergelmer it follows that the mighty well was conceived as situated on a high water-shed, far up in a subterranean mountain range, whence those rivers of which it is the source flow down in different directions to different realms of Hades. Of several of these rivers it is said that they in their upper courses, before they reach Hel, flow in the vicinity of mankind (*gumnom nær*—str. 28, 7), which naturally can have no other meaning than that the high land through which they flow after leaving Hvergelmer has been conceived as lying not very deep below the crust of Midgard (the earth). Hvergelmer and this high land are not to be referred to that division of the lower world which in Grimnersmal is called Hel, for not until after the rivers have flowed through the mountain landscape, where their source is, are they said to *falla til Heljar.*

Thus (1) there is in the lower world a mountain ridge, a high land, where is found Hvergelmer, the source of all waters; (2) this mountain, which we for the present may call Mount Hvergelmer, is the watershed of the lower world, from which rivers flow in different directions; and (3) that division of the lower world which is called Hel lies below one side of Mount Hvergelmer, and thence receives many rivers. What that division of the lower world which lies below the other side of Mount Hvergelmer is called is not stated in Grimnersmal. But from Vafthrudnersmal and Vegtamskvida we already know that Hel is bounded by Nifelhel. In Vegtamskvida Odin rides through Nifelhel to Hel; in Vafthrudnersmal *halir* die from Hel to Nifelhel. Hel and Nifelhel thus appear to be each other's opposites, and to complement each other, and combined they form the whole lower world. Hence it follows that the land on the other side of the Hvergelmer mountain is Nifelhel.

It also seems necessary that both these Hades realms should in the mythology be separated from each other not only by an abstract boundary line, but also by a natural boundary—a mountain or a body of water—which might prohibit the crossing of the boundary by persons who neither had a right nor were obliged to cross. The tradition on which Saxo's account of Gorm's journey to the lower world is based makes Gorm and his men, when from Gudmund-Mimer's realm they wish to visit the abodes of the damned, first cross a river and then come to a boundary which cannot be crossed, excepting by *scalæ*, steps on the mountain wall, or ladders, above which the gates are placed, that open to a city "resembling most a cloud of vapour" (*vaporanti maxime nubi simile*—i. 425). This is Saxo's way of translating the name *Nifelhel*, just as he in the story about Hadding's journey to the lower world translated *Glæsisvellir* (the Glittering Fields) with *loca aprica*.

In regard to the topography and eschatology of the Teutonic lower world, it is now of importance to find out on which opposite sides of the Hvergelmer mountain Hel and Nifelhel were conceived to be situated.

Nifl, an ancient word, related to *nebula* and *nephek* means fog, mist, cloud, darkness. Nifelhel means *that* Hel which is enveloped in fog and twilight. The name *Hel* alone has evidently had partly a more general application to a territory embracing the whole kingdom of death—else it could not be used as a part of the compound word *Nifelhel*—partly a more limited meaning, in which *Hel*, as in Vafthrudnersmal and Vegtamskvida, forms a sharp contrast to *Nifelhel*, and from the latter point of view it is that division of the lower world which is *not* enveloped in mist and fog.

According to the cosmography of the mythology there was, before the time when "Ymer lived," Nifelheim, a world of fog, darkness, and cold, north of Ginungagap, and an opposite world, that of fire and heat, south of the empty abyss. Unfortunately it is only Gylfaginning that has preserved for our time these cosmographical outlines, but there is no suspicion that the author of Gylfaginning invented them. The fact that his cosmographic description also mentions the ancient cow Audhumla, which is nowhere else named in our mythic records, but is not utterly forgotten in our popular traditions, and which is a genuine Aryan conception, this is the strongest argument in favour of his having had genuine authorities for his theo-cosmogony at hand, though he used them in an arbitrary manner. The Teutons may also be said to have been compelled to construct a cosmogony in harmony with their conception of that world with which they were best acquainted, their own home between the cold North and the warmer South.

Nifelhel in the lower world has its counterpart in Nifelheim in chaos. Gylfaginning identifies the two (ch. 6 and 34). Forspjallsljod does the same, and locates Nifelheim far to the north in the lower world (*nordr at Nifelheim*—str. 26), behind Ygdrasil's farthest root, under which the poem makes the goddess of night, after completing her journey around the heavens, rest for a new journey. When Night has completed such a journey and come to the lower world, she goes northward in the direction towards Nifelheim, to remain in her hall, until Dag with his chariot gets down to the western horizon and in his turn rides through the "horse doors" of Hades into the lower world.

From this it follows that Nifelhel is to be referred to the north of the mountain Hvergelmer, Hel to the south of it. Thus this mountain is the wall separating Hel from Nifelhel. On that mountain in the gate, or gates, which in the Gorm story separates Gudmund-Mimer's abode from those dwellings which resemble a "cloud of vapour," and up there is the death boundary, at which "halir" die for the second time, when they are transferred from Hel to Nifelhel.

The immense water-reservoir on the brow of the mountain, which stands under Ygdrasil's northern root, sends, as already stated, rivers down to both sides—to Nifelhel in the North and to Hel in the South. Of the most of these rivers we now know only the names. But those of which we do know more are characterised in such a manner that we find that it is a sacred land to which those flowing to the South towards Hel hasten their course, and that it is an unholy land which is sought by those which send their streams to the north down into Nifelhel. The rivers *Gjöll* and *Leiptr* fall down into Hel, and *Gjöll* is, as already indicated, characterised by a bridge of gold, Leiptr by a shining, clear, and most holy water. Down there in the South are found the mystic Hodd-goda, surrounded by other Hel-rivers; Balder's and the *ásmegir's* citadel (perhaps identical with Hodd-goda); Mimer's fountain, seven times overlaid with gold, the fountain of inspiration and of the creative force, over which the "overshadowing holy tree" spreads its branches (Völuspa), and around whose reed-wreathed edge the seed of poetry grows (Eilif Gudrunson); the Glittering Fields, with flowers which never fade and with harvests which never are gathered; Urd's fountain, over which Ygdrasil stands for ever green (Völuspa), and in whose silver-white waters swans swim; and the sacred thing-stead of the Asas, to which they daily ride down over Bifrost. North of the mountain roars the weapon-hurling Slid, and doubtless is the same river as that in whose "heavy streams" the souls of nithings must wade. In the North *solú fjarri* stands, also at Nastrands, that hall, the walls of which are braided of serpents (Völuspa). Thus Hel is described as an Elysium, Nifelhel with its subject regions as a realm of unhappiness.

Yet a few words about Hvergelmer, from and to which "all waters find their way." This statement in Grimnersmal is of course true of the greatest of all waters, the ocean. The myth about Hvergelmer and its subterranean connection with the ocean gave our ancestors the explanation of ebb- and flood-tide. High up in the northern channels the bottom of the ocean opened itself in a hollow tunnel, which led down to the "kettle-roarer," "the one roaring in his basin" (this seems to be the meaning of *Hvergelmir: hverr=*kettle; *galm=*Anglo-

Saxon *gealm,* a roaring). When the waters of the ocean poured through this tunnel down into the Hades-well there was ebb-tide; when it returned water from its super-abundance there was flood-tide (see Nos. 79, 80, 81).

Adam of Bremen had heard this tunnel mentioned in connection with the story about the Frisian noblemen who went by sea to the furthest north, came to the land of subterranean giants, and plundered their treasures (see No. 48). On the way up some of the ships of the Frisians got into the eddy caused by the tunnel, and were sucked with terrible violence down into the lower world.*

Charlemagne's contemporary, Paul Varnefrid (Diaconus), relates in his history of the Longobardians that he had talked with men who had been in Scandinavia. Among remarkable reports which they gave him of the regions of the far north was also that of a maelstrom, which swallows ships, and sometimes even casts them up again (see Nos. 15, 79, 80, 81).

Between the death-kingdom and the ocean there was, therefore, one connecting link, perhaps several. Most of the people who drowned did not remain with *Ran.* Ægir's wife received them hospitably, according to the Icelandic sagas of the middle age. She had a hall in the bottom of the sea, where they were welcomed and offered *sess ok rekkju* (seat and bed). Her realm was only an ante-chamber to the realms of death (Kormak, Sona-torrek).

---

*"Et ecce instabilis Oceani Euripus, ad initia quædam fontis sui arcana recurrens, infelices nautas jam desperatos, immo de morte sola cogitantes, vehementissimo in petu traxit ad Chaos. Hanc dicunt esse voraginem abyssi, illud profundum, in quo fama est omnes maris recursus, qui decrescere videntur, absorberi et denuo removi, quod fluctuatio dici solet" (*De situ Daniæ,* ed. Mad., p. 159).

The demon Nidhog, which by Gylfaginning is thrown
into Hvergelmer is, according to the ancient records, a
winged dragon flying about, one of several similar monsters which have their abode in Nifelhel and those lower
regions, and which seek to injure that root of the world-
tree which is nearest to them, that is the northern one,
which stands over Nifelhel and stretches its rootlets southward over Mount Hvergelmer and down into its great
water-reservoir (Grimnersmal, 34, 35). Like all the
Aryan mythologies, the Teutonic also knew this sort of
monsters, and did so long before the word "dragon"
(*drake*) was borrowed from southern kinsmen as a name
for them. Nidhog abides now on Nastrands, where, by
the side of a wolf-demon, it tortures *náir* (corpses), now
on the Nida Mountains, whence the vala in Völuspa sees
him flying away with *náir* under his wings. Nowhere
(except in Gylfaginning) is it said that he lives in the well
Hvergelmer, though it is possible that he, in spite of his
wings, was conceived as an amphibious being which also
could subsist in the water. Tradition tells of dragons
who dwell in marshes and swamps.

The other two subterranean fountains, Urd's and
Mimer's, and the roots of Ygdrasil standing over them,
are well protected against the influence of the foes of
creation, and have their separate guardians. Mimer, with
his sons and the beings subject to him, protects and guards
his root of the tree, Urd and her sisters hers, and to the
latter all the victorious gods of Asgard come every day
to hold counsel. Was the northern root of Ygdrasil,
which spreads over the realms of the frost-giants, of the

demons, and of the damned, and was Hvergelmer, which waters this root and received so important a position in the economy of the world-tree, left in the mythology without protection and without a guardian? Hvergelmer we know is situated on the watershed, where we have the death-borders between Hel and Nifelhel fortified with abysses and gates, and is consequently situated in the immediate vicinity of beings hostile to gods and men. Here, if anywhere, there was need of valiant and vigilant watchers. Ygdrasil needs its northern root as well as the others, and if Hvergelmer was not allowed undisturbed to conduct the circuitous flow of all waters, the world would be either dried up or drowned.

Already, long before the creation of the world, there flowed from Hvergelmer that broad river called *Elivágar,* which in its extreme north froze into that ice, which, when it melted, formed out of its dropping venom the primeval giant Ymer (Vafthr., 31; Gylfag., 5). After creation this river like Hvergelmer, whence it rises and Nifelhel, into which it empties, become integral parts of the northern regions of the lower world. *Elivágar,* also called *Hraunn Hrönn,* sends in its upper course, where it runs near the crust of the earth, a portion of its waters up to it, and forms between Midgard and the upper Jotunheim proper, the river Vimur, which is also called *Elivágar* and *Hraunn,* like the parent stream (cp. Hymerskv., 5, 38; Grimnersm., 28; Skaldskaparm., ch. 3, 16, 18, 19, and Helg. Hj., 25). Elivágar separates the realm of the giants and frost-giants from the other "worlds."

South of Elivágar the gods have an "outgard," a

"sæter" which is inhabited by valiant watchers—*snotrir vikingar* they are called in Thorsdrapa, 8—who are bound by oaths to serve the gods. Their chief is Egil, the most famous archer in the mythology (Thorsdrapa, 1, 8; cp. Hymiskv., 7, 38; Skaldskap., ch. 16). As such he is also called Orvandel (the one busy with the arrow). This Egil is the guardian entrusted with the care of Hvergelmer and Elivágar. Perhaps it is for this reason that he has a brother and fellow-warrior who is called Ide (*Idi* from *ida*, a fountain with eddying waters). The "sæter" is called "Ides sæter" (Thorsdrapa, 1). The services which he as watcher on Mt. Hvergelmer and on the Elivágar renders to the regions of bliss in the lower world are so great that, although he does not belong to the race of the gods by birth or by adoption, he still enjoys among the inhabitants of Hel so great honour and gratitude that they confer divine honours on him. He is "the one worshipped in Hel who scatters the clouds which rise storm-threatening over the mountain of the lower world," *hel-blotinn hneitr undir-fjálfrs bliku* (Thorsdr., 19). The storm-clouds which Are, *Hræsvelgr,* and other storm-demons of Nifelheim send to the elysian fields of the death-kingdom, must, in order to get there, surmount Mt. Hvergelmer, but there they are scattered by the faithful watchman. Now in company with Thor, and now alone, Egil-Orvandel has made many remarkable journeys to Jotunheim. Next after Thor, he was the most formidable foe of the giants, and in connection with Heimdal he zealously watched their every movement. The myth in regard to him is fully discussed in the treatise on the

Ivalde-sons which forms a part of this work, and there the proofs will be presented for the identity of Orvandel and Egil. I simply desire to point out here, in order to present complete evidence later, that Ygdrasil's northern root and the corresponding part of the lower world also had their defenders and watchmen, and I also wished to call attention to the manner in which the name *Hel* is employed in the word *Helblótinn*. We find it to be in harmony with the use of the same word in those passages of the poetic Edda which we have hitherto examined.

60.

THE WORD HEL IN SKIRNERSMAL. DESCRIPTION OF NIFELHEL. THE MYTHIC MEANING OF NÁR, NÁIR. THE HADES-DIVISION OF THE FROST-GIANTS AND SPIRITS OF DISEASE.

In Skirnersmal (strophe 21) occurs the expression *horfa ok snugga Heljar til*. It is of importance to our theme to investigate and explain the connection in which it is found.

The poem tells that Frey sat alone, silent and longing, ever since he had seen the giant Gymer's wonderfully beautiful daughter Gerd. He wasted with love for her; but he said nothing, since he was convinced in advance that neither Asas nor Elves would ever consent to a union between him and her. But when the friend of his youth, who resided in Asgard, and in the poem is called Skirner, succeeded in getting him to confess the cause of his longing, it was, in Asgard, found necessary to do something to relieve it, and so Skirner was sent to the home of the giant to ask for the hand of Gerd on Frey's behalf. As bridal gifts he took with him eleven golden apples and the ring *Draupnir.* He received one of the best horses of Asgard to ride, and for his defence Frey's magnificient sword, "which fights of itself against the race of giants." In the poem this sword receives the epithets *Tams-vöndr* (str. 26) and *Gambanteinn* (str. 32). *Tams-vöndr,* means the "staff that subdues;" *Gambanteinn* means the "rod of revenge" (see Nos. 105, 116). Both epithets are formed in accordance with the common poetic usage of describing swords by compound words of which the latter part is *vöndr or teinn.* We find, as names for swords, *benvondr, blodvondr, hjaltvondr, hridvondr, hvitvondr, mordvondr, sarvondr, benteinn, eggteinn, hævateinn, hjorteinn, hræteinn, sarteinn, valteinn, mistelteinn.*

Skirner rides over damp fells and the fields of giants, leaps, after a quarrel with the watchman of Gymer's citadel, over the fence, comes in to Gerd, is welcomed with ancient mead, and presents his errand of courtship, supported by the eleven golden apples. Gerd refuses both the apples and the object of the errand. Skirner then offers her the most precious treasure, the ring *Draupnir,* but in vain. Then he resorts to threats, He exhibits the sword so dangerous to her kinsmen; with it he will cut off her head if she refuses her consent. Gerd answers that she is not to be frightened, and that she has a father who is not afraid to fight. Once more Skirner shows her the sword, which also may fell her father (*ser thu thenna mæki, mey,* &c.), and he threatens to strike her with the "subduing staff," so that her heart shall soften, but too late for her happiness, for a blow from the staff will remove her thither, where sons of men never more shall see her.

> Tamsvendi ec t1ic drep,
> enn ec t1ic temia mun,
> mer! at minom munom;
> t1ar skaltu ganga
> er t1ic gumna synir
> sit1an eva se (str. 26).

This is the former threat of death repeated in another form. The former did not frighten her. But that which now overwhelms her with dismay is the description Skirner gives her of the lot that awaits her in the realm of death, whither she is destined—s1e, the giant maid, if she dies by the avenging wrath of the gods (*gamban-reidi*). She shall then come to that region which is situated below the Na-gates (*fyr nágrindr nethan*—str. 35), and which is inhabited by frost-giants who, as we shall find, do not deserve the name *mannasynir*, even though the word *menn* be taken in its most common sense, and made to embrace giants of the masculine kind.

This phrase *fyr nágrindr nethan* must have been a stereotyped eschatological term applied to a particular division, a particular realm in the lower world. In Lokasenna (str. 63), Thor says to Loke, after the latter has emptied his phials of rash insults upon the gods, that if he does not hold his tongue the hammer Mjolner shall send him to Hel *fyr nágrindr nethan*. Hel is here used in its widest sense, and this is limited by the addition of

the words "below the Na-gates," so as to refer to a particular division of the lower world. As we find by the
application of the phrase to Loke, this division is of such
a character that it is intended to receive the foes of the
Asas and the insulters of the gods.

The word *Nagrind,* which is always used in the plural,
and accordingly refers to more than one gate of the kind,
has as its first part *nár* (pl. *náir*), which means corpse,
dead body. Thus Na-gates means Corpse-gates.

The name must seem strange, for it is not dead bodies,
but souls, released from their bodies left on earth, which
descend to the kingdom of death and get their various
abodes there. How far our heathen ancestors had a
more or less *material* conception of the soul is a question
which it is not necessary to discuss here (see on this point
No. 95). Howsoever they may have regarded it, the
very existence of a Hades in their mythology demonstrates that they believed that a conscious and sentient
element in man was in death separated from the body
with which it had been united in life, and went down to
the lower world. That the body from which this conscious, sentient element fled was not removed to Hades, but
went in this upper earth to its disintegration, whether it
was burnt or buried in a mound or sunk to the bottom of
the sea, this our heathen ancestors knew just as well as
we know it. The people of the stone-age already knew
this.

The phrase Na-gates does not stand alone in our mythological eschatology. One of the abodes of torture lying
within the Na-gate is called Nastrands (*Nástrandir*), and

is described in Völuspa as filled with terrors. And the victims, which Nidhog, the winged demon of the lower world, there sucks, are called *náir framgenga*, "the corpses of those departed."

It is manifest that the word *nár* thus used cannot have its common meaning, but must be used in a special mythological sense, which had its justification and its explanation in the heathen doctrine in regard to the lower world.

It not unfrequently happens that law-books preserve ancient significations of words not found elsewhere in literature. The Icelandic law-book Grágás (ii. 185) enumerates four categories within which the word *nár* is applicable to a person yet living. Gallows-*nár*, can be called, even while living, the person who is hung; grave-*nár*, the person placed in a grave; skerry-*nár* or rock-*nár* may, while yet alive, he be called who has been exposed to die on a skerry or rock. Here the word *nár* is accordingly applied to persons who are conscious and capable of suffering, but on the supposition that they are such persons as have been condemned to a punishment which is not to cease so long as they are sensitive to it.

And this is the idea on the basis of which the word *náir* is mythologically applied to the damned and tortured beings in the lower world.

If we now take into account that our ancestors believed in a *second* death, in a slaying of souls in Hades, then we find that this same use of the word in question, which at first sight could not but seem strange, is a consistent development of the idea that those banished from Hel's realms of bliss die a second time, when they are transferred across the border to Nifelhel and the world of torture. When they are overtaken by this second deati they are for the second time *náir*. And, as this occurs at the gates of Nifelhel, it was perfectly proper to call the gates *nágrindr*.

We may imagine that it is terror, despair, or rage which, at the sight of the Na-gates, severs the bond between the damned spirit and his Hades-body, and that the former is anxious to soar away from its terrible destination. But however this may be, the avenging powers have runes, which capture the fugitive, put chains on his Hades-body, and force him to feel with it. The Sun-song, a Christian song standing on the scarcely crossed border of heathendom, speaks of damned ones whose breasts were risted (carved) with bloody runes, and Havamál of runes which restore consciousness to *náir*. Such runes are known by Odin. If he sees in a tree a gallows-*nár* (*virgil-nár*), then he can rist runes so that the body comes down to him and talks with him (see No. 70).

Ef cc se a tre uppi
vafa virgilná,
sva cc rist
oc i runom fác,
at sa gengr gumi
oc mælir viti mic (Havamál, 157).

Some of the subterranean *náir* have the power of motion, and are doomed to wade in "heavy streams." Among them are perjurers, murderers, and adulterers (Völuspa, 38). Among these streams is Vadgelmer, in which they who have slandered others find their far-reaching retribution (Sigurdarkv., ii. 4). Other *nâir* have the peculiarity which their appellation suggests, and receive quiet and immovable, stretched on iron benches, their punishment (see below). Saxo, who had more elaborate descriptions of the Hades of heathendom than those which have been handed down to our time, translated or reproduced in his accounts of Hadding's and Gorm's journeys in the lower world the word *nâir* with *exsanguia simulacra* (p. 426).

That place after death with which Skirner threatens the stubborn Gerd is also situated within the Na-gates, but still it has another character than Nastrands and the other abodes of torture which are situated below Nifelhel. It would also have been unreasonable to threaten a person who rejects a marriage proposal with those punishments which overtake criminals and nithings. The Hades division, which Skirner describes as awaiting the giant-daughter, is a subterranean Jotunheim, inhabited by deceased ancestors and kinsmen of Gerd.

Mythology has given to the giants as well as to men a life hereafter. As a matter of fact, mythology never destroys life. The horse which was cremated with its master on his funeral pyre, and was buried with him in his grave-mound, afterwards brings the hero down to Hel. When the giant who built the Asgard wall got into conflict with the gods, Thor's hammer sent him "down below Nifelhel" (*nidr undir Niflhel*—Gylfag., ch. 43.) King Gorm saw in the lower world the giant Geirrod and both his daughters. According to Grimnersmal (str. 31), frost-giants dwell under one of Ygdrasil's roots—consequently in the lower world; and Forspjalls-ljod says that hags (giantesses) and thurses (giants), *náir,* dwarfs, and swartıy elves go to sleep under the world-tree's fartıest root on the north border of Jormun-grund* (the lower world), when Dag on a chariot spark-ling with precious stones leaves the lower world, and when Nat after her journey on the heavens has returned to her home (str. 24, 28). It is therefore quite in order if we, in Skirner's description of the realm which after death awaits the giant-daughter offending the gods, rediscover that part of the lower world to which the drowned prime-val ancestors of the giant-maid were relegated when Bor's sons opened the veins of Ymer's throat (Sonatorr., str. 3) and then let the billows of the ocean wash clean the rocky ground of earth, before tıey raised the latter from the sea and there created the inhabitable Midgard.

The frost-giants (rimethurses) are the primeval giants (*gigantes*) of the Teutonic mythology, so called because they sprang from the frost-being Ymer, whose feet by contact with each other begat their progenitor, the "strange-headed" monster Thrudgelmer (Vafthr. 29, 33). Their original home in chaos was Nifelheim. From the Hvergelmer fountain there the Elivagar rivers flowed to the north and became hoar-frost and ice, wıich, melted by warmth from the south, were changed into drops of venom, which again became Ymer, called by the giants Aurgelmer (Vafthr., 31; Gylfag., 5). Thrudgelmer

---

*With this name of the lower world compare Gudmund-Mimer's abode *á Grund* (see No. 45), and *Hellıgrund* (Heliand., 44, 22), and *neowla grund* (Caedmon, 267, 1, 270, 16).

begat Bergelmer countless winters before the earth was made (Vafthr., 29; Gylf., ch. 7). Those members of the giant race living in Jotunheim on the surface of the earth, whose memory goes farthest back in time, can remember Bergelmer when he *a var ludr um lagidr*. At least Vafthrudmer is able to do this (Vafthr., 35).

When the original giants had to abandon the fields populated by Bor's sons (Völuspa, 4), they received an abode corresponding as nearly as possible to their first home, and, as it seems, identical with it, excepting that Nifelheim now, instead of being a part of chaos, is an integral part of the cosmic universe, and the extreme north of its Hades. As a Hades-realm it is also called Nifelhel.

In the subterranean land with which Skirner threatens Gerd, and which he paints for her in appalling colours, he mentions three kinds of beings—(1) frost-giants, the ancient race of giants; (2) demons; (3) giants of the later race.

The frost-giants occupy together one abode, which, judging from its epithet, hall (*höll*), is the largest and most important there; while those members of the younger giant clan who are there, dwell in single scattered abodes, called gards.* Gerd is also there to have a separate abode (str. 28).

Two frost-giants are mentioned by name, which shows that they are representatives of their clan. One is named Rimgrimner (*Hrimgrimnir*—str. 35), the other Rimner (*Hrimnir*—str. 28).

Grimner is one of Odin's many surnames (Grimners-

*Compare the phrase *iotna gaurthum i* (str. 30, 3) with *til hrimthursa hallar* (30, 4).

mal, 47, and several other places; cp. Egilsson's Lex. Poet.). Rimgrimner means the same as if Odin had said Rim-Odin, for Odin's many epitiets could without hesitation be used by the poets in paraphrases, even when these referred to a giant. But the name Odin was too sacred for such a purpose. Upon the whole the skalds seem piously to have abstained from using that name in paraphrases, even when the latter referred to celebrated princes and heroes. Glum Geirason is the first known exception to the rule. He calls a king *Málm-Odinn*. The above epitiet places Rimgrimner in the same relation to the frost-giants as Odin-Grimner sustains to the asas; it characterises him as the race-chief and clan-head of the former, and in this respect gives him the same place as Thrudgelmer occupies in Vafthrudnersmal. Ymer cannot be regarded as the special clan-chief of the frost-giants, since he is also the progenitor of other classes of beings (see Vafthr., 33, and Völuspa, 9; cp. Gylfag., ci. 14). But they have other points of resemblance. Thrudgelmer is "strange-headed" in Vafthrudnersmal; Rimgrimner is "three-headed" in Skirnersmal (str. 31; cp. with str. 35). Thus we have in one poem a "strangeheaded" Thrudgelmer as progenitor of the frost-giants; in the other poem a "three-headed" Rimgrimner as progenitor of the same frost-giants. The "strange-headed" giant of the former poem, which is a somewhat indefinite or obscure phrase, thus finds in "three-headed" of the latter poem its further definition. To this is to be added a power which is possessed both by Thrudgelmer and Rimgrimner, and also a weakness for which both Thrud-

435

gelmer and Rimgrimner are blamed. Thrudgelmer's father begat children without possessing *gygjar gaman* (Vafthr., 32). That Thrudgelmer inherited this power from his strange origin and handed it down to the clan of frost-giants, and that he also inherited the inability to provide for the perpetuation of the race in any other way, is evident from Allvismal, str. 2. If we make a careful examination, we find that Skirnersmal presupposes this same positive and negative quality in Rimgrimner, and consequently Thrudgelmer and Rimgrimner must be identical.

Gerd, who tries to reject the love of the fair and blithe Vana-god, will, according to Skirner's threats, be punished therefor in the lower world with the complete loss of all that is called love, tenderness, and sympathy. Skirner says that she either must live alone and without a husband in the lower world, or else vegetate in a useless cohabitation (*nara*) with the three-headed giant (str. 31). The threat is gradually emphasised to the effect that she *shall* be possessed by Rimgrimner, and this threat is made immediately after the solemn conjuration (str. 34) in which Skirner invokes the inhabitants of Nifelhel and also of the regions of bliss, as witnesses, that she shall never gladden or be gladdened by a man in the physical sense of this word.

Hear, ye giants,	Heyri iotnar,
Hear, frost-giants,	heyri hrimthursar,
Ye sons of Suttung—	synir Suttunga,
Nay, thou race of the Asa-god!*—	sjalfir áslithar

---

*With race of the Asa-god *áslidar* there can hardly be meant others than the *ásmegir* gathered in the lower world around Balder. This is the only place where the word *áslidar* occurs.

how I forbid,	hve cc fyr byd,
how I banis1	hve cc fyrir banna
man's gladness from the maid,	manna glaum mani
man's enjoyment from the maid!	manna nyt mani.
Rimgrimner is the giant's name	Hrímgrimner heiter t1urs,
who s1all possess t1ee	er t1ic 1afa scal
below the Na-gates.	fyr nagrindr nedan.

More plainly, it seems to me, Skirner in speaking to Gerd could not have expressed the negative quality of Rimgrimner in question. Thor also expresses himself clearly on the same subject when he meets the dwarf Alvis carrying home a maid over whom Thor has the right of marriage. Thor says scornfully that he thinks he discovers in Alvis something which reminds him of the nature of thurses, although Alvis is a dwarf and the thurses are giants, and he further defines wherein this similarity consists: *thursa lici thicci mér á ther vera; erat thu till brudar borinn*: "Thurs' likeness you seem to me to have; you were not born to have a bride." So far as the positive quality is concerned it is evident from the fact that Rimgrimner is the progenitor of the frost-giants.

Descended to Nifelhel, Gerd must not count on a shadow of friendship and sympathy from her kinsmen there. It would be best for her to confine herself in the solitary abode which there awaits her, for if she but looks out of the gate, staring gazes shall meet her from Rimner and all the others down there; and she shall there be looked upon with more hatred than Heimdal, the watchman of the gods, who is the wise, always vigilant foe of the rime-thurses and giants. But whether she is at home or abroad, demons and tormenting spirits shall never leave her in peace. She shall be bowed to the earth by *tramar* (evil witches). *Morn* (a Teutonic Eumenides, the agony of the soul personified) shall fill her with his being. The spirits of sickness—such also dwell there; they once took an oath not to harm Balder (Gylf., ch. 50)—shall increase her woe and the flood of her tears. Tope (insanity), Ope (hysteria), Tjausul and Othale (constant restlessness), shall not leave her in peace. These spirits are also counted as belonging to the race of thurses, and hence it is said in the rune-song that *thurs veldr kvenna kvillu,* "thurs causes sickness of women." In this connection it should be remembered that the daughter of Loke, the ruler of Nifelhel, is also the queen of diseases. Gerd's food shall be more loathsome to her than the poisonous serpent is to man, and her drink shall be the most disgusting. Miserable she shall crawl among the homes of the Hades giants, and up to a mountain top, where Are, a subterranean eagle-demon has his perch (doubtless the same Are which, according to Völuspa [47], is to join with his screeches in Rymer's shield-song, when the Midgard-serpent writhes in giant-rage, and the ship of death, Naglfar, gets loose). Up there she shall sit early in the morning, and constantly turn her face in the same direction—in the direction where Hel is situated, that is, south over Mt. Hvergelmer, toward the subterranean regions of bliss. Toward Hel she shall long to come in vain:

> Ara tiufo á
> scaltu ár sitja
> horfa ok snugga Heljar til.

"On Are's perch thou shalt early sit, turn toward Hel, and long to get to Hel."

By the phrase *snugga Heljar til,* the skald has meant something far more concrete than to "long for death." Gerd is here supposed to be dead, and within the Na-gates. To long for death, she does not need to crawl up to "Are's perch." She must subject herself to these nightly exertions, so that when it dawns in the foggy Nifelhel, she may get a glimpse of that land of bliss to which she may never come; she who rejected a higher happiness—that of being with the gods and possessing Frey's love.

I have been somewhat elaborate in the presentation of this description in Skirnersmal, which has not hitherto been understood. I have done so, because it is the only evidence left to us of how life was conceived in the fore-court of the regions of torture, Nifelhel, the land situated below Ygdrasil's northern root, beyond and below the mountain, where the root is watered by Hvergelmer. It is plain that the author of Skirnersmal, like that of Vafthrudnersmal, Grimnersmal, Vegtamskvida, and Thorsdrapa (as we have already seen), has used the word Hel in the sense of a place of bliss in the lower world. It is also evident that with the root under which the frost-giant dwells that one, referred to by Gylfaginning, can impossibly be meant under which Mimer's glorious fountain, and Mimer's grove, and all his treasures stored for a future world, are situated.

61.

THE WORD HEL IN VOLUSPA.   WHO THE INHABITANTS OF
HEL ARE.

We now pass to Völuspa, 40 (Hauk's Codex), where
the word *Helvegir* occurs.

One of the signs that Ragnarok and the fall of the
world are at hand, is that the mighty ash Ygdrasil
trembles, and that a fettered giant-monster thereby gets
loose from its chains.   Which this monster is, whether
it is Garm, bound above the Gnipa cave, or some other,
we will not now discuss.   The astonishment and confusion caused by these events among all the beings of the
world, are described in the poem with but few words,
but they are sufficient for the purpose and well calculated
to make a deep impression upon the hearers.   Terror is
the predominating feeling in those beings which are not
chosen to take part in the impending conflict.   They, on
the other hand, for whom the quaking of Ygdrasil is the
signal of battle for life or death, either arm themselves
amid a terrible war-cry for the battle (the giants, str. 41),
or they assemble to hold the last council (the Asas), and
then rush to arms.

Two classes of beings are mentioned as seized by terror
—the dwarfs, who stood breathless outside of their stone-
doors, and those beings which are *á Helvegum*.   *Helvegir*
may mean the paths or ways in Hel: there are many paths,
just as there are many gates and many rivers.   *Helvegir*
may also mean the regions, districts in Hel (cp. *Austr-
vegr, Sudrvegr, Norvegr;* and Allvism., 10, according to

which the Vans call the earth *vegir*, ways). The author may have used the word in either of these senses or in both, for in this case it amounts to the same. At all events it is stated that the inhabitants in Hel are terrified when Ygdrasil quakes and the unnamed giant-monster gets loose.

Skelfr Yggdrasils	Quakes Ygdrasil's
askr standandi,	Ash standing,
ymr hid alldna tre	The old tree trembles,
enn iotunn losnar;	The giant gets loose;
hrædaz allir	All are frightened
a Helvegum	On the Helways (in Hel's regions)
adr Surtar thann	ere Surt's spirit (or kinsman)
sevi of gleypir.	swallows him (namely, the giant).

Surt's spirit, or kinsman (*sevi, sefi* may mean either), is, as has also hitherto been supposed, the fire. The final episode in the conflict on Vigrid's plain is that the Muspel-flames destroy the last remnant of the contending giants. The terror which, when the world-tree quaked and the unnamed giant got loose, took possession of the inhabitants of Hel continues so long as the conflict is undecided. Valfather falls, Frey and Thor likewise; no one can know who is to be victorious. But the terror ceases when on the one hand the liberated giant-monster is destroyed, and on the other hand Vidar and Vale, Mode and Magne, survive the conflict and survive the flames, which do not penetrate to Balder and *Hödr* and their protegés in Hel. The word *thann* (him), which occurs in the seventh line of the strophe (in the last of the translation) can impossibly refer to any other than the giant mentioned in the fourth line (*iotunn*). There are in the strophe only two masculine words to which tıe masculine *thann* can be referred—*iotunn* and *Yggdrasils askr*. *Iotunn*, which stands nearest to *thann,* thus has the preference; and as we have seen tıat the world-tree falls by neither fire nor edge (Fjolsv., 20), and as it, in fact, survives the conflagration of Surt, then *thann* must naturally be referred to the *iotunn*.

Here Völuspa has furnished us witı evidence in regard to the position of Hel's inhabitants towards tıe contending parties in Ragnarok. They who are frigıtened when a giant-monster—a most dangerous one, as it hitherto had been chained—gets free from its fetters, and they whose frigıt is allayed when the monster is destroyed in the conflagration of the world, such beings can impossibly follow this monster and its fellow warriors with their good wisıes. Their hearts are on the side of the good powers, which are friendly to mankind. But they do not take an active part in their behalf; tıey take no part wıatever in the conflict. This is manifest from the fact tıat their fright does not cease before the conflict is ended. Now we know that among the inhabitants in Hel are tıe *ásmegir* Lif and Leifthraser and their offspring, and that they are not *hertharfir;* they are not to be employed in war, since their very destiny forbids their taking an active part in the events of this period of the world (see No. 53). But the text does not permit us to think of them alone when we are to determine who the beings *á Helvegum* are. For the text says that *all,* who are *á Helvegum,* are alarmed until the conflict is happily ended. What the interpreters of this much abused passage have failed to see, the seeress in Völuspa has not forgotten, that, namely, during the lapse of countless thousands of years, innumerable children and women, and men who never wielded the sword, have descended to the kingdom of death and received dwellings in Hel, and that Hel—in the limited local sense which the word hitherto has appeared to have in the songs of the gods—does not contain warlike inhabitants. Those who have fallen on the battle-field come, indeed, as shall be shown later, to Hel, but not to remain there; they continue their journey to Asgard, for Odin chooses one half of those slain on the battlefield for his dwelling, and Freyja the other half (Grimnersmal, 14). The chosen accordingly have Asgard as their place of destination, which they reach in case they are not found guilty by a sentence which neutralises the force and effect of the previous choice (see below), and sends them to die the second death on crossing the boundary to Nifelhel. Warriors who have not fallen on the battle-field are as much entitled to Asgard as those fallen by the sword, provided they as heroes have acquired fame and honour. It might, of course, happen to the greatest general and the most distinguished hero, the conqueror in hundreds of battles, that he might die from sickness or an accident, while, on the other hand, it might be that a man who never wielded a sword in earnest might fall on the field of battle before he had given a blow. That the mythology should make the latter entitled to Asgard, but not the former, is an absurdity as void of support in the records—on the contrary, these give the opposite testimony—as it is of sound sense. The election contained for the chosen ones no exclusive privilege. It did not even imply additional favour to one who, independently of the election, could count on a place among the einherjes. The election made the person going to battle *feigr,* which was not a favour, nor could it be considered the opposite. It might play a royal crown from the head of the chosen one to that of his enemy, and this could not well be regarded as a kindness. But for the electing powers of Asgard themselves the election implied a privilege. The dispensation of life and death regularly belonged to the norns; but the election partly supplied the gods with an exception to this rule, and partly it left to Odin the right to determine the fortunes and issues of battles. The question of the relation between the power of the gods and that of fate—a question which seemed to the Greeks and Romans dangerous to meddle with and well-nigh impossible to dispose of—was partly solved by the Teutonic mythology by the naïve and simple means of dividing the dispensation of life and death between the divinity and fate, which, of course, did not hinder that fate always stood as the dark, inscrutable power in the background of all events. (On election see further, No. 66).

It follows that in Hel's regions of bliss there remained none that were warriors by profession. Those among them who were not guilty of any of the sins which the Asa-doctrine stamped as sins unto death passed through Hel to Asgard, the others through Hel to Nifelhel. All the inhabitants on Hel's elysian fields accordingly are the *ásmegir,* and the women, children, and the agents of the

444

peaceful arts who have died during countless centuries, and who unused to the sword, have no place in the ranks of the einherjes, and therefore with the anxiety of those waiting abide the issue of the conflict. Such is the background and contents of the Völuspa strophe. This would long since have been understood, had not the doctrine constructed by Gylfaginning in regard to the lower world, with Troy as the starting-point, bewildered the judgment.

62.

THE WORD HEL IN ALLVISMAL. THE CLASSES OF BEINGS IN HEL.

In Allvismal occurs the phrases: those *i helio* and *halir*. The premise of the poem is that such objects as earth, heaven, moon, sun, night, wind, fire, &c., are expressed in six different ways, and that each one of these ways of expression is, with the exclusion of the others, applicable within one or two of the classes of beings found in the world. For example, Heaven is called—

> Himinn among men,
> Lyrner among gods,
> Vindofner among Vans,
> Uppheim among giants.
> Elves say Fager-tak (Fairy-roof),
> dwarfs Drypsal (dropping-hall) (str. 12).

In this manner thirteen objects are mentioned, each one with its six names. In all of the thirteen cases man has a way of his own of naming the objects. Likewise the giants. No other class of beings has any of the thirteen appellations in common with them. On the other hand, the Asas and Vans have the same name for two objects (moon and sun) ; elves and dwarfs have names in common for no less than six objects (cloud, wind, fire, tree, seed, mead) ; the dwarfs and the inhabitants of the lower world for three (heaven, sea, and calm). Nine times it is stated how those in the lower world express themselves. In six of these nine cases Allvismal refers to the inhabitants of the lower world by the general expression "those in Hel;" in three cases the poem lets "those in Hel" be represented by some one of those classes of beings that reside in Hel. These three are *upregin* (str. 10), *ásasynir* (str. 16), and *halir* (str. 28).

The very name *upregin* suggests that it refers to beings of a certain divine rank (the Vans are in Allvismal called *ginnregin,* str. 20, 30) that have their sphere of activity in the upper world. As they none the less dwell in the lower world, the appellation must have reference to beings which have their homes and abiding places in Hel when they are not occupied with .their affairs in the world above. These beings are Nat, Dag, Mane, Sol.

Ásasynir has the same signification as *ásmegir.* As this is the case, and as the *ásmegir* dwell in the lower world and the *ásasynir* likewise, then they must be identical, unless we should be credulous enough to assume that there were in the lower world two categories of beings, both called sons of Asas.

Halir, when the question is about the lower world, means the souls of the dead (Vafthr., 43 ; see above).

From this we find that Allvismal employs the word

Hel in such a manner that it embraces those regions where
Nat and Dag, Mane and Sol, the living human inhabitants
of Mimer's grove, and the souls of departed human beings
dwell. Among the last-named are included also souls of
the damned, which are found in the abodes of torture
below Nifelhel, and it is within the limits of possibility
that the author of the poem also had them in mind,
though there is not much probability that he should conceive them as having a nomenclature in common with
gods, *ásmegir,* and the happy departed. At all events,
he has particularly—and probably exclusively—had in his
mind the regions of bliss when he used the word Hel, in
which case he has conformed in the use of the word to
Völuspa, Vafthrudnersmal, Grimnersmal, Skirnersmal,
Vegtamskvida, and Thorsdrapa.

63.

THE WORD HEL IN OTHER PASSAGES. THE RESULT OF THE
INVESTIGATION FOR THE COSMOGRAPHY AND FOR THE
MEANING OF THE WORD HEL. HEL IN A LOCAL
SENSE THE KINGDOM OF DEATH, PARTICULARLY ITS
REALMS OF BLISS. HEL IN A PERSONAL SENSE IDEN-
TICAL WITH THE GODDESS OF FATE AND DEATH, THAT
IS, URD.

While a terrible winter is raging, the gods, according
to Forspjallsljod,* send messengers, with Heimdal as
chief, down to a lower-world goddess (dis), who is

*Of the age and genuineness of Forspjallsljod I propose to publish a
separate treatise.

designated as *Gjöll's* (the lower world river's) *Sunna* (Sol, sun) and as the distributor of the divine liquids (str. 9, 11) to beseech her to explain to them the mystery of creation, the beginning of heaven, of Hel, and of the world, life and death, if she is able (*hlyrnis, heliar, heims of vissi, ártith, æfi, aldrtila*). The messengers get only tears as an answer. The poem divides the universe into three great divisions: heaven, Hel, and the part lying between Hel and heaven, the world inhabited by mortals. Thus Hel is here used in its general sense, and refers to the whole lower world. But here, as wherever Hel has this general signification, it appears that the idea of regions of punishment is not thought of, but is kept in the background by the definite antithesis in which the word Hel, used in its more common and special sense of the subterranean regions of bliss, stands to Nifelhel and the regions subject to it. It must be admitted that what the anxious gods wish to learn from the wise goddess of the lower world must, so far as their desire to know and their fears concern the fate of Hel, refer particularly to the regions where Urd's and Mimer's holy wells are situated, for if the latter, which water the world-tree, pass away, it would mean nothing less than the end of the world. That the author should make the gods anxious concerning Loke's daughter, whom they had hurled into the deep abysses of Nifelhel, and that he should make the wise goddess by *Gjöll* weep bitter tears over the future of the sister of the Fenris-wolf, is possible in the sense that it cannot be refuted by any definite words of the old records; but we may be permitted to regard it as highly improbable.

448

Among the passages in which the word Hel occurs in the poetic Edda's mythological songs we have yet to mention Harbardsljod (str. 27); where the expression *drcpa i Hel* is employed in the same abstract manner as the Swedes use the expression "at slå ihjäl," which means simply "to kill" (it is Thor who threatens to kill the insulting Harbard); and also Völuspa (str. 42), Fjölls-vinnsmal (str. 25), and Grimnersmal (str. 31).

Völuspa (str. 42), speaks of Goldcomb, the cock which, with its crowing, wakes those who sleep in Herfather's abode, and of a sooty-red cock which crows under the earth near Hel's halls. In Fjöllsvinnsmal (str. 25), Svipdag asks with what weapon one might be able to bring down to Hel's home (*á Heljar sjöt*) that golden cock Vidofner, which sits in Mimer's tree (the world-tree). and doubtless is identical with Goldcomb. That Vidolner has done nothing for which he deserves to be punished in the home of Loke's daughter may be regarded as probable. *Hel* is here used to designate the kingdom of death in general, and all that Spivdag seems to mean is that Vidofner, in case such a weapon could be found, might be transferred to his kinsman, the sooty-red cock which crows below the earth. Saxo also speaks of a cock which is found in Hades, and is with the goddess who has the cowbane stalks when she shows Hadding the flower-meadows of the lower world, the Elysian fields of those fallen by the sword, and the citadel within which death does not seem able to enter (see No. 47). Thus there is at least one cock in the lower world's realm of bliss. That there should be one also in Nifelhel and in the abode

449

of Loke's daughter is nowhere mentioned, and is hardly credible, since the cock, according to an ancient and wide-spread Aryan belief, is a sacred bird, which is the special foe of demons and the powers of darkness. According to Swedish popular belief, even of the present time, the crowing of the cock puts ghosts and spirits to flight; and a similar idea is found in Avesta (Vendidad, 18), where, in str. 15, Ahuramazda himself translates the morning song of the cock with the following words: "Rise, ye men, and praise the justice which is the most perfect! Behold the demons are put to flight!" Avesta is naïvely out of patience with thoughtless persons who call this sacred bird (*Parodarsch*) by the so little respect-inspiring name "Cockadoodledoo" (*Kahrkatâs*). The idea of the sacredness of the cock and its hostility to demons was also found among the Aryans of South Europe and survived the introduction of Christianity. Aurelius Prudentius wrote a *Hymnus ad galli cantum,* and the cock has as a token of Christian vigilance received the same place on the church spires as formerly on the world-tree. Nor have the May-poles forgotten him. But in the North the poets and the popular language have made the red cock a symbol of fire. Fire has two characters—it is sacred, purifying, and beneficent, when it is handled carefully and for lawful purposes. In the opposite case it is destructive. With the exception of this special instance, nothing but good is reported of the cocks of mythology and poetry.

Grimnersmal (str. 31) is remarkable from two points of view. It contains information—brief and scant, it is true, but nevertheless valuable—in regard to Ygdrasil's three roots, and it speaks of Hel in an unmistakable, distinctly personal sense.

In regard to the roots of the world-tree and their position, our investigation so far, regardless of Grimnersmal (str. 31), has produced the following result:

Ygdrasil has a northern root. This stands over the vast reservoir Hvergelmer and spreads over Nifelhel, situated north of Hvergelmer and inhabited by frostgiants. There nine regions of punishment are situated, among them Nastrands.

Ygdrasil's second root is watered by Mimer's fountain and spreads over the land where Mimer's fountain and grove are located. In Mimer's grove dwell those living (not dead) beings called *Ásmegir* and *Ásasynir,* Lif and Leifthraser and their offspring, whose destiny it is to people the regenerated earth.

Ygdrasil's third root stands over Urd's fountain and the subterranean thingstead of the gods.

The lower world consists of two chief divisions · Nifelhel (with the regions thereto belonging) and Hel,— Nifelhel situated north of the Hvergelmer mountain, and Hel south of it. Accordingly both the land where Mimer's well and grove are situated and the land where Urd's fountain is found are within the domain Hel.

In regard to the zones or climates, in which the roots are located, they have been conceived as having a southern and northern. We have already shown that the root over Hvergelmer is the northern one. That the root over Urd's fountain has been conceived as the southern one is manifest from the following circumstances. Eilif Gud-runson, who was converted to Christianity—the same skald who wrote the purely heathen Thorsdrapa—says in one of his poems, written after his conversion, that Christ sits *sunnr at Urdarbrunni,* in the south near Urd's fountain, an expression which he could not have used unless his hearers had retained from the faith of their childhood the idea that Urd's fountain was situated south of the other fountains. Forspjallsljod puts upon Urd's fountain the task of protecting the world-tree against the devastating cold during the terrible winter which the poem describes. *Othhrærir skyldi Urthar geyma mættk at veria mestum thorra.*—"Urd's Odreirer (mead-fountain) proved not to retain strength enough to protect against the terrible cold." This idea shows that the sap which Ygdrasil's southern root drew from Urd's fountain was thought to be warmer than the saps of the other wells. As, accordingly, the root over Urd's well was the southern, and that over Hvergelmer and the frost-giants the northern, it follows that Mimer's well was conceived as situated between those two. The memory of this fact Gylfaginning has in its fashion preserved, where in chapter 15 it says that Mimer's fountain is situated where Ginungagap formerly was—that is, between the northern Nifelheim and the southern warmer region (Gylfaginning's "Muspelheim").

Grimnersmal (str. 31) says:

Thrir rætr standa	Three roots stand
a thria vega	on three ways
undan asci Yggdrasils:	below Ygdrasil's ash:

Hel byr und einni,	Hel dwells under one,
annari hrimthursar,	under another frost-giants,
thridio mennzkir menn.	under a third human-"men."

The root under which the frost-giants dwell we already know as the root over Hvergelmer and the Nifelhel inhabited by frost-giants.

The root under which human beings, living persons, *mennskir menn,* dwell we also know as the one over Mimer's well and Mimer's grove, where the human beings Lif and Leifthraser and their offspring have their abode, where *jörd lifanda manna* is situated.

There remains one root: the one under which the goddess of fate, Urd, has her dwelling. Of this Grimnersmal says that she who dwells there is named Hel.

Hence it follows of necessity that the goddess of fate, Urd, is identical with the personal Hel, the queen of the realm of death, particularly of its regions of bliss. We have seen that Hel in its local sense has the general signification, the realm of death, and the special but most frequent signification, the elysium of the kingdom of death. As a person, the meaning of the word Hel must be analogous to its signification as a place. It is the same idea having a personal as well as a local form.

The conclusion that Urd is Hel is inevitable, unless we assume that Urd, though queen of her fountain, is not the regent of the land where her fountain is situated. One might then assume Hel to be one of Urd's sisters, but these have no prominence as compared with herself. One of them, Skuld, who is the more known of the two, is at the same time one of Urd's maid-servants, a valkyrie, who on the battlefield does her errands, a feminine psycho-messenger who shows the fallen the way to Hel, the realm of her sisters, where they are to report themselves ere they get to their destination. Of *Verdandi* the records tell us nothing but the name, which seems to preclude the idea that she should be the personal Hel.

This result, that Urd is identical with Hel; that she who dispenses life also dispenses death; that she who with her serving sisters is the ruler of the past, the present, and the future, also governs and gathers in her kingdom all generations of the past, present, and future—this result may seem unexpected to those who, on the authority of Gylfaginning, have assumed that the daughter of Loke cast into the abyss of Nifelhel is the queen of the kingdom of death; that she whose threshold is called Precipice (Gylfag., 34) was the one who conducted Balder over the threshold to the subterranean citadel glittering with gold; that she whose table is called Hunger and whose knife is called Famine was the one who ordered the clear, invigorating mead to be placed before him; that the sister of those foes of the gods and of the world, the Midgard-serpent and the Fenris-wolf, was entrusted with the care of at least one of Ygdrasil's roots; and that she whose bed is called Sickness, jointly with Urd and Mimer, has the task of caring for the world-tree and seeing that it is kept green and gets the liquids from their fountains.

Colossal as this absurdity is, it has been believed for centuries. And in dealing with an absurdity which is centuries old, we must consider that it is a force which does not yield to objections simply stated, but must be conquered by clear and convincing arguments. Without the necessity of travelling the path by which I have reached the result indicated, scholars would long since have come to the conviction that Urd and the personal Hel are identical, if Gylfaginning and the text-books based thereon had not confounded the judgment, and that for the following reasons:

The name *Urdr* corresponds to the Old English *Vurd, Vyrd, Vird,* to the Old Low German *Wurth,* and to the Old High German *Wurt.* The fact that the word is found in the dialects of several Teutonic branches indicates, or is thought by the linguists to indicate, that it belongs to the most ancient Teutonic times, when it probably had the form *Vorthi.*

There can be no doubt that Urd also among other Teutonic branches than the Scandinavian has had the meaning of goddess of fate. Expressions handed down from the heathen time and preserved in Old English documents characterise Vyrd as tying the threads or weaving the web of fate (Cod. Ex., 355; Beowulf, 2420), and as the one who writes that which is to happen (Beowulf, 4836). Here the plural form is also employed, *Vyrde,* the urds, the norns, which demonstrates that she in England, as in the North, was conceived as having sisters or assistants. In the Old Low German poem "Heliand," Wurth's personality is equally plain.

But at the same time as *Vyrd, Wurth,* was the goddess of fate, she was also that of death. In Beowulf (4831, 4453) we find the parallel expressions:

him vas Vyrd ungemete nea1: Urd was exceedingly near ·
  to him;
vas deád ungemete nea1: deat1 was exceedingly near.

And in Heliand, 146, 2; 92, 2:

Thiu Wurt1 is at 1andun: Urd is near;
Dód is at 1endi: deat1 is near.

And there are also other expressions, as *Thiu Wurth
nâhida thus*: Urd (death) then approached; *Wurth ina
benam*: Urd (death) took him away (cp. J. Grimm,
Deutsche Myth., i. 373).

Thus Urd, the goddess of fate, was, among the Teutonic branches in Germany and England, identical with
death, conceived as a queen. So also in the North. The
norns made laws and chose life and *örlög* (fate) for the
children of time (Völuspa). The word *örlög* (Nom. Pl.;
the original meaning seems to be *urlagarne,* that is, the
original laws) frequently has a decided leaning to the
idea of death (cp. Völuspa: *Ek sá Baldri örlög fólgin*).
Hakon Jarl's *örlög* was that Kark cut his throat (Nj.,
156). To receive the "judgment of the norns" was identical with being doomed to die (Yng., Heimskringla, ch.
52). Fate and death were in the idea and in usage so
closely related, that they were blended into one personality in the mythology. The ruler of death was that one
who could resolve death; but the one who could determine the length of life, and so also could resolve death,
and the kind of death, was, of course, the goddess of fate.
They must blend into one.

In the ancient Norse documents we also find the name

him was Vyrd ungemete neah   Urd was exceedingly near
to him;
was dead ungemete neah   death was exceedingly near.

> Thiu Wurth is at handun: Urd is near;
> Dod is at hendi: death is near.

456

Urd used to designate death, just as in Heliand and Beowulf, and this, too, in such a manner that Urd's personal
character is not emphasised. Ynglingatal (Heimskr.,
ch. 44) calls Ingjald's manner of death his *Urdr,* and to
determine death for anyone was to *draga Urdr at* him.

Far down in the Christian centuries the memory survived that Urd was the goddess of the realm of death
and of death.   When a bright spot, which was called
Urd's moon, appeared on the wall it meant the breaking
out of an epidemic (Eyrbyggia Saga, 270).   Even as
late as the year 1237 Urd is supposed to have revealed
herself, the night before Christmas, to Snobjorn to predict a bloody conflict, and she then sang a song in which
she said that she went mournfully to the contest to choose
a man for death.   Saxo translates *Urdr* or *Hel* with
"Proserpina" (*Hist.,* i. 43).

64.

URD'S MAID-SERVANTS: (1) MAID-SERVANTS OF LIFE—
NORNS, DISES OF BIRTH, HAMINGJES, GIPTES,
FYLGIES; (2) MAID-SERVANTS OF DEATH—VAL-
KYRIES, THE PSYCHO-MESSENGERS OF DISEASES AND
ACCIDENTS.

As those beings for whom Urd determines birth, position in life, and death, are countless, so her servants, who
perform the tasks commanded by her as queen, must also
be innumerable.   They belong to two large classes: the
one class is active in her service in regard to life, the other
in regard to death.

Most intimately associated with her are her two sisters. With her they have the authority of judges. Compare Völuspa, 19, 20, and the expressions *norna dómr, norna kvidr.* And they dwell with her under the world-tree, which stands for ever green over her gold-clad fountain.

As maid-servants under Urd there are countless hamingjes (fylgjes) and giptes (also called gafes, audnes, heilles). The hamingjes are fostered among beings of giant-race (who hardly can be others than the norns and Mimer). Three mighty rivers fall down into the world, in which they have their origin, and they come wise in their hearts, soaring over the waters to our upper world (Vafthr., 48, 49). There every child of man is to have a hamingje as a companion and guardian spirit. The testimony of the Icelandic sagas of the middle ages in this regard are confirmed by phrases and forms of speech which have their root in heathendom. The hamingjes belong to that large circle of feminine beings which are called dises, and they seem to have been especially so styled. What Urd is on a grand scale as the guardian of the mighty Ygdrasil, this the hamingje is on a smaller scale when she protects the separate fruit produced on the world-tree and placed in her care. She does not appear to her favourite excepting perhaps in dreams or shortly before his death (the latter according to Helgakv. Hjörv. the prose; Njal, 62; Hallf, ch. 11; proofs from purely heathen records are wanting). In strophes which occur in Gisle Surson's saga, and which are attributed (though on doubtful grounds) to this heathen skald, the hero of the saga, but the origin of which (from a time when the details of the myth were still remembered) is fully confirmed by a careful criticism, it is mentioned how he stood between good and evil inspirations, and how the *draumkona* (dream-woman) of the good inspirations said to him in sleep: "Be not the first cause of a murder! excite not peaceful men against yourself!—promise me this, thou charitable man! Aid the blind, scorn not the lame, and insult not a Tyr robbed of his hand!" These are noble counsels, and that the hamingjes were noble beings was a belief preserved through the Christian centuries in Iceland, where, according to Vigfusson, the word *hamingja* is still used in the sense of Providence. They did not usually leave their favourite before death. But there are certain phrases preserved in the spoken language which show that they could leave him before death. He who was abandoned by his hamingje and gipte was a lost man. If the favourite became a hideous and bad man, then his *hamingja* and *gipta* might even turn her benevolence into wrath, and cause his well-deserved ruin. *Uvar 'ro disir,* angry at you are the dises! cries Odin to the royal nithing Geirrod, and immediately thereupon the latter stumbles and falls pierced by his own sword. That the invisible hamingje could cause one to stumble and fall is shown in Fornm., iii.

The *giptes* seem to have carried out such of Urd's resolves, on account of which the favourite received an unexpected, as it were accidental, good fortune.

Not only for separate individuals, but also for families and clans, there were guardian spirits (*kynfylgjur, ættarfylgjur*).

8 459

Another division of this class of maid-servants under Urd are those who attend the entrance of the child into the world, and who have to weave the threads of the new-born babe into the web of the families and events. Like Urd and her sisters, they too are called norns. If it is a child who is to be a great and famous man, Urd herself and her sisters may be present for the above purpose (see No. 30 in regard to Halfdan's birth).

A few strophes incorporated in Fafnersmal from a heathen didactic poem, now lost (Fafn., 12-15), speak of norns whose task it is to determine and assist the arrival of the child into this world. *Nornir, er naudgaunglar 'ro oc kjósa mædr frá maugum.* The expression *kjósa mædr frá maugum,* "to choose mothers from descendants," seems obscure, and can under all circumstances not mean simply "to deliver mothers of children." The word *kjósa* is never used in any other sense than to choose, elect, select. Here it must then mean to choose, elect as mothers; and the expression "from descendants" is incomprehensible, if we do not on the one hand conceive a crowd of eventual descendants, who at the threshold of life are waiting for mothers in order to become born into this world, and on the other hand women who are to be mothers, but in reference to whom it has not yet been determined which descendant each one is to call hers among the great waiting crowd, until those norns which we are here discussing resolve on that point, and *from* the indefinite crowd of waiting *megir* choose mothers *for* those children which are especially destined for them.

These norns are, according to Fafn., 13, of different

birth. Some are Asa-kinswomen, others of elf-race, and again others are daughters of Dvalin. In regard to the last-named it should be remembered that Dvalin, their father, through artists of his circle, decorated the citadel, within which a future generation of men await the regeneration of the world, and that the mythology has associated him intimately with the elf of the morning dawn, Delling, who guards the citadel of the race of regeneration against all that is evil and all that ought not to enter (see No. 53). There are reasons (see No. 95) for assuming that these dises of birth were Honer's maid-servants at the same time as they were Urd's, just as the valkyries are Urd's and Odin's maid-servants at the same time (see below).

To the other class of Urd's maid-servants belong those lower-world beings which execute her resolves of death, and conduct the souls of the dead to the lower world.

Foremost among the psycho-messengers (psycho-pomps), the attendants of the dead, we note that group of shield-maids called valkyries. As Odin and Freyja got the right of choosing on the battlefield, the valkyries have received Asgard as their abode. There they bring the mead-horns to the Asas and einherjes, when they do not ride on Valfather's errands (Völuspa, 31; Grimnersmal, 36; Eiriksm., 1; Ulf Ugges. Skaldsk., 238). But the third of the norns, Skuld, is the chief one in this group (Völuspa, 31), and, as shall be shown below, they for ever remain in the most intimate association with Urd and the lower world.

461

65.

ON THE COSMOGRAPHY. THE WAY OF THOSE FALLEN BY THE SWORD TO VALHAL IS THROUGH THE LOWER WORLD.

The modern conception of the removal of those fallen by the sword to Asgard is that the valkyries carried them immediately through blue space to the halls above. The heathens did not conceive the matter in this manner.

It is true that the mythological horses might carry their riders through the air without pressing a firm foundation with their hoofs. But such a mode of travel was not the rule, even among the gods, and, when it did happen, it attracted attention even among them. Compare Gylfaginning, i. 118, which quotes strophes from a heathen source. The bridge Bifrost would not have been built or established for the daily connection between Asgard and Urd's subterranean realm if it had been unnecessary in the mythological world of fancy. Mane's way in space would not have been regarded as a road in the concrete sense, that quakes and rattles when Thor's thunder-chariot passes over it (Haustl., Skaldsk., ch. 16), had it not been thought that Mane was safer on a firm road than without one of that sort. To every child that grew up in the homes of our heathen fathers the question must have lain near at hand, what such roads and bridges were for, if the gods had no advantage from them. The mythology had to be prepared for such questions, and in this, as in others cases, it had answers wherewith to satisfy that claim on causality and consistency which even the most naïve view of the world presents. The answer was: If the Bifrost bridge breaks under its riders, as is to happen in course of time, then their horses would have to *swim* in the sea of air (*Bilraust brotnar, er their á bru fara, oc svima i modo marir*—Fafn., 15., compare a strophe of Kormak, Kormak's Saga, p. 259, where the atmosphere is called the fjord of the gods, *Dia fjördr*). A horse does not swim as fast and easily as it runs. The different possibilities of travel are associated with different kinds of exertion and swiftness. The one method is more adequate to the purpose than the other. The solid connections which were used by the gods and which the mythology built in space are, accordingly, objects of advantage and convenience. The valkyries, riding at the head of their chosen heroes, as well as the gods, have found solid roads advantageous, and the course they took with their favourites was not the one presented in our mythological text-books. Grimnersmal (str. 21 ; see No. 93) informs us that the breadth of the atmospheric sea is too great and its currents too strong for those riding on their horses from the battlefield to wade across.

In the 45th chapter of Egil Skallagrimson's saga we read how Egil saved himself from men, whom King Erik Blood-axe sent in pursuit of him to Saud Isle. While they were searching for him there, he had stolen to the vicinity of the place where the boat lay in which those in pursuit had rowed across. Three warriors guarded the boat. Egil succeeded in surprising them, and in giving one of them his death-wound ere the latter was able to defend himself. The second fell in a duel on the strand. The third, who sprang into the boat to make it loose, fell there after an exchange of blows. The saga has preserved a strophe in which Egil mentions this exploit to his brother Thorolf and his friend Arinbjorn, whom he met after his flight from Saud Isle. There he says:

> at thrymreynis thjónar
> thrir nökkurrir Hlakkar,
> til hásalar Heljar
> helgengnir, för dvelja.

"Three of those who serve the tester of the valkyriedin (the warlike Erik Blood-axe) will late return; they have gone to the lower world, to Hel's high hall."

The fallen ones were king's men and warriors. They were slain by weapons and fell at their posts of duty, one from a sudden, unexpected wound, the others in open conflict. According to the conception of the mythological text-books, these sword-slain men should have beeen conducted by valkyries through the air to Valhal. But the skald Egil, who as a heathen born about the year 904, and who as a contemporary of the sons of Harald Fairhair must have known the mythological views of his fellow-heathen believers better than the people of our time, assures us positively that these men from King Erik's body-guard, instead of going immediately to Valhal, went to the lower world and to Hel's high hall there. He certainly would not have said anything of the sort, if those for whom he composed the strophe had not regarded this idea as both possible and correct.

The question now is: Does this Egil's statement stand

alone and is it in conflict with those other statements touching the same point which the ancient heathen records have preserved for us? The answer is, that in these ancient records there is not found a single passage in conflict with Egil's idea, but that they all, on the contrary, fully agree with his words, and that this harmony continues in the reports of the first Christian centuries in regard to this subject.

All the dead and also those fallen by the sword come first to Hel. Thence the sword-slain come to Asgard, if they have deserved this destiny.

In Gisle Surson's saga (ch. 24) is mentioned the custom of binding Hel-shoes on the feet of the dead. Warriors in regard to whom there was no doubt that Valhal was their final destiny received Hel-shoes like all others, *that er tidska at binda mönnum helskó, sem menn, skulo á ganga till Valhallar.* It would be impossible to explain this custom if it had not been believed that those who were chosen for the joys of Valhal were obliged, like all others, to travel *á Helvegum.* Wherever this custom prevailed, Egil's view in regard to the fate which immediately awaited sword-fallen men was general.

When Hermod betook himself to the lower world to find Balder he came, as we know, to the golden bridge across the river *Gjöll.* Urd's maid-servant, who watches the bridge, mentioned to him that the day before five *fylki* of dead men had rode across the same bridge. Consequently all these dead are on horseback and they do not come separately or a few at a time, but in large troops called *fylki,* an expression which, in the Icelandic litera-

465

ture, denotes larger or smaller divisions of an army—legions, cohorts, maniples or companies in battle array; and with *fylki* the verb *fylkja*, to form an army or a division of an army in line of battle, is most intimately connected. This indicates with sufficient clearness that the dead here in question are men who have fallen on the field of battle and are on their way to Hel, each one riding, in company with his fallen brothers in arms, with those who belonged to his own *fylki*. The account presupposes that men fallen by the sword, whose final destination is Asgard, first have to ride down to the lower world. Else we would not find these *fylkes* on a Helway galloping across a subterranean bridge, into the same realm as had received Balder and Nanna after death.

It has already been pointed out that Bifrost is the only connecting link between Asgard and the lower regions of the universe. The air was regarded as an ether sea which the bridge spanned, and although the horses of mythology were able to swim in this sea, the solid connection was of the greatest importance. The gods used the bridge every day (Grimnismal, Gylfaginning). Frost giants and mountain-giants are anxious to get possession of it, for it is the key to Asgard. It therefore has its special watchman in the keen-eyed and vigilant Heimdal. When in Ragnarok the gods ride to the last conflict they pass over Bifrost (Fafnersmal). The bridge does not lead to Midgard. Its lower ends were not conceived as situated among mortal men. It stood outside and below the edge of the earth's crust both in the north and in the south. In the south it descended to Urd's fountain and to the thingstead of the gods in the lower world (see the accompanying drawing, intended to make these facts intelligible). From this mythological topographical arrangement it follows of necessity that the valkyries at the head of the chosen slain must take their course through the lower world, by the way of Urd's fountain and the thingstead of the gods, if they are to ride on Bifrost bridge to Asgard, and not be obliged to betake themselves thither on swimming horses.

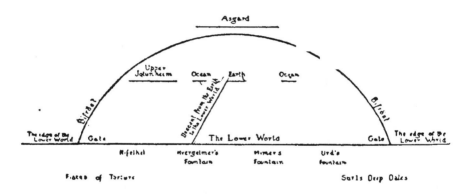

There are still two poems extant from the heathen time, which describe the reception of sword-fallen kings in Valhal. The one describes the reception of Erik Blood-axe, the other that of Hakon the Good.

When King Erik, with five other kings and their attendants of fallen warriors, come riding up thither, the gods hear on their approach a mighty din, as if the foundations of Asgard trembled. All the benches of Valhal quake and tremble. What single probability can we now conceive as to what the skald presupposed? Did he suppose that the chosen heroes came on horses that swim in the air, and that the movements of the horses in this element produced a noise that made Valhal tremble? Or that it is Bifrost which thunders under the hoofs of hundreds of horses, and quakes beneath their weight? There is scarcely need of an answer to this alternative. Meanwhile the skald himself gives the answer. For the skald makes Brage say that from the din and quaking it might be presumed that it was Balder who was returning to the halls of the gods. Balder dwells in the lower world; the connection between Asgard and the lower world is Bifrost: this connection is of such a nature that it quakes and trembles beneath the weight of horses and riders, and it is predicted in regard to Bifrost that in Ragnarok it shall break under the weight of the host of riders. Thus Brage's words show that it is Bifrost from which the noise is heard when Erik and his men ride up to Valhal. But to get to the southern end of Bifrost, Erik and his riders must have journeyed in Hel, across Gjoll, and past the thingstead of the gods near Urd's well. Thus it is by this road that the psychopomps of the heroes conduct their favourites to their final destination.

In his grand poem "Hákonármal," Eyvind Skaldaspiller makes Odin send the valkyries Gandul and Skagul "to choose among the kings of Yngve's race some who are to come to Odin and abide in Valhal." It is not said by which road the two valkyries betake themselves to Midgard, but when they have arrived there they find that a battle is imminent between the Yngve descendants, Hakon the Good, and the sons of Erik. Hakon is just putting on his coat-of-mail, and immediately thereupon begins the brilliantly-described battle. The sons of Erik are put to flight, but the victor Hakon is wounded by an arrow, and after the end of the battle he sits on the battlefield, surrounded by his heroes, "with shields cut by swords and with byrnies pierced by arrows." Gandul and Ska-gul, "maids on horseback, with wisdom in their countenances, with helmets on their heads, and with shields before them," are near the king. The latter hears that Gandul, "leaning on her spear," says to Skagul that the wound is to cause the king's death, and now a conversation begins between Hakon and Skagul, who confirms what Gandul has said, and does so with the following words :

> Rida vit nú skulum,
> kvad hin rika Skagul,
> græna 1eima goda
> Odni at segja,
> at un mun allvaldr koma
> á 1ann sjálfan at sjá.

"We two (Gandul and Skagul) shall now, quoth the mighty Skagul, *ride o'er green realms* (or worlds) *of the gods* in order to say to Odin that now a great king is coming to see him."

Here we get definite information in regard to whic1 way the valkyries journey between Asgard and Midgard. The fields through which the road goes, and which are beaten by the hoofs of their horses, are *green realms of the gods* (worlds, *heimar*).

With these green realms Eyvind has not meant the

469

blue ether.   He distinguishes between blue and green.
The sea he calls blue (*blámœr*—see Heimskringla).
What he expressly states, and to which we must confine
ourselves, is that, according to his cosmological conception and that of his heathen fellow-believers, there were
realms clothed in green and inhabited by divinities on the
route the valkyries had to take when they from a battle-
field in Midgard betook themselves back to Valhal and
Asgard.   But as valkyries and the elect ride on Bifrost
up to Valhal, Bifrost, which goes down to Urd's well,
must be the connecting link between the realms decked
with green and Asgard.   The *grœnar heimar* through
which the valkyries have to pass are therefore the realms
of the lower world.

Among the realms or "worlds" which constituted the
mythological universe, the realms of bliss in the lower
world were those which might particularly be characterised as the green.   Their groves and blooming meadows
and fields of waving grain were never touched by decay
or frost, and as such they were cherished by the popular
fancy for centuries after the introduction of Christianity.
The Low German language has also rescued the memory
thereof in the 'expression *gróni godes wang* (Hel., 94,
24).   That the green realms of the lower world are called
realms of the gods is also proper, for they have contained
and do contain many beings of a higher or lower divine
rank.   There dwells the divine mother Nat, worshipped
by the Teutons; there Thor's mother and her brother and
sister Njord and Fulla are fostered; there Balder, Nanna,
and *Hödr* are to dwell until Ragnarok; there Delling,

Billing, Rind, Dag, Mane, and Sol, and all the clan of
artists gathered around Mimer, they who "smithy" living beings, vegetation, and ornaments, have their halls;
there was born Odin's son Vale. Of the mythological
divinities, only a small number were fostered in Asgard.
When Gandul and Skagul at the head of sword-fallen
men ride "o'er the green worlds of the gods," this agrees
with the statement in the myth about Hermod's journey to
Hel, that "fylkes" of dead riders gallop over the subterranean gold-bridge, on the other side of which glorious regions are situated, and with the statement in Vegtamskvida that Odin, when he had left Nifelhel behind
him, came to a *foldvegr,* a way over green plains, by
which he reaches the hall that awaits Balder.

In the heroic songs of the Elder Edda, and in other
poems from the centuries immediately succeeding the introduction of Christianity, the memory survives that the
heroes journey to the lower world. Sigurd Fafners-
bane comes to Hel. Of one of Atle's brothers who fell
by Gudrun's sword it is said, *i Helju hon thana hafdi*
(Atlam., 51). In the same poem, strophe 54, one of
the Niflungs says of a sword-fallen foe that they had
him *lamdan til Heljar.*

The mythic tradition is supported by linguistic usage,
which, in such phrases as *berja i Hel, drepa i Hel, drepa
til Heljar, færa til Heljar,* indicated that those fallen by
the sword also had to descend to the realm of death.

The memory of valkyries, subordinate to the goddess
of fate and death, and belonging with her to the class of
norns, continued to flourish in Christian times both among

Anglo-Saxons and Scandinavians. Among the former *välcyrge, välcyrre* (valkyrie) could be used to express the Latin *parca,* and in Beowulf occur phrases in which *Hild* and *Gud* (the valkyries *Hildr* and *Gunnr*) perform the tasks of *Vyrd*. In Atlamal (28), the valkyries are changed into "dead women," inhabitants of the lower world, who came to choose the hero and invite him to their halls. The basis of the transformation is the recollection that the valkyries were not only in Odin's service, but also in that of the lower world goddess Urd (compare Atlamal, 16, where they are called norns), and that they as psychopomps conducted the chosen Heroes to Hel on their way to Asgard.

66.

THE CHOOSING. THE MIDDLE-AGE FABLE ABOUT "RIST-
ING WITH THE SPEAR-POINT."

If death on the battle-field, or as the result of wounds received on the field of battle, had been regarded as an inevitable condition for the admittance of the dead into Asgard, and for the honour of sitting at Odin's table, then the choosing would under all circumstances have been regarded as a favour from Odin. But this was by no means the case, nor could it be so when regarded from a psychological point of view (see above, No. 61). The poems mentioned above, "Eiriksmál" and "Hakonarmal," give us examples of choosing from a standpoint quite different from that of favour. When one of the einherjes, Sigmund, learns from Odin that Erik Blood-axe has fallen and is expected in Valhal, he asks why Odin robbed Erik of victory and life, *although* he, Erik, possessed Odin's friendship. From Odin's answer to the question we learn that the skald did not wish to make Sigmund express any surprise that a king, whom Odin loves above other kings and heroes, has died in a lost instead of a won battle. What Sigmund emphasises is, that Odin did not rather take unto himself a less loved king than the so highly appreciated Erik, and permit the latter to conquer and live. Odin's answer is that he is hourly expecting Ragnarok, and that he therefore made haste to secure as soon as possible so valiant a hero as Erik among his einherjes. But Odin does not say that he feared that he might have to relinquish the hero for ever, in case the latter, not being chosen on this battle-field, should be snatched away by some other death than that by the sword.

Hakonarmal gives us an example of a king who is chosen in a battle in which he is the victor. As conqueror the wounded Hakon remained on the battlefield; still he looks upon the choosing as a disfavour. When he had learned from Gandul's words to Skagul that the number of the einherjes is to be increased with him, he blames the valkyries for dispensing to him this fate, and says he had deserved a better lot from the gods (*várun thó verdir gagns frá godum*). When he enters Valhal he has a keener reproach on his lips to the welcoming Odin: *illúdigr mjók thykkir oss Odinn vera, sjám ver hans of hugi*.

473

Doubtless it was for our ancestors a glorious prospect to be permitted to come to Odin after death, and a person who saw inevitable death before his eyes might comfort himself with the thought of soon seeing "the benches of Balder's father decked for the feast" (Ragnar's death-song). But it is no less certain from all the evidences we have from the heathen time, that honourable life was preferred to honourable death, although between the wars there was a chance of death from sickness. Under these circumstances, the mythical eschatology could not have made death from disease an insurmountable obstacle for warriors and heroes on their way to Valhal. In the ancient records there is not the faintest allusion to such an idea. It is too absurd to have existed. It would have robbed Valhal of many of Midgard's most brilliant heroes, and it would have demanded from faithful believers that they should prefer death even with defeat to victory and life, since the latter lot was coupled with the possibility of death from disease. With such a view no army goes to battle, and no warlike race endowed with normal instincts has ever entertained it and given it expression in their doctrine in regard to future life.

The absurdity of the theory is so manifest that the mythologists who have entertained it have found it necessary to find some way of making it less inadmissible than it really is. They have suggested that Odin did not necessarily fail to get those heroes whom sickness and age threatened with a straw-death, nor did they need to relinquish the joys of Valhal, for there remained to them an expedient to which they under such circumstances resorted: they risted (marked, scratched) themselves with the spear-point (*marka sik geirs-oddi*).

If there was such a custom, we may conceive it as springing from a sacredness attending a voluntary death as a sacrifice—a sacredness which in all ages has been more or less alluring to religious minds. But all the descriptions we have from Latin records in regard to Teutonic customs, all our own ancient records from heathen times, all Northern and German heroic songs, are unanimously and stubbornly silent about the existence of the supposed custom of "risting with the spear-point," although, if it ever existed, it would have been just such a thing as would on the one hand be noticed by·strangers, and on the other hand be remembered, at least for a time, by the generations converted to Christianity. But the well-informed persons interviewed by Tacitus, they who presented so many characteristic traits of the Teutons, knew nothing of such a practice; otherwise they certainly would have mentioned it as something very remarkable and peculiar to the Teutons. None of the later classical Latin or middle age Latin records which have made contributions to our knowledge of the Teutons have a single word to say about it; nor the heroic poems. The Scandinavian records, and the more or less historical sagas, tell of many heathen kings, chiefs, and warriors who have died on a bed of straw, but not of a single one who "risted himself with the spear-point." The fable about this "risting with the spear-point" has its origin in Ynglingasaga, ch. 10, where Odin, changed to a king in Svithiod, is said, when death was approaching, to have let *marka sik geirs-oddi*. Out of this statement has been constructed a custom among kings and heroes of anticipating a straw-death by "risting with the spear-point," and this for the purpose of getting admittance to Valhal. Vigfusson (Dictionary) has already pointed out the fact that the author of Ynglingasaga had no other authority for his statement than the passage in Havamál, where Odin relates that he wounded with a spear, hungering and thirsting, voluntarily inflicted on himself pain, which moved Bestla's brother to give him runes and a drink from the fountain of wisdom. The fable about the spear-point risting, and its purpose, is therefore quite unlike the source from which, through ignorance and random writing, it sprang.

67.

THE PSYCHO-MESSENGERS OF THOSE NOT FALLEN BY THE SWORD. LOKE'S DAUGHTER (PSEUDO-HEL IN GYLFAGINNING) IDENTICAL WITH LEIKIN.

The psychopomps of those fallen by the sword are, as we have seen, stately dises, sitting high in the saddle, with helmet, shield, and spear. To those not destined to fall by the sword Urd sends other maid-servants, who, like the former, may come on horseback, and who, as it appears, are of very different appearance, varying in accordance with the manner of death of those persons whose departure they attend. She who comes to those who sink beneath the weight of years has been conceived as a very benevolent dis, to judge from the solitary passage where she is ciaracterised, that is in Ynglingatal and in Ynglingasaga, ch. 49, wiere it is said of the aged and just king Halfdan Whiteleg, that ie was taken hence by the woman, who is helpful to those bowed and stooping (*hallvarps hlífinauma*). Tie burden which Elli (age), Utgard-Loke's foster-mother (Gylfag., 47), puts on men, and which gradually gets too heavy for them to bear, is removed by this kind-hearted dis.

Other psychopomps are of a terrible kind. The most of them belong to tie spirits of disease dwelling in Nifel-hel (see No. 60). King Vanlande is tortured to death by a being whose epithet, *vitta vættr* and *trollkund*, shows tiat she belongs to the same group as *Heidr,* the prototype of witches, and who is contrasted with the valkyrie Hild by the appellation *ljóna lids bága Grim-hildr* (Yngl., ch. 16). The same *vitta vættr* came to King Adils when his horse fell and he himself struck his head against a stone (Yngl., ch. 33). Two kings, who die on a bed of straw, are mentioned in Ynglingasaga's Thjodolf-strophes (ch. 20 and 52) as visited by a being called in the one instance Loke's kinswoman (*Loka mær*), and in the other Hvedrung's kinswoman (*Hved-rungs mær*). That this Loke's kinswoman has no au-thority to determine life and death, but only carries out the dispensations of the norns, is definitely stated in the Thjodolf-strophe (ch. 52), and also that her activity, as one who brings the invitation to the realm of deati, does not imply that the person invited is to be counted among the damned, although she herself, the kinswoman of Loke, the daughter of Loke, surely does not belong to the regions of bliss.

Ok til tlings
thridja jöfri
hvedrungs mær
or heimi baud,
thá er Hálfdan,
sa er á Holti bjó
norna dóms
um notit lafdi.

As *all* the dead, whether they are destined for Valhal
or for Hel (in the sense of the subterranean realms of
bliss), or for Nifelhel, must first report themselves in
Hel, their psychopomps, whether they dwell in Valhal,
Hel, or Nifelhel, must do the same. This arrangement
is necessary also from the point of view that the unhappy who "die from Hel into Nifelhel" (Grimnersmal)
must have attendants who conduct them from the realms
of bliss to the Na-gates, and thence to the realms of torture. Those dead from disease, who have the subterranean kinswoman of Loke as a guide, may be destined
for the realms of bliss—then she delivers them there; or
be destined for Nifelhel—then they die under her care
and are brought by her through the Na-gates to the
worlds of torture in Nifelhel.

Far down in Christian times the participle *leikinn* was
used in a manner which points to something mythical as
the original reason for its application. In Biskupas.
(i. 464) it is said of a man that he was *leikinn* by some
magic being (*flagd*). Of another person who sought
solitude and talked with himself, it is said in Eyrbyggja
(270) that he was believed to be *leikinn*. Ynglingatal
gives us the mythical explanation of this word.

478

In its strophe about King Dyggve, who died from disease, this poem says (Yngling., cı. 20) tıat, as the lower world dis had chosen him, Loke's kinswoman came and made him *leikinn* (*Allvald Yngva thjodar Loka mær um leikinn hefir*). The person who became *leikinn* is accordingly visited by Loke's kinswoman, or, if others have had the same task to perform, by some being who resembled her, and who brought psychical or physical disease.

In our mythical records there is mention made of a giantess whose very name, *Leikin, Leikn,* is immediately connected with that activity which Loke's kinswoman— and she too is a giantess—exercises when she makes a person *leikinn*. Of this personal *Leikin* we get the following information in our old records:

1. She is, as stated, of giant race (Younger Edda, i. 552).

2. She has once fared badly at Thor's hands. He broke her leg (*Leggi brauzt thu Leiknar*—Skaldsk., ch. 4, after a song by Vetrlidi).

3. She is *kveldrida*. The original and mythological meaning of *kveldrida* is a horsewoman of torture or death (from *kvelja,* to torture, to kill). The meaning, a horsewoman of the night, is a misunderstanding. Compare Vigfusson's Dict., *sub voce* "Kveld."

4. The horse which this woman of torture and death rides is black, untamed, difficult to manage (*styggr*), and ugly-grown (*ljótvaxinn*). It drinks human blood, and is accompanied by other horses belonging to Leikin, black and bloodthirsty like it. (All this is stated by Hallfred

479

Vandradaskald.)* Perhaps these loose horses are intended for those persons whom the horsewomen of torture causes to die from disease, and whom she is to conduct to the lower world.

Popular traditions have preserved for our times the remembrance of the "ugly-grown" horse, that is, of a three-legged horse, which on its appearance brings sickness, epidemics, and plagues. The Danish popular belief (Thiele i. 137, 138) knows this monster and the word Hel-horse has been preserved in the vocabulary of the Danish language. The diseases brought by the Hel-horse are extremely dangerous, but not always fatal. When they are not fatal the convalescent is regarded as having ransomed his life with that tribute of loss of strength and of torture which the disease caused him, and in a symbolic sense he has then "given death a bushel of oats" (that is, to its horse). According to popular belief in Slesvik (Arnkiel, i. 55; cp. J. Grimm, *Deutsche Myth,* 804), Hel rides in the time of a plague on a three-legged horse and kills people. Thus the ugly-grown horse is not forgotten in traditions from the heathen time.

Völuspa inform us that in the primal age of man, the sorceress Heid went from house to house and was a welcome guest with evil women, since she *seid Leikin* (*sida* means to practise sorcery). Now, as Leikin is the "horse-woman of torture and death," and rides the Hel-horse, then the expression *sida Leikin* can mean nothing else

---

*Tidhöggvit lét tiggi
Tryggvar sonr fyrir styggvan
Leiknar hest á leiti
ljotvaxinn hræ Saxa.*

*Vinhrödigr gaf vida
visi margra Frisa
blökku brúnt at derkka
blöd kvellridu stódi.*

480

than by sorcery to send Leikin, the messenger of disease and death, to those persons who are the victims of the evil wishes of "evil women;" or, more abstractly, to bring by sorcery dangerous diseases to men.*

From all this follows that Leikin is either a side-figure to the daughter of Loke, and like her in all respects, or she and the Loke-daughter are one and the same person. To determine the question whether they are identical, we must observe (1) the definitely representative manner in which Völuspa, by the use of the name Leikin, makes the possessor of this name a mythic person, who visits men with diseases and death; (2) the manner in which Ynglingatal characterises the activity of Loke's daughter with a person doomed to die from disease; sie makes him *leikinn,* an expression which, without doubt, is in its sense connected with the feminine name Leikn, and which was preserved in the vernacular far down in Christian times, and there designated a supernatural visitation bringing the symptoms of mental or physical illness; (3)

---

*Völuspa 23, Cod. Reg., says of Heid :
> *seid hon kuni,*
> *seid hon Leikin.*

The letter *u* is in this manuscript used for both *u* and *y* (compare Bugge, Sæmund Edd., Preface x., xi.), and hence *kuni* may be read both *kuni* and *kyni.* The latter reading makes logical sense. *Kyni* is dative of *kyn,* a neuter noun, meaning something sorcerous, supernatural, a monster. *Kynjamein* and *kynjasott* mean diseases brought on by sorcery. *Seid* in both the above lines is past tense of the verb *sida,* and not in either one of them the noun *seidr.*

There was a sacred sorcery and an unholy one, according to the purpose for which it was practised, and according to the attending ceremonies. The object of the holy sorcery was to bring about something good either for the sorcerer or for others, or to find out the will of the gods and future things. The sorcery practised by *Heidr* is the unholy one, hated by the gods, and again and again forbidden in the laws, and this kind of sorcery is designated in Voluspa by the term *sida kyni* Of a thing practised with improper means it is said that it is not *kynja-lauss,* kyn-free.

The reading in Cod. Hauk., *seid hon hvars hon kunni, seid hon hugleikin,* evidently has some "emendator" to thank for its existence who did not understand the passage and wished to substitute something easily understood for the obscure lines he thought he had found.

the Christian popular tradition in which the deformed and disease-bringing horse, which Leikin rides in the myth, is represented as the steed of "death" or "Hel;" (4) that change of meaning by which the name Hel, which in the mythical poems of the Elder Edda designates the whole heathen realm of death, and especially its regions of bliss, or their queen, got to mean the abode of torture and misery and its ruler—a transmutation by which the name Hel, as in Gylfaginning and in the Slesvik traditions, was transferred from Urd to Loke's daughter.

Finally, it should be observed that it is told of Leikin, as of Loke's daughter, that she once fared badly at the hands of the gods, who did not, however, take her life. Loke's daughter is not slain, but is cast into Nifelhel (Gylfaginning, ch. 34). From that time she is *gnúpleit* —that is to say, she has a stooping form, as if her bones had been broken and were unable to keep her in an upright position. Leikin is not slain, but gets her legs broken.

All that we learn of Leikin thus points to the Lokemaid, the Hel, not of the **myth,** but of Christian tradition.

68.

THE WAY TO HADES COMMON TO THE DEAD.

It has already been demonstrated that all the dead must go to Hel—not only they whose destination is the realm of bliss, but also those who are to dwell in Asgard or in the regions of torture in Nifelheim. Thus the dead tread at the outset the same road. One and the same route is prescribed to them all, and the same Helgate daily opens for hosts of souls destined for different lots. Women and children, men and the aged, they who have practised the arts of peace and they who have stained the weapons with blood, those who have lived in accordance with the sacred commandments of the norns and gods and they who have broken them—all have to journey the same way as Balder went before them, down to the fields of the fountains of the world. They come on foot and on horseback—nay, even in chariots, if we may believe *Helreid Brynhildar,* a very unreliable source— guided by various psychopomps: the beautifully equipped valkyries, the blue-white daughter of Loke, the sombre spirits of disease, and the gentle maid-servant of old age. Possibly the souls of children had their special psycho- pomps. Traditions of mythic origin seem to suggest this; but the fragments of the myths themselves preserved to our time give us no information on this subject.

The Hel-gate here in question was situated below the eastern horizon of the earth. When Thor threatens to kill Loke he says (Lokas., 59) that he will send him *á austrvega.* When the author of the Sol-song sees the sunset for the last time, he hears in the opposite dircetion—that is, in the east—the Hel-gate grating dismally on its hinges (str. 39). The gate has a watchman and a key. The key is called *gillingr, gyllingr* (Younger Edda, ii. 494); and hence a skald who celebrates his ancestors in his songs, and thus recalls to those living the shades of those in Hades, may say that he brings to the light of day the tribute paid to Gilling (*yppa gillings gjöldum*. See Eyvind's strophe, Younger Edda, i. 248. The paraphrase has hitherto been misunderstood, on account of the pseudo-myth *Bragarædur* about the mead.) From the gate the highway of the dead went below the earth in a westerly direction through deep and dark dales (Gylfag., ch. 52), and it required several days—for Hermod nine days and nights—before they came to light regions and to the golden bridge across the river Gjoll, flowing from north to south (see No. 59). On the other side of the river the roads forked. One road went directly north. This led to Balder's abode (Gylfag., ch. 52) ; in other words, to Mimer's realm, to Mimer's grove, and to the sacred citadel of the *ásmegir*, where death and decay cannot enter (see No. 53). This northern road was not, therefore, the road common to all the dead. Another road went to the south. As Urd's realm is situated south of Mimer's (see Nos. 59, 63), this second road must have led to Urd's fountain and to the thingstead of the gods there. From the Sun-song we learn that the departed had to continue their journey by that road. The deceased skald of the Sun-song came to the norns, that is to say, to Urd and her sisters, after he had left this road behind him, and he sat for nine days and nights *á norna stoli* before he was permitted to continue his journey (str. 51). Here, then, is the end of the road common to all, and right here, at Urd's fountain and at the thingstead of the gods something must happen, on which account the dead are divided into different groups, some

destined for Asgard, others for the subterranean regions
of bliss, and a third lot for Nifelhel's regions of torture.
We shall now see whether the mythic fragments preserved to our time contain any suggestions as to what
occurs in this connection. It must be admitted that this
dividing must take place somewhere in the lower world,
that it was done on the basis of the laws which in mythological ethics distinguish between right and wrong, innocence and guilt, that which is pardonable and that
which is unpardonable, and that the happiness and unhappiness of the dead is determined by this division

69.

THE TWO THINGSTEADS OF THE ASAS. THE EXTENT OF
THE AUTHORITY OF THE ASAS AND OF THE DIS OF
FATE. THE DOOM OF THE DEAD.

The Asas have two thingsteads: the one in Asgard, the
other in the lower world.

In the former a council is held and resolutions passed
in such matters as pertain more particularly to the clan
of the Asas and to their relation to other divine clans and
other powers. When Balder is visited by ugly dreams,
Valfather assembles the gods to hold counsel, and all the
Asas assemble *á thingi,* and all the asynjes *á máli* (Vegtamskv., 1; Balder's Dr., 4). In assemblies here the
gods resolved to exact an oath from all things for Balder's safety, and to send a messenger to the lower world
to get knowledge partly about Balder, partly about future events. On this thingstead efforts are made of

reconciliation between the Asas and the Vans, after Gulveig had been slain in Odin's hall (Völuspa, 23, 24). Hither (á thing goda) comes Thor with the kettle captured from Hymer, and intended for the feasts of the gods (Hymerskv., 39) ; and here the Asas hold their last deliberations, when Ragnarok is at hand (Völuspa, 49: *Æsir 'ro a thingi*). No matters are mentioned as discussed in this thingstead in which any person is interested who does not dwell in Asgard, or which are not of such a nature that they have reference to how the gods themselves are to act under particular circumstances. That the thingstead where such questions are discussed must be situated in Asgard itself is a matter of convenience, and is suggested by the very nature of the case.

It follows that the gods assemble in the Asgard thingstead more for the purpose of discussing their own interests than for that of judging in the affairs of others. They also gather there to amuse themselves and to exercise themselves in arms (Gylfaginning, 50).

Of the other thingstead of the Asas, of the one in the lower world, it is on the other hand expressly stated that they go thither to sit in judgment, to act as judges; and there is no reason for taking this word *dœma,* when as here it means activity at a thingstead, in any other than its judicial and common sense.

What matters are settled there? We might take this to be the proper place for exercising Odin's privilege of choosing heroes to be slain by the sword, since this right is co-ordinate with that of the norns to determine life and dispense fate, whence it might seem that the domain of the

486

authority of the gods and that of the norns here approached each other sufficiently to require deliberations and decisions in common. Still it is not on the thingstead at Urd's fountain that Odin elects persons for death by the sword. It is expressly stated that it is in his own home in Valhal that Odin exercises his right of electing (Grimnersmal, 8), and this right he holds so independently and so absolutely that he does not need to ask for the opinion of the norns. On the other hand, the gods have no authority to determine the life and death of the other mortals. This belongs exclusively to the norns. The norns elect for every other death but that by weapons, and their decision in this domain is never called a decision by the gods, but *norna domr, norna kvidr, freigdar ord, Dauda ord.*

If Asas and norns did have a common voice in deciding certain questions which *could* be settled in Asgard, then it would not be in accordance with the high rank given to the Asas in mythology to have them go to the norns for the decision of such questions. On the contrary, the norns would have to come to them. Urd and her sisters are beings of high rank, but nevertheless they are of giant descent, like Mimer. The power they have is immense; and on a closer investigation we find how the mythology in more than one way has sought to maintain in the fancy of its believers the independence (at least apparent and well defined, within certain limits) of the gods—an independence united with the high rank which they have. It may have been for this very reason that the youngest of the dises of fate, Skuld, was selected as a valkyrie, and as a maid-servant both of Odin and of her sister Urd.

Tıe questions in which the Asas are judges near Urd's fountain must be such as *cannot* be settled in Asgard, as tıe lower world is their proper forum, where both the parties concerned and the witnesses are to be found. Tıe questions are of great importance. This is evident already from the fact that the journey to the thingstead is a troublesome one for the gods, at least for Thor, who, to get thither, must wade across four rivers. Moreover, the questions are of such a character that they occur every day (Grimnersmal, 29, 31).

At this point of the investigation the results hitherto gained from the various premises unite themselves in the following manner

The Asas *daily* go to the thingstead near Urd's fountain. At the thingstead near Urd's fountain there *daily* arrive hosts of the dead.

The task of the Asas near Urd's fountain is to judge in questions of which the lower world is the proper forum. When the dead arrive at Urd's fountain their final doom is not yet sealed. They have not yet been separated into the groups which are to be divided between Asgard, Hel, and Nifelhel.

The question now is, Can we conceive that the daily journey of the Asas to Urd's fountain and the daily arrival there of the dead have no connection with each other?—That the judgments daily pronounced by the Asas at this thingstead, and that the daily event in accordance with which the dead at this thingstead are di-

vided between the realms of bliss and those of torture
have nothing in common?

That these mythological facts should have no connection with each other is hard to conceive for anyone who,
in doubtful questions, clings to that which is probable
rather than to the opposite. The probability becomes a
certainty by the following circumstances:

Of the kings Vanlande and Halfdan, Ynglingatal says
that after death they met Odin. According to the common view presented in our mythological text-books, this
should not have happened to either of them, since both of
them died from disease. One of them was visited and
fetched by that choking spirit of disease called *vitta vættr*,
and in this way he was permitted "to meet Odin" (*kom
a vit Vilja brodur*). The other was visited by *Hvedrungs
mær*, the daughter of Loke, who "called him from this
world to Odin's Thing."

> Ok til things
> thridja jöfri
> Hvedrungs mær
> or heimi baud.

Thing-bod means a legal summons to appear at a Thing,
at the seat of judgment. *Bjoda til things* is to perform
this legal summons. Here it is Hvedrung's kinswoman
who comes with sickness and death and *thing-bod* to King
Halfdan, and summons him to appear before the judgment-seat of Odin. As, according to mythology, all the
dead, and as, according to the mythological text-books,
at least all those who have died from disease must go to
Hel, then certainly King Halfdan, who died from dis-

ease, must descend to the lower world; and as there is a Thing at which Odin and the Asas daily sit in judgment, it must have been this to which Halfdan was summoned. Otherwise we would be obliged to assume that Hvedrung's kinswoman, Loke's daughter, is a messenger, not from the lower world and Urd, but from Asgard, although the strophe further on expressly states that she comes to Halfdan on account of "the doom of the norns;" and furthermore we would be obliged to assume that the king, who had died from sickness, after arriving in the lower world, did not present himself at Odin's court there, but continued his journey to Asgard, to appear at some of the accidental deliberations which are held at the thingstead there. The passage proves that at least those who have died from sickness have to appear at the court which is held by Odin in the lower world.

70.

THE DOOM OF THE DEAD (*continued*). SPEECH-RUNES
ORDS TÍRR NÁMÆLI.

In Sigrdrifumal (str. 12) we read:

Málrunar skaltu kunna,
vilt-ar magni ther
heiptom gjaldi harm;
thær um vindr,
thær um vefr,
thær um setr allat saman
a thvi thingi,
er thjothir scolo
i fulla doma fara.

"Speech-runes you must know, if you do not wish that the strong one with consuming woe shall requite you for the injury you have caused. All those runes you must wind, weave, and place together in that Thing where the host of people go into the full judgments."

In order to make the significance of this passage clear, it is necessary to explain the meaning of speech-runes or mal-runes.

Several kinds of runes are mentioned in Sigrdrifumal, all of a magic and wonderful kind. Among them are mal-runes (speech-runes). They have their name from the fact that they are able to restore to a tongue mute or silenced in death the power to *mæla* (speak). Odin employs mal-runes when he rists *i runom,* so that a corpse from the gallows comes and *mælir* with him (Havam., 157). According to Saxo (i. 38), Hadding places a piece of wood risted with runes under the tongue of a dead man. The latter then recovers consciousness and the power of speech, and sings a terrible song. This is a reference to mal-runes. In Gudrunarkvida (i.) it is mentioned how Gudrun, mute and almost lifeless (*hon gordiz at deyja*), sat near Sigurd's dead body. One of the kinswomen present lifts the napkin off from Sigurd's head. By the sight of the features of the loved one Gudrun awakens again to life, bursts into tears, and is able to speak. The evil Brynhild then curses the being (*vettr*) which "gave mal-runes to Gudrun," that is to say, freed her tongue, until then sealed as in death.

Those who are able to apply these mighty runes are very few. Odin boasts that he knows them. Sigrdrifva, who also is skilled in them, is a dis, not a daughter of man. The runes which Hadding applied were risted by Hardgrep, a giantess who protected him. But within the court here in question men come in great numbers (*thjódir*), and among them there must be but a small number who have penetrated so deeply into the secret knowledge of runes. For those who have done so it is of importance and advantage. For by them they are able to defend themselves against complaints, the purpose of which is "to requite with consuming woe the harm they have done." In the court they are able to *mæla* (speak) in their own defence.

Thus it follows that those hosts of people who enter this thingstead stand there with speechless tongues. They are and remain mute before their judges unless they know the mal-runes which are able to loosen the fetters of their tongues. Of the dead man's tongue it is said in Solarljod (44) that it is *til trés metin ok kolnat alt fyr utan.*

The sorrow or harm one has caused is requited in this Thing by *heiptir,* unless the accused is able—thanks to the mal-runes—to speak and give reasons in his defence. In Havamál (151) the word *heiptir* has the meaning of something supernatural and magical. It has a similar meaning here, as Vigfusson has already pointed out. The magical mal-runes, wound, woven, and placed together, form as it were a garb of protection around the defendant against the magic *heiptir.* In the Havamál strophe mentioned the skald makes Odin paraphrase, or at least partly explain, the word *heiptir* with *mein,* which "eat" their victims. It is in the nature of the myth to regard such forces as personal beings. We have already seen the spirits of disease appear in this manner (see No. 60). The *heiptir* were also personified. They were the Erinnyes of the Teutonic mythology, armed with scourges of thorns (see below).

He who at the Thing particularly dispenses the law of requital is called *magni*. The word has a double meaning, which appears in the verb *magna,* which means both to make strong and to operate with supernatural means.

From all this it must be sufficiently plain that the Thing here referred to is not the Althing in Iceland or the Gulathing in Norway, or any other Thing held on the surface of the earth. The thingstead here discussed must be situated in one of the mythical realms, between which the earth was established. And it must be superhuman beings of higher or lower rank who there occupy the judgment-seats and requite the sins of men with *heiptir*. But in Asgard men do not enter with their tongues sealed in death. For the einherjes who are invited to the joys of Valhal there are no *heiptir* prepared. Inasmuch as the mythology gives us information about only two thingsteads where superhuman beings deliberate and judge— namely, the Thing in Asgard and the Thing near Urd's fountain—and inasmuch as it is, in fact, only in the latter that the gods act as judges, we are driven by all the evidences to the conclusion that Sigrdrifumal has described to us that very thingstead at which Hvedrung's kinswoman summoned King Halfdan to appear after death.

Sigrdrifumal, using the expression *á thvi,* sharply distinguished this thingstead or court from all others. The poem declares that it means *that* Thing where hosts of people go into *full* judgments. "Full" are those judgments against which no formal or real protests can be made—decisions which are irrevocably valid. The only kind of judgments of which the mythology speaks in this manner, that is, characterises as judgments that "never die," are those "over each one dead."

This brings us to the well-known and frequently-quoted strophes in Havamál:

> Str. 76. Deyr fæ,
> deyja frændr,
> deyr sialfr it sama;
> enn orztirr
> deyr aldregi
> hveim er ser godan getr.
>
> Str. 77. Deyr fæ,
> deyja frændr,
> deyr sialfr it sama;
> ec veit einn
> at aldri deyr:
> domr um daudan hvern.

(76) "Your cattle shall die; your kindred shall die; you yourself shall die; but the fair fame of him who has earned it never dies."

(77) "Your cattle shall die; your kindred shall die; you yourself shall die; one thing I know which never dies: the judgment on each one dead."

Hitherto these passages have been interpreted as if Odin or Havamál's skald meant to say—What you have of earthly possessions is perishable; your kindred and yourself shall die. But I know one thing that never dies: the reputation you acquired among men, the posthumous fame pronounced on your character and on your deeds: that reputation is immortal, that fame is imperishable.

But can this have been the meaning intended to be conveyed by the skald? And could these strophes, which, as it seems, were widely known in the heathendom of the North, have been thus understood by their hearers and readers? Did not Havamál's author, and the many who listened to and treasured in their memories these words of his, know as well as all other persons who have some age and experience, that in the great majority of cases the fame acquired by a person scarcely survives a generation, and passes away together with the very memory of the deceased?

Could it have escaped the attention of the Havamál skald and his hearers that the number of mortals is so large and increases so immensely with the lapse of centuries that the capacity of the survivors to remember them is utterly insufficient?

Was it not a well-established fact, especially among the Germans, before they got a written literature, that the skaldic art waged, so to speak, a desperate conflict with the power of oblivion, in order to rescue at least the names of the most distinguished heroes and kings, but that nevertheless thousands of chiefs and warriors were after the lapse of a few generations entirely forgotten?

Did not Havamál's author know that millions of men have, in the course of thousands of years, left this world without leaving so deep footprints in the sands of time that they could last even through one generation?

Every person of some age and experience has known this, and Havamál's author too. The lofty strains above quoted do not seem to be written by a person wholly destitute of worldly experience.

The assumption that Havamál with that judgment on each one dead, which is said to be imperishable, had reference to the opinion of the survivors in regard to the deceased attains its climax of absurdity when we consider that the poem expressly states that it means the judgment on *every* dead person--"*domr um daudan hvern.*" In the cottage lying far, far in the deep forest dies a child, hardly known by others than by its parents, who, too, are soon to be harvested by death. But the judgment of the survivors in regard to this child's character and deeds is to be imperishable, and the good fame it acquired during its brief life is to live for ever on the lips of posterity! Perhaps it is the sense of the absurdity to which the current assumption leads on this point that has induced some of the translators to conceal the word *hvern* (every) and led them to translate the words *domr um daudan hvern* in an arbitrary manner with "judgment on the dead man."

If we now add that the judgment of posterity on one deceased, particularly if he was a person of great influence, very seldom is so unanimous, reliable, well-considered, and free from prejudice that in these respects it ought to be entitled to permanent validity, then we find that the words of the Havamál strophes attributed to Odin's lips, when interpreted as hitherto, are not words of wisdom, but t1e most stupid.twaddle ever heard declaimed in a solemn manner.

There are two reasons for the misunderstanding—the one is formal, and is found in the word *ords-tirr* (str. 76); the other reason is that Gylfaginning, which too long has had the reputation of being a reliable and exhaustive codification of the scattered statements of the mythic sources, has nothing to say about a court for the dead. It knows that, according to the doctrine of the heathen fathers, good people come to regions of bliss, the wicked to Nifelhel; but who he or they were who determined how far a dead person was worthy of the one fate or the other, on this point Gylfaginning has not a word to say. From the silence of this authority, the conclusion has been drawn that a court summoning the dead within its forum was not to be found in Teutonic mythology, although other Aryan and non-Aryan mythologies have presented such a judgment-seat, and that the Teutonic fancy, though always much occupied with the affairs of the lower world and with the conditions of the dead in the various realms of death, never felt the necessity of conceiving for itself clear and concrete ideas of how and through whom the deceased were determined for bliss or misery. The ecclesiastical conception, which postpones the judgment to the last day of time and permits the souls of the dead to be transferred, without any special act of judgment, to heaven, to purgatory, or to hell, has to some extent contributed to making us familiar with this idea which was foreign to the heathens. From this it followed that scholars have been blind to the passages in our mythical records whici speak of a court in the lower world, and they have either read them without sufficient attention (as, for instance, the above-quoted statements of Ynglingatal, which it is impossible to harmonise with the current conception), or interpreted them in an utterly absurd manner (which is the case with Sigrdrifumal, str. 12), or they have interpolated assumptions, which, on a closer inspection, are reduced to nonsense (as is the case with the Havamál strophes), or given them a possible, but improbable, interpretation (thus Sonatorrek, 19). The compound *ordstirr* is composed of *ord, gen, ords,* and *tirr.* The composition is of so loose a character that the two parts are not blended into a *new* word. The sign of the gen. *-s* is retained, and shows that *ordstirr,* like *lofstirr,* is not in its sense and in its origin a compound, but is written as one word, probably on account of the laws of accentuation. The more original meaning of *ordstirr* is, therefore, to be found in the sense of *ords tirr.*

Tirr means reputation in a good sense, but still not in a sense so decidedly good but that a qualifying word, which makes the good meaning absolute, is sometimes added. Thus in *lofs-tirr,* laudatory reputation; *góðr tirr,* good reputation. In the Havamál strophe 76, above-quoted, the possibility of an *ords tirr* which is not good is presupposed. See the last line of the strophe.

So far as the meaning of *ord* is concerned, we must leave its relatively more modern and grammatical sense (word) entirely out of the question. Its older signification is an utterance (one which may consist of many "words" in a grammatical sense), a command, a result, a judgment; and these older significations have long had a conscious existence in the language. Compare Fornmanna, ii. 237: "The first word: All shall be Christians; the second word: All heathen temples and idols shall be unholy," &c.

In Völuspa (str. 27) *ord* is employed in the sense of an established law or judgment among the divine powers, *a gengoz eidar, ord oc særi,* where the treaties between the Asas and gods, solemnised by oaths, were broken.

When *ord* occurs in purely mythical sources, it is most frequently connected with judgments pronounced in the lower world, and sent from Urd's fountain to their destination. *Urdar ord* is Urd's judgment, which must come to pass (Fjölsvinnsm., str. 48), no matter whether it concerns life or death. *Feigdar ord,* a judgment determining death, comes to Fjolner, and is fulfilled "where Frode dwelt" (Yng.-tal, Heimskr., 14). *Dauda ord,* the judgment of death, awaited Dag the Wise, when he came to Vorva (Yng.-tal, Heimskr., 21). To a subterranean judgment refers also the expression *bana-ord,* which frequently ocurs.

Vigfusson (Dict., 466) points out the possibility of an etymological connection between *ord* and *Urdr.* He compares *word* (*ord*) and *wurdr* (*urdr*), *word* and *weird* (fate, goddess of fate). Doubtless there was, in the most ancient time, a mythical idea-association between them.

These circumstances are to be remembered in connection with the interpretation of *ordstirr, ords-tirr* in Havamál, 76. The real meaning of the phrase to be; reputation based on a decision, on an utterance of authority.

When *ordstirr* had blended into a compound word, there arose by t1e side of its literal meaning another, in which the accent fell so 1eavily on *tirr* that *ord* is superfluous and gives no additional meaning of a judgment on which this *tirr* is based.   Already in Hofudlausn (str. 26) *ordstirr* is used as a compound, meaning simply honourable reputation, honour.   There is mention of a victory which Erik Blood-axe won, and it is said that he thereby gained *ordstirr* (renown).

In interpreting Havamál (76) it would therefore seem that we must choose between the proper and figurative sense of *ordstirr*.   The age of the Havamál strophe is not known.   If it was from it Eyvind Skaldaspiller drew his *deyr fé, deyja frændr,* which he incorporated in his drapa on Hakon the Good, who died in 960, then the Havamál strophe could not be composed later than the middle of the tenth century.   Hofudlausn was composed by Egil Skallagrimson in the year 936 or thereabout.   From a chronological point of view there is therefore nothing to hinder our aplying the less strict sense, "honourable reputation, honour," to the passage in question.

But there are other hindrances.   If the Havamál skald with *ords-tirr* meant "honourable reputation, honour," he could, not, as he has done, have added the condition which he makes in the last line of the strophe: *hveim er ser godan getr,* for the idea "good" would then already be contained in ordstirr.   If in spite of this we would take the less strict sense, we must subtract from *ordstirr* the meaning of *honourable* reputation, *honour,* and conceive the expression to mean simply reputation in general, a meaning which the word never had.

We are therefore forced to the conclusion that the meaning of court-decision, judgment, which *ord* has not only in Ynglingatal and Fjölsvinnsmal, but also in linguistic usage, was clear to the author of the Havamál strophe, and that he applied *ords tirr* in its original sense and was speaking of imperishable judgments.

It should also have been regarded as a matter of course that the judgment which, according to the Havamál strophe (77), is passed on everyone dead, and which itself never dies, must have been prepared by a court whose decision could not be questioned or set aside, and that the judgment must have been one whose influence is eternal, for the infinity of the judgment itself can only depend on the infinity of its operation. That the more or less vague opinions sooner or later committed to oblivion in regard to a deceased person should be supposed to contain such a judgment, and to have been meant by the immortal doom over the dead, I venture to include among the most extraordinary interpretations ever produced.

Both the strophes are, as is evident from the first glance, most intimately connected with each other. Both begin: *deyr fæ, deyja frændr.* *Ord* in the one strophe corresponds to *domr* in the other. The latter strophe declares that the judgment on *every* dead person is imperishable, and thus completes the more limited statement of the foregoing strophe, that the judgment which gives a good renown is everlasting. The former strophe speaks of only *one* category of men who have been subjected to an ever-valid judgment. namely of that category to whose honour the eternal judgment is pronounced. The second strophe speaks of both the categories, and assures us that the judgment on the one as on the other category is everlasting.

The strophes are by the skald attributed to Odin's lips. Odin pronounces judgment every day near Urd's fountain at the court to which King Halfdan was summoned, and where hosts of people with fettered tongues await their final destiny (see above.) The assurances in regard to the validity of the judgment on everyone dead are thus given by a being who really may be said to know what he talks about (*ec veit*, &c.), namely, by the judge himself.

In the poem Sonatorrek the old Egil Skallagrimson laments the loss of sons and kindred, and his thoughts are occupied with the fate of his children after death. When he speaks of his son Gunnar, who in his tender years was snatched away by a sickness, he says (str. 19):

> Son minn
> sóttar brimi
> heiptuligr
> ór heimi nam,
> þann ec veit
> at varnadi
> vamma varr
> vid námæli.

"A fatal fire of disease (fever?) snatched from this world a son of mine, of whom I know that he, careful as he was in regard to sinful deeds, took care of himself for *námæli*."

To understand this strophe correctly, we must know that the skald in the preceding 17th, as in the succeeding 20th, strophe, speaks of Gunnar's fate in the lower world.

The word *námæli* occurs now iere else, and its meaning is not known. It is of importance to our subject to find it out.

In those compounds of which the first part is *ná-*, *ná* may be the adverbial prefix, which means *near by*, *by the side of*, or it may be the substantive *nár*, which means a corpse, dead body, and in a mythical sense one damned, one who dies for the second time and comes to Nifelhel (see No. 60). The question is now, to begin with, w iether it is the adverbial prefix or the substantive *ná-* which we have in *námæli*.

Compounds which have the adverbial *ná* as the first part of the word are very common. In all of them the prefix *ná-* implies nearness in space or in kinship, or it has the signification of some thing correct or exact.

(1) In regard to space: *nábúd, nábúi, nábýli, nágranna, nágranni, nágrennd, nágrenni, nákommin, nákvæma, nákvæmd, nákvæmr, náleid, nálægd, nálægjast, nálægr, námunda, násessi, náseta, násettr, násæti, návera, náverukona, náverandi, návist, návistarkona, návistarmadr, návistarvitni.*

(2) In regard to friendship: *náborinn, náfrændi, náfrændkona, námagr, náskyldr, nástædr, náongr.*

(3) In regard to correctness, exactness: *nákvæmi, nákvæmliga, nákvæmr.*

The idea of correctness comes from the combination of *ná-* and *kvæmi, kvæmliga, kvæmr*. The exact meaning is—*that which comes near to*, and which in that sense is precise, exact, to the point.

These three cases ex iaust the meanings of the adverbial prefix *ná-*. I should consider it perilous, and as the abandoning of solid ground under the feet, if we, without evidence from the language tried, as has been done, to give it another hitherto unknown signification.

But none of these meanings can be applied to *námæli*. In analogy with the words under (1) it can indeed mean "An oration held near by;" but this signification produces no sense in the above passage, the only place where it is found.

In another group of words the prefix *ná-* is the noun *nár*. Here belong *nábjargir, nábleikr, nágrindr, nágöll, náreid, nástrandir,* and other words.

Mæli means a declamation, an oration, an utterance, a reading, or the proclamation of a law. *Mæla, mælandi, formælandi, formæli, nymæli,* are used in legal language. *Formælandi* is a defendant in court. *Formæli* is his speech or plea. *Nymæli* is a law read or published for the first time.

Mæli can take either a substantive or adjective as prefix. Examples: *Gudmæli, fullmæli. Ná* from *nár* can be used as a prefix both to a noun and to an adjective. Examples: *nágrindr, nábleikr.*

Námæli should acordingly be an oration, a declaration, a proclamation, in regard to *nár*. From the context we find that *námæli* is something dangerous, something to look out for. Gunnar is dead and is gone to the lower world, which contains not only happiness but also terrors; but his aged father, who in another strophe of the poem gives to understand that he had adhered faithfully to the religious doctrines of his fathers, is convinced that his son has avoided the dangers implied in *námæli,* as he had no sinful deed to blame himself for. In the following strophe (20) he expressed his confidence that the deceased had been adopted by *Gauta spjalli,* a friend of Odin in the lower world, and had landed in the realm of happiness. (In regard to *Gauta spjalli* see further on. The expression is applicable both to Mimer and Honer).

Námæli must, therefore, mean a declaration (1) that is dangerous; (2) which does not affect a person who has lived a blameless life; (3) which refers to the dead and affects those who have not been *vamma varir,* on the lookout against blameworthy and criminal deeds.

The passage furnishes additional evidence that the dead in the lower world make their appearance in order to be judged, and it enriches our knowledge of the mythological eschatology with a technical term (*námæli*) for that judgment which sends sinners to travel through the Na-gates to Nifelhel. The opposite of *námæli* is *ords tirr,* that judgment which gives the dead fair renown, and both kinds of judgments are embraced in the phrase *domr um daudan. Námæli* is a proclamation for *náir,* just as *nágrindr* are gates and *nástrandir* are strands for *náir.*

71.

THE DOOM OF THE DEAD (*continued*). THE LOOKS OF THE THINGSTEAD. THE DUTY OF TAKING CARE OF THE ASHES OF THE DEAD. THE HAMINGJE AT THE JUDGMENT. SINS OF WEAKNESS. SINS UNTO DEATH.

Those hosts which are conducted by their psychopomps

to the Thing near Urd's fountain proceed noiselessly. It is a silent journey. The bridge over *Gjöll* scarcely resounds under the feet of the death-horses and of the dead (Gylfaginning). The tongues of the shades are sealed (see No. 70).

This thingstead has, like all others, had its judgment-seats. Here are seats (in Völuspa called *rökstólar*) for the holy powers acting as judges. There is also a rostrum (*á thularstóli at Urdar brunni*—Havam., 111) and benches or chairs for the dead (compare the phrase, *falla á Helpalla*—Fornald., i. 397, and the sitting of the dead one, *á nornastóli*—Solarlj., 51). Silent they must receive their doom unless they possess mal-runes (see No. 70).

The dead should come well clad and ornamented. Warriors bring their weapons of attack and defence. The women and children bring ornaments that they were fond of in life. Hades-pictures of those things which kinsmen and friends placed in the grave-mounds accompany the dead (Hakonarm., 17; Gylfaginning, 52) as evidence to the judge that they enjoyed the devotion and respect of their survivors. The appearance presented by the shades assembled in the Thing indicates to what extent the survivors heed the law, which commands respect for the dead and care for the ashes of the departed.

Many die under circumstances which make it impossible for their kinsmen to observe these duties. Then strangers should take the place of kindred. The condition in which these shades come to the Thing shows best whether piety prevails in Midgard; for noble minds take to heart the advices found as follows in Sigrdrifumal, 33, 34: "Render the last service to the corpses you find on the ground, whether from sickness they have died, or are drowned, or are from weapons dead. Make a bath for those who are dead, wash their hands and their head, comb them and wipe them dry, ere in the coffin you lay them, and pray for their happy sleep."

It was, however, not necessary to wipe the blood off from the byrnie of one fallen by the sword. It was not improper for the elect to make their entrance in Valhal in a bloody coat of mail. Eyvind Skaldaspiller makes King Hakon come all stained with blood (*allr i dreyra drifinn*) into the presence of Odin.

When the gods have arrived from Asgard, dismounted from their horses (Gylfag.) and taken their judges' seats, the proceedings begin, for the dead are then in their places, and we may be sure that their psychopomps have not been slow on their Thing-journey. Somewhere on the way the Hel-shoes must have been tried; those who ride to Valhal must then have been obliged to dismount. The popular tradition first pointed out by Walter Scott and J. Grimm about the need of such shoes for the dead and about a thorn-grown heath, which they have to cross, is not of Christian but of heathen origin. Those who have shown mercy to fellowmen that in this life, in a figurative sense, had to travel thorny paths, do not need to fear torn shoes and bloody feet (W. Scott, *Minstrelsy*, ii.) ; and when they are seated on Urd's benches, their very shoes are, by their condition, a conspicuous proof in the eyes of the court that they who have exercised mercy are worthy of mercy.

11

507

The Norse tradition preserved in Gisle Surson's saga in regard to the importance for the dead to be provided with shoes reappears as a popular tradition, first in England, and then several places (Müllenhoff, *Deutsche Alt.*, v. 1, 114; J. Grimm., *Myth.*, iii. 697; nachtr., 349; Weinhold, *Altn. Leb.*, 494; Mannhardt in *zeitschr. f. deutsch. Myth.*, iv. 420; Simrock, *Myth.*, v. 127). *Visio Godeschalci* describes a journey which the pious Holstein peasant Godeskalk, belonging to the generation immediately preceding that which by Vicelin was converted to Christianity, believed he had made in the lower world. There is mentioned an immensely large and beautiful linden-tree hanging full of shoes, which were handed down to such dead travellers as had exercised mercy during their lives. When the dead had passed this tree they had to cross a heath two miles wide, thickly grown with thorns, and then they came to a river full of irons with sharp edges. The unjust had to wade through this river, and suffered immensely. They were cut and mangled in every limb; but when they reached the other strand, their bodies were the same as they had been when they began crossing the river. Compare with this statement Solarljod, 42, where the dying skald hears the roaring of subterranean streams mixed with much blood—*Gylfar straumar grenjudu, blandnir mjök ved blód.* The just are able to cross the river by putting their feet on boards a foot wide and fourteen feet long, which floated on the water. This is the first day's journey. On the second day they come to a point where the road forked into three ways—one to heaven, one to hell, and one between these realms (compare

Müllenhoff, *D. Alt.*, v. 113, 114). These are all mythic traditions, but little corrupted by time and change of religion. That in the lower world itself Hel-shoes were to be had for those who were not supplied with them, but still deserved them, is probably a genuine mythological idea.

Proofs and witnesses are necessary before the above-named tribunal, for Odin is far from omniscient. He is not even the one who knows the most among the beings of mythology. Urd and Mimer know more than he. With judges on the one hand who, in spite of all their loftiness, and with all their superhuman keenness, nevertheless are not infallible, and with defendants on the other hand whose tongues refuse to serve them, it might happen, if there were no proofs and witnesses, that a judgment, everlasting in its operations, not founded on exhaustive knowledge and on well-considered premises, might be proclaimed. But the judgment on human souls proclaimed by their final irrevocable fate could not in the sight of the pious and believing bear the stamp of uncertain justice. There must be no doubt that the judicial proceedings in the court of death were so managed that the wisdom and justice of the *dicta* were raised high above every suspicion of being mistaken.

The heathen fancy shrank from the idea of a knowledge able of itself to embrace all, the greatest and the least, that which has been, is doing, and shall be in the world of thoughts, purposes, and deeds. It hesitated at all events to endow its gods made in the image of man with omniscience. It was easier to conceive a divine insight

which was secured by a net of messengers and spies
stretched throughout the world. Such a net was cast
over the human race by Urd, and it is doubtless for this
reason that the subterranean Thing of the gods was
located near her fountain and not near Mimer's. Urd
has given to every human soul, already before the hour of
birth, a maid-servant, a hamingje, a norn of lower rank,
to watch over and protect its earthly life. And so there
was a wide-spread organization of watching and protecting spirits, each one of whom knew the motives and deeds
of a special individual. As such an organisation was at
the service of the court, there was no danger that the
judgment over each one dead would not be as just as it
was unappealable and everlasting.

The hamingje hears of it before anyone else when her
mistress has announced *dauda ord*—the doom of death,
against her favourite. She (and the *gipte, heille,* see No.
64) leaves him then. She is *horfin,* gone, which can be
perceived in dreams (Balder's Dream, 4) or by revelations
in other ways, and this is an unmistakable sign of death.
But if the death-doomed person is not a nithing, whom
she in sorrow and wrath has left, then she by no means
abandons him. They are like members of the same body,
which can only be separated by mortal sins (see below).
The hamingje goes to the lower world, the home of her
nativity (see No. 64), to prepare an abode there for her
favourite, which also is to belong to her (Gisle Surson's
saga.) It is as if a spiritual marriage was entered into
between her and the human soul.

But on the dictum of the court of death it depends

where the dead person is to find his haven. The judgment, although not pronounced on the hamingje, touches her most closely. When the most important of all questions, that of eternal happiness or unhappiness, is to be determined in regard to her favourite, she must be there where her duty and inclination bid her be—with him whose guardian-spirit she is. The great question for her is whether she is to continue to share his fate or not. During his earthly life she has always defended him. It is of paramount importance that she should do so now. His lips are sealed, but she is able to speak, and is his other ego. And she is not only a witness friendly to him, but, from the standpoint of the court, she is a more reliable one than he would be himself.

In Atlamal (str. 28) there occurs a phrase which has its origin in heathendom, where it has been employed in a clearer and more limited sense than in the Christian poem. The phrase is *ec qued aflima ordnar ther disir,* and it means, as Atlamal uses it, that he to whom the dises (the hamingje and gipte) have become *aflima* is destined, in spite of all warnings, to go to his ruin. In its very nature the phrase suggests that there can occur between the hamingje and the human soul another separation than the accidental and transient one which is expressed by saying that the hamingje is *horfin. Aflima* means "amputated," separated by a sharp instrument from the body of which one has been a member. The person from whom his dises have been cut off has no longer any close relation with them. He is for ever separated from them, and his fate is no longer theirs. Hence there are persons doomed to die and persons dead who do not have hamingjes by them. They are those whom the hamingjes in sorrow and wrath have abandoned, and with whom they are unable to dwell in the lower world, as they are nithings and are awaited in Nifelhel.

The fact that a dead man sat *á nornastóli* or *á Helpalli* without having a hamingje to defend him doubtless was regarded by the gods as a conclusive proof that he had been a criminal.

If we may judge from a heathen expression preserved in strophe 16 of Atlakvida, and there used in an arbitrary manner, then the hamingjes who were "cut off" from their unworthy favourite continue to feel sorrow and sympathy for them to the last. The expression is *nornir gráta nái,* "the norns (hamingjes) bewail the *náir.*" If the *námæli,* the na-dictum, the sentence to Nifelhel which turns dead criminals into *nair,* in the eschatological sense of the word, has been announced, the judgment is attended with tears on the part of the former guardian-spirits of the convicts. This corresponds, at all events, with the character of the hamingjes.

Those fallen on the battlefield are not brought to the fountain of Urd while the Thing is in session. This follows from the fact that Odin is in Valhal when they ride across Bifrost, and sends Asas or einherjes to meet them with the goblet of mead at Asgard's gate (Eiriksm., Hakonarmal). But on the way there has been a separation of the good and bad elements among them. Those who have no hamingjes must, *á nornastóli,* wait for the next Thing-day and their judgment. The Christian age well remembered that brave warriors who had committed nithing acts did not come to Valhal (see Hakon Jarl's word in Njála). The heathen records confirm that men slain by the sword who had lived a wicked life were sent to the world of torture (see Harald Harfager's saga, ch. 27—the verses about the viking Tborer Wood-beard, who fell in a naval battle with Einar Ragnvaldson, and who had been scourge to the Orkneyings).

The high court must have judged very leniently in regard to certain human faults and frailties. Sitting long by and looking diligently into the drinking-horn certainly did not lead to any punishment worth mentioning. The same was the case with fondness for female beauty, if care was taken not to meddle with the sacred ties of matrimony. With a pleasing frankness, and with much humour, the Asa-father has told to the children of men adventures which he himself has had in that line. He warns against too much drinking, but admits without reservation and hypocrisy that he himself once was drunk, nay, very drunk, at Fjalar's and what he had to suffer, on account of his uncontrollable longing for Billing's maid, should be to men a hint not to judge each other too severely in such matters (see Havamál.) All the less he will do so as judge. Those who are summoned to the Thing and against whom there are no other charges, may surely count on a good *ords tirr,* if they in other respects have conducted themselves in accordance with the wishes of Odin and his associate judges: if they have lived lives free from deceit, honourable, helpful, and without fear of death. This, in connection with respect for the gods, for the temples, for their duties to kindred and to the dead, is the alpha and the omega of the heathen Teutonic moral code, and the sure way to Hel's regions of bliss and to Valhal. He who has observed these virtues may, as the old skald sings of himself, "glad, with serenity and without discouragement, wait for Hel."

> Skal ek thó gladr
> med godan vilja
> ok úhryggr
> Heljar bida (Sonatorrek, 24).

If the judgment on the dead is lenient in these respects, it is inexorably severe in other matters. Lies uttered to injure others, perjury, murder (secret murder, assassination, not justified as blood-revenge), adultery, the profaning of temples, the opening of grave-mounds, treason, cannot escape their awful punishment. Unutterable terrors await those who are guilty of these sins. Those psychopomps that belong to Nifelhel await the adjournment of the Thing in order to take them to the world of torture, and Urd has chains (*Heljar reip*—Solarljod, 27; *Des Todes Seil*—J. Grimm, *D. Myth.*, 805) which make every escape impossible.

72.

THE HADES-DRINK.

Before the dead leave the thingstead near Urd's fountain, something which obliterated the marks of earthly death has happened to those who are judged happy.

Pale, cold, mute, and with the marks of the spirits of disease, they left Midgard and started on the Hel-way. They leave the death-Thing full of the warmth of life, with health, with speech, and more robust than they were on earth. The shades have become corporal. When those slain by the sword ride over the Gjoll to Urd's fountain, scarcely a sound is heard under the hoofs of their horses; when they ride away from the fountain over Bifrost, the bridge resounds under the trampling horses. The sagas of the middle ages have preserved, but at the same time demonised, the memory of how Hel's inhabitants were endowed with more than human strength (Gretla, 134, and several other passages).

The life of bliss presupposes health, but also forgetfulness of the earthly sorrows and cares. The heroic poems and the sagas of the middle ages have known that there was a Hades-potion which brings freedom from sorrow and care, without obliterating dear memories or making one forget that which can be remembered without longing or worrying. In the mythology this drink was, as shall be shown, one that produced at the same time vigour of life and the forgetfulness of sorrows.

In Saxo, and in the heroic poems of the Elder Edda, which belong to the Gjukung group of songs, there reappear many mythical details, though they are sometimes taken out of their true connection and put in a light which does not originally belong to them. Among the mythical reminiscences is the Hades-potion.

In his account of King Gorm's and Thorkil's journey to the lower world, Saxo (see No 46) makes Thorkil warn his travelling companions from tasting the drinks offered them by the prince of the lower world, for the reason that they produce forgetfulness, and make one desire to remain in Gudmund's realm (*Hist., Dan.,* i. 424—*amissa memoria . . . pocalis abstinendum edocuit*).

The Gudrun song (ii. 21) places the drinking-horn of the lower world in Grimhild's hands.   In connection with later additions, the description of this horn and its contents contains purely mythical and very instructive details in regard to the *pharmakon nepenthes* of the Teutonic lower world.

> Str. 21. Færdi mer Grimildr
> full at drecka
> svalt oc sarlict,
> ne ec sacar mundac;
> tIar var um aukit
> Urdar magni,
> svalcauldom sæ
> oc Sonar dreyra.

> Str. 22. Voro i Iorni
> hverskyns stafir
> ristnir oc rodnir,
> ratIa ec ne mattac,
> lyngfiscr langr
> lands Haddingja,
> ax oscorit,
> innleid dyra.

"Grimhild handed me in a filled horn to drink a cool, bitter drink, in order that I might forget my past afflictions.   This drink was prepared from *Urd's strength, cool-cold sea, and the liquor of Son.*"

"On the horn were all kinds of staves engraved and

painted, which I could not interpret: *the Hadding-land's long heath-fish, unharvested ears of grain, and animals' entrances."*

The Hadding-land is, as Sv. Egilsson has already pointed out, a paraphrase of the lower world. The paraphrase is based on the mythic account known and mentioned by Saxo in regard to Hadding's journey in Hel's realm (see No. 47).

Heath-fish is a paraphrase of the usual sort for serpent, dragon. Hence a lower-world dragon was engraved on the horn. More than one of the kind has been mentioned already: Nidhog, who has his abode in Nifelhel, and the dragon, which, according to Erik Vidforle's saga, obstructs the way to Odain's-acre. The dragon engraved on the horn is that of the Hadding-land. Hadding-land, on the other hand, does not mean the whole lower world, but the regions of bliss visited by Hadding. Thus the dragon is such an one as Erik Vidforle's saga had in mind. That the author did not himself invent his dragon, but found it in mythic records extant at the time, is demonstrated by Solarljod (54), where it is said that immense subterranena dragons come flying from the west—the opposite direction of that the shades have to take when they descend into the lower world—and obstruct "the street of the prince of splendour" (*glævalds götu*). The ruler of splendour is Mimer, the prince of the Glittering Fields (see Nos. 45-51).

The Hadding-land's "unharvested ears of grain" belong to the flora inaccessible to the devastations of frost, the flowers seen by Hadding in the blooming meadows of the world below (see No. 47). The expression refers to the fact that the Hadding-land has not only imperishable flowers and fruits, but also fields of grain which do not require harvesting. Compare herewith what Völuspa says about the Odain's-acre which in the regeneration of the earth rises from the lap of the sea: "unsown the fields yield the grain."

Beside the heath-fish and the unharvested ears of grain, there were also seen on the Hadding-land horn *dyra-innleid*. Some interpreters assume that "animals entrails" are meant by this expression; others have translated it with "animal gaps." There is no authority that *innleid* ever meant entrails, nor could it be so used in a rhetorical-poetical sense, except by a very poor poet. Where we meet with the word it means a way, a way in, in contrast with *útleid,* a way out. As both Gorms saga and that of Erik Vidforle use it in regard to animals watching entrances in the lower world, this gives the expression its natural interpretation.

So much for the staves risted on the horn. They all refer to the lower world. Now as to the drink which is mixed in this Hades-horn. It consists of three liquids:

Urdar Magn,	Urd's strength,
svalkaldr sær,	cool-cold sea,
Sonar dreyri.	Son's liquid.

Son has already been mentioned above (No. 21) as one of the names of Mimer's fountain, the well of creative power and of poetry. Of Son Eilif Gudrunson sings that it is enwreathed by bulrushes and is surrounded by a border of meadow on which grows the seed of poetry.

As Urd's strength is a liquid mixed in the horn, nothing else can be meant thereby than the liquid in Urd's fountain, which gives the warmth of life to the world-tree, and gives it strength to resist the cold (see No. 63).

From this it is certain that at least two of the three subterranean fountains made their contributions to the drink. There remains the well Hvergelmer, and the question now is, whether it and the liquid it contains can be recognised as the *cool-cold sea*. Hvergelmer is, as we know, the mother-fountain of all waters, even of the ocean (see No. 59). That this immense cistern is called a sea is not strange, since also Urd's fountain is so styled (in Völuspa, Cod. Reg., 19.) Hvergelmer is situated under the northern root of the world-tree near the borders of the subterranean realm of the rime-thurses—that is, the powers of frost; and the Elivagar rivers flowing thence formed the ice in Nifelheim. Cool (*Svöl*) is the name of one of the rivers which have their source in Hvergelmer (Grimnersmal). Cool-cold sea is therefore the most suitable word with which to designate Hvergelmer when its own name is not to be used.

All those fountains whose liquids are sucked up by the roots of the world-tree, and in its stem blend into the sap which gives the tree imperishable strength of life, are accordingly mixed in the lower-world horn (cp. No. 21).

That Grimhild, a human being dwelling on earth, should have access to and free control of these fountains is, of course, from a mythological standpoint, an absurdity. From the standpoint of the Christian time the absurdity becomes probable. The sacred things and forces of the lower world are then changed into deviltry and arts of magic, which are at the service of witches. So the author of Gudrunarkvida (ii.) has regarded the matter. But in his time there was still extant a tradition, or a heathen song, which spoke of the elements of the drink which gave to the dead who had descended to Hel, and were destined for happiness, a higher and more enduring power of life ,and also soothed the longing and sorrow which accompanied the recollection of the life on earth, and this tradition was used in the description of Grimhild's drink of forgetfulness.

Magn is the name of the liquid from Urd's fountain, since it *magnar,* gives strength. The word *magna* has preserved from the days of heathendom the sense of strengthening in a supernatural manner by magical or superhuman means. Vigfusson (Dict., 408) gives a number of examples of this meaning. In Heimskringla (ch. 8) Odin "magus" Mimer's head, which is chopped off, in such a manner that it recovers the power of speech. In Sigrdrifumal (str. 12) Odin himself is, as we have seen, called *magni,* "the one magning," as the highest judge of the lower world, who gives *magn* to the dead from the Hades-horn.

The author of the second song about Helge Hundings-bane has known of *dyrar veilgar,* precious liquids of which those who have gone to Hel partake. The dead Helge says that when his beloved Sigrun is to share them with him, then it is of no consequence that they have lost earthly joy and kingdoms, and that no one must lament that his breast was tortured with wounds (Helge Hund., ii. 46.) The touching finale of this song, though preserved only in fragments, and no doubt borrowed from a heathen source, shows that the power of the subterranean potion to allay longing and sorrow had its limits. The survivors should mourn over departed loved ones with moderation, and not forget that they are to meet again, for too bitter tears of sorrow fall as a cold dew on the breast of the dead one and penetrate it with pain (str. 45).

73.

THE HADES-DRINK (*continued*), THE HADES-HORN EMBELLISHED WITH SERPENTS.

In Sonatorrek (str. 18) the skald (Egil Skallagrimson) conceives himself with the claims of a father to keep his children opposed to a stronger power which has also made a claim on them. This power is firm in its resolutions against Egil (*stendr á föstum thokk á hendi mér*) ; but, at the same time, it is lenient toward his children, and bestows on them the lot of happiness. The mythic person who possesses this power is by the skald called *Fáns hrosta hilmir*, "the lord of *Fánn's* brewing."

Fánn is a mythical serpent- and dragon-name (Younger Edda, ii. 487, 570). The serpent or dragon which possessed this name in the myths or sagas must have been one which was engraved or painted somewhere. This is evident from the word itself, which is a contraction of *fáinn,* engraved, painted (cp. Egilsson's Lex. Poet., and Vigfusson's Dict., *sub voce*). Its character as such does not hinder it from being endowed with a magic life (see below.) The object on which it was engraved or painted must have been a drinking-horn, whose contents (brewing) is called by Egil *Fánn's,* either because the serpent encircled the horn which contained the drink, or because the horn, on which it was engraved, was named after it. In no other way can the expression, *Fánn's* brewing, be explained, for an artificial serpent or dragon is neither the one who brews the drink nor the malt from which it is brewed.

The possessor of the horn, embellished with *Fánn's* image, is the mythical person who, to Egil's vexation, has insisted on the claim of the lower world to his sons. If the skald has paraphrased correctly, that is to say, if he has produced a paraphrase which refers to the character here in question of the person indicated by the paraphrase, then it follows that *"Fánn's* brewing" and *Fánn* himself, like their possessor, must have been in some way connected with the lower world.

From the mythic tradition in Gudrunarkvida (ii.), we already know that a serpent, "a long heath-fish," is engraved and painted on the subterranean horn, whose sorrow-allaying mead is composed of the liquid of the three Hades-fountains.

When King Gorm (*Hist., Dan.,* 427; cp. No. 46) made his journey of discovery in the lower world, he saw a vast ox-horn (*ingens bubali cornu*) there. It lay near the gold-clad mead-cisterns, the fountains of the lower world. Its purpose of being filled with their liquids is sufficiently clear from its location. We are also told that it was carved with figures (*nec cælaturæ artificio vacuum*), like the subterranean horn in Gudrunarkvida. One of Gorm's men is anxious to secure the treasure. Then the horn lengthens into a dragon who kills the would-be robber (*cornu in draconem extractum sui spiritum latoris eripuit.*) Like Slidrugtanne and other subterranean treasures, the serpent or dragon on the drinking-horn of the lower world is endowed with life when necessary, or the horn itself acquires life in the form of a dragon, and punishes with death him who has no right to touch it. The horn itself is accordingly a *Fánn*, an artificial serpent or dragon, and its contents is *Fánn's hrosti* (*Fánn's* brewing).

The Icelandic middle-age sagas have handed down the memory of an aurocks-horn (*úrarhorn*), which was found in the lower world, and was there used to drink from (Fornald., iii. 616).

Thus it follows that the *hilmir Fán's hrosta*, "the lord of Fán's brewing," mentioned by Egil, is the master of the Hades-horn, he who determines to whom it is to be handed, in order that they may imbibe vigour and forgetfulness of sorrow from "Urd's strength, cool sea, and Son's liquid." And thus the meaning of the strophe here discussed (Sonatorrek, 18) is made perfectly clear. Egil's deceased sons have drunk from this horn, and thus they have been initiated as dwellers for ever in the lower world. Hence the skald can say that *Hilmir Fán's hrosta* was inexorably firm against him, their father, who desired to keep his sons with him.*

From Völuspa (str. 28, 29), and from Gylfaginning (ch. 15), it appears that the mythology knew of a drinking horn which belonged at the same time, so to speak, both to Asgard and to the lower world. Odin is its possessor, Mimer its keeper. A compact is made between the Asas dwelling in heaven and the powers dwelling in the lower world, and a security (*ved*) is given for the keeping of the agreement. On the part of the Asas and their clan patriarch Odin, the security given is a drinking-horn. From this "Valfather's pledge" Mimer every morning drinks mead from his fountain of wisdom (Völuspa, 29), and from the same horn he waters the root of the world-tree (Völuspa, 28). As Müllenhoff has already pointed out (*D. Alterth.,* v. 100 ff.), this drinking-horn is not to be confounded with Heimdal's war-trumpet, the Gjallar-horn, though Gylfaginning is also guilty of this mistake.

---

*The interpretation of the passage, which has hitherto prevailed, begins with a text emendation. *Fánn* is changed to Finn. Finn is the name of a dwarf. *Finns hrosti* is "the dwarf's drink," and "the dwarf's drink' is, on the authority of the Younger Edda, synonymous with poetry. The possessor of *Finns hrosti* is Odin, the lord of poetry. With text emendations of this sort (they are numerous, are based on false notions in regard to the adaptability of the Icelandic Christian poetics to the heathen poetry and usually quote Gylfaginning as authority) we can produce anything we like from the statements of the ancient records. Odin's character as the Lord of poetry has not the faintest idea in common with the contents of the strophe. His character as judge at the court near Urd's fountain, and as the one who, as the judge of the dead, has authority over the liquor in the subterranean horn, is on the other hand closely connected with the contents of the strophe, and is alone able to make it consistent and intelligible. Further on in the poem, Egil speaks of Odin as the lord of poetry. Odin, he says, has not only been severe against him (in the capacity of *hilmir Fáns hrosta*), but he has also been kind in bestowing the gift of poetry, and therewith consolation in sorrow (*bölva bœtr*). The paraphrase here used by Egil for Odin's name is *Mims vinr* (Mimer's friend). From Mimer Odin received the drink of inspiration, and thus the paraphrase is in harmony with the sense. As *hilmir Fáns hrosta* Odin has wounded Egil's heart; as *Mims vinr* (Mimer's friend) he has given him balsam for the wounds inflicted. This two-sided conception of Odin's relation to the poet permeates the whole poem.

Thus the drinking-horn given to Mimer by Valfather represents a treaty between the powers of heaven and of the lower world. Can it be any other than the Hades-horn, which, at the thingstead near Urd's fountain, is employed in the service both of the Asa-gods and of the lower world? The Asas determine the happiness or unhappiness of the dead, and consequently decide what persons are to taste the strength-giving mead of the horn. But the horn has its place in the lower world, is kept there —there performs a task of the greatest importance, and gets its liquid from the fountains of the lower world.

What Mimer gave Odin in exchange is that drink of wisdom, without which he would not have been able to act as judge in matters concerning eternity, but after receiving the which he was able to find and proclaim the right decisions (*ord*) (*ord mér af ordi ordz leitadi*—Hav., 141). Both the things exchanged are, therefore, used at the Thing near Urd's fountain. The treaty concerned the lower world, and secured to the Asas the power necessary, in connection with their control of mankind and with their claim to be worshipped, to dispense happiness and unhappiness in accordance with the laws of religion and morality. Without this power the Asas would have been of but little significance. Urd and Mimer would have been supreme.

With the *dyrar veigar* (precious liquids), of which the dead Helge speaks, we must compare the *skírar veigar* (clear liquids), which, according to Vegtamskvida, awaited the dead Balder in the lower world. After tasting of it, the god who had descended to Hades regained

his broken strength, and the earth again grew green (see
No. 53).

In *dyrar veigar, skirar veigar,* the plural form must not
be passed over without notice. The contents of one and
the same drink are referred to by the plural *veigar*—

Her stendr Balldri	Here stands for Balder
of brugginn miœdr	mead brewed
skirar veigar	clear "veigar" (Vegt., 7)—

which can only be explained as referring to a drink prepared by a mixing of several liquids, each one of which
is a *veig*. Originally *veigar* seems always to have designated a drink of the dead, allaying their sorrows and giving
them new life. In Hyndluljod (50) *dyrar veigar* has the
meaning of a potion of bliss which Ottar, beloved by
Freyja, is to drink. In strophe 48, Freyja threatens the
sorceress Hyndla with a fire, which is to take her hence
for ever. In strophe 49, Hyndla answers the threat with
a similar and worse one. She says she already sees the
conflagration of the world; there shall nearly all beings
"suffer the loss of life" (*verda flestir fjörlausn thola*),
Freyja and her Ottar of course included, and their final
destiny, according to Hyndla's wish, is indicated by
Freyja's handing Ottar a pain-foreboding, venomous
drink. Hyndla invokes on Freyja and Ottar the flames of
Ragnarok and damnation. Freyja answers by including
Ottar in the protection of the gods, and foretelling that he
is to drink *dyrar veigar.*

Besides in these passages *veigar* occurs in a strophe
composed by Ref Gestson, quoted in Skaldskaparmal, ch.

2. Only half of the strophe is quoted, so that it is impossible to determine definitely the meaning of the *veigar* referred to by the skald. We only see that they are given by Odin, and that "we" must be grateful to him for them. The half strophe is possibly a part of a death-song which Ref Gestson is known to have composed on his foster-father, Gissur.

Veig in the singular means not only drink, but also power, strength. Perhaps Bugge is right in claiming that this was the original meaning of the word. The plural *veigar* accordingly means strengths. That this expression "strengths" should come to designate in a rational manner a special drink must be explained by the fact that "the strengths" was the current expression for the liquids of which the invigorating mythical drink was composed. The three fountains of the lower world are the strength-givers of the universe, and as we have already seen, it is the liquids of these wells that are mixed into the wonderful brewing in the subterranean horn.

When Eilif Gudrunson, the skald converted to Christianity, makes Christ, who gives the water of eternal life, sit near Urd's fountain, then this is a Christianised heathen idea, and refers to the power of this fountain's water to give, through the judge of the world, to the pious a less troublesome life than that on earth. The water which gives warmth to the world-tree and heals its wounds is to be found in the immediate vicinity of the thingstead, and has also served to strengthen and heal the souls of the dead.

To judge from Hyndluljod (49), those doomed to

527

unhappiness must also partake of some drink. It is
"much mixed with venom" (*citri blandinn miok*), and
forebodes tiem evil (*illu heilli*). They must, therefore,
be compelled to drink it *before* they enter the world of
misery, and accordingly, no doubt, while they sit *á norna-
stoli* on the very thingstead. The Icelandic sagas of the
middle ages know the venom drink as a potion of misery.

It appears that this potion of unhappiness did not loosen
the speechless tongues of the damned. *Eitr* means the
lowest degree of cold and poison at the same time, and
would not, therefore, be serviceable for that purpose, since
the tongues were made speechless with cold. In Saxo's
descriptions of the regions of misery in the lower world,
it is only the torturing demons that speak. The dead
are speechless, and suffer their agonies without uttering a
sound; but, when the spirits of torture so desire, and
force and egg them on they can produce a howl (*mug-
itus.*) There broods a sort of muteness over the forecourt
of the domain of torture, the Nifelheim inhabited by the
frost-giants, acording to Skirnersmal's description thereof
(see No. 60.) Skirner threatens Gerd that she, among
ier kindred there, shall be more widely hated tian Heimdal himself; but the manner in which they express this
hate is with staring eyes, not with words (*a thic Hrimnir
hari, a thic hotvetna stari*—str. 28).

74.

AFTER THE JUDGMENT. THE LOT OF THE BLESSED.

When a deceased who has received a good *ords tirr*

leaves the Thing, he is awaited in a home which his ham-ingje has arranged for her favourite somewhere in "the green worlds of the gods." But what he first has to do is to *leita kynnis,* that is, visit kinsmen and friends who have gone before him to their final destination (Sonatorr., 17). Here he finds not only those with whom he became per-sonally acquainted on earth, but he may also visit and converse with ancestors from the beginning of time, and he may hear the history of his race, nay, the history of all past generations, told by persons who were eye-wit-nesses. The ways he travels are *munvegar* (Sonatorr., 10), paths of pleasure, where the wonderful regions of Urd's and Mimer's realms lie open before his eyes.

Those who have died in their tender years are received by a being friendly to children, which Egil Skallagrimson (Sonatorrek, 20) calls *Gauta spjalli.* The expression means "the one with whom Odin counsels," "Odin's friend." As the same poem (str. 22) calls Odin Mimer's friend, and as in the next place *Gauta spjalli* is charac-terised as a ruler in *Godheim* (compare *grænar heimar goda*—Hakonarmal, 12), he must either be Mimer, who is Odin's friend and adviser from his youth until his death, or he must be Honer, who also is styled Odin's friend, his *sessi* and *máli.* That Mimer was regarded as the friend of dead children corresponds with his vocation as the keeper in his grove of immortality *Mimisholt,* of the Asa-children, the *ásmegir,* who are to be the mankind of the regenerated world. But Honer too has an important calling in regard to children (see No. 95), and it must therefore be left undecided which one of the two is here meant.

Egil is convinced that his drowned son Bodvar found
a harbour in the subterranean regions of bliss.* The
land to which Bodvar comes is called by Egil "the home
of the bee-ship" (*býskips bær.*) The poetical figure is
taken from the experience of seamen, that birds who have
grown tired on their way across the sea alight on ships to
recuperate their strength. In Egil's paraphrase the bee
corresponds to the bird, and the honey-blossom where the
bee alights corresponds to the ship. The fields of bliss
are the haven of the ship laden with honey. The figure
may be criticised on the point of poetic logic, but is of a
charming kind on the lips of the hardy old viking, and it
is at the same time very appropriate in regard to a characteristic quality ascribed to the fields of bliss. For they
are the proper home of the honey-dew which falls early
in the morning from the world-tree into the dales near
Urd's fountain (Völuspa). Lif and Leifthraser live
through ages on this dew (see Nos. 52, 53), and doubtless this same Teutonic ambrosia is the food of the happy
dead. The dales of the earth also unquestionably get
their share of the honey-dew, which was regarded as the
fertilising and nourishing element of the ground. But
the earth gets her share directly from Rimfaxe, the steed
of the Hades-goddess Nat. This steed, satiated with the
grass of the subterranean meadows, produces with his
mouth a froth which is honey-dew, and from his bridle the
dew drops "in the dales" in the morning (Vafthr., 14).
The same is true of the horses of the valkyries coming

---

*Likewise the warlike skald Kormak is certain that he would have come
to Valhal in case he had been drowned under circumstances described in
his saga, a work which is, however, very unreliable.

from the lower world. From their manes, when they shake them, falls dew "in deep dales," and thence come harvests among the peoples (Helge Hjorv., 28.)

75.

AFTER THE JUDGMENT (*continued*). THE FATE OF THE DAMNED. THEIR PATH. ARRIVAL AT THE NA-GATES.

When the na-dictum (the judgment of those who have committed sins unto death) has been proclaimed, they must take their departure for their terrible destination. They cannot take flight. The locks and fetters of the norns (*Urdar lokur, Heljar reip*) hold them prisoners, and amid the tears of their former hamingjes (*nornir gráta nái*) they are driven along their path by *heiptir*, armed with rods of thorns, who without mercy beat their lazy heels. The technical term for these instruments of torture is *limar,* which seems to have become a word for eschatological punishment in general. In Sigrdrifumal (23) it is said that horrible *limar* shall fall heavy on those who have broken oaths and promises, or betrayed confidence. In Sigurd Fafnesb. (ii. 3) it is stated that everyone who has lied about another shall long be tortured with *limar.* Both the expressions *troll brutu, hrís i hæla theim* and *troll visi ydr til búrs* have their root in the recollection of the myth concerning the march of the damned under the rod of the Eumenides to Nifelhel (see further on this point Nos. 91 and 123).

Their way from Urd's well goes to the north (see No. 63) through Mimer's domain. It is ordained that before their arrival at the home of torture they are to see the regions of bliss. Thus they know what they have forfeited. Then their course is past Mimer's fountain, the splendid dwellings of Balder and the *ásmegir,* the golden hall of Sindre's race (see Nos. 93, 94), and to those regions where mother Nat rests in a hall built on the southern spur of the Nida mountains (Forspjallsljod). The procession proceeds up this mountain region through valleys and gorges in which the rivers flowing from Hvergelmer find their way to the south. The damned leave Hvergelmer in their rear and cross the border rivers *Hraunn* (the subterranean Elivagar rivers, see No. 59), on the other side of which rise Nifelhel's black, perpendicular mountain-walls (Saxo, *Hist., Dan.;* see No. 46). Ladders or stairways lead across giddying precipices to the Na-gates. Howls and barking from the monstrous Nifelheim dogs watching the gates (see Nos. 46, 58) announce the arrival of the damned. Then hasten, in compact winged flocks, monsters, Nifelheim's birds of prey, Nidhog, Are, *Hræsvelger,* and their like to the south, and alight on the rocks around the Na-gates (see below). When the latter are opened on creaking hinges, the damned have died their second death. To that event, which is called "the second death," and to what this consists of, I shall return below (see No. 95).

Those who have thus marched to a terrible fate are sinners of various classes. Below Nifelheim there are nine regions of punishment. That these correspond to nine kinds of unpardonable sins is in itself probable, and is to some extent confirmed by Solarljod, if this poem, standing almost on the border-line between heathendom and Christianity, may be taken as a witness. Solarljod enumerates nine or ten kinds of punishments for as many different kinds of sins. From the purely heathen records we know that enemies of the gods (Loke), perjurers, murderers, adulterers (see Völuspa), those who have violated faith and the laws, and those who have lied about others, are doomed to Nifelhel for ever, or at least for a very long time (*oflengi*—Sig. Fafn., ii. 3). Of the unmerciful we know that they have already suffered great agony on their way to Urd's fountain. Both in reference to them and to others, it doubtless depended on the investigation at the Thing whether they could be ransomed or not.

The sacredness of the bond of kinship was strongly emphasised in the eschatological conceptions. *Niflgódr*, "good for the realm of damnation," is he who slays kinsmen and sells the dead body of his brother for rings (Sonatorrek, 15); but he who in all respects has conducted himself in a blameless manner toward his kinsmen and is slow to take revenge if they have wronged him, shall reap advantage therefrom after death (Sigrdr., 22).

When the damned come within the Na-gates, the winged demons rush at the victims designated for them, press them under their wings, and fly with them through Nifelheim's foggy space to the departments of torture appointed for them. The seeress in Völuspa (str. 62) sees Nidhog, loaded with *náir* under his wings, soar away from the Nida mountains. Whither he was accustomed to fly with them appears from strophe 38, where he in Nastrands is sucking his prey. When King Gorm, beyond the above-mentioned boundary river, and by the Nida mountains' ladders, had reached the Na-gates opened for him, he sees dismal monsters (*larvæ atræ;* cp. Völuspa's *in dimmi·dreki*) in dense crowds, and hears the air filled with their horrible screeches (cp. Völuspa's *Ari hlaccar, slitr nai neffaulr,* 47). When Solarljod's skald enters the realm of torture he sees "scorched" birds which are not birds but souls (*sálir*), flying "numerous as gnats."

76.

THE PLACES OF PUNISHMENT.

The regions over which the flocks of demons fly are the same as those which the author of Skirnersmal has in view when Skirner threatens Gerd with sending her to the realms of death. It is the home of the frost-giants, of the subterranean giants, and of the spirits of disease. Here live the offspring of Ymer's feet, the primeval giants strangely born and strangely bearing, who are waiting for the quaking of Ygdrasil and for the liberation of their chained leader, in order that they may take revenge on the gods in Ragnarok, and who in the meantime contrive futile plans of attack on Hvergelmer's fountain or on the north end of tie Bifrost bridge. Here the demons of restless uneasiness, of mental agony, of convulsive weeping, and of insanity (Othale, Morn. Ope, and Tope) have their home; and here dwells also their queen, Loke's daughter, Leikin, whose threshold is precipice and whose bed is disease. According to the authority used by Saxo in the description of Gorm's journey, the country is thickly populated. Saxo calls it *urbs, oppidum* (cp. Skir-nismal's words about the giant-homes, among w ich Gerd is to drag herself hopeless from house to house). The ground is a marsh with putrid water (*putidum cœnum*), which diffuses a horrible stench. The river Slid flowing north out of Hvergelmer there seeks its way in a muddy stream to the abyss which leads down to the nine places of punishment. Over all hovers Nifelheim's dismal sky.

The mortals who, like Gorm and his men, have been permitted to see these regions, and who have conceived the idea of descending into those worlds which lie below Nifelheim, or the most of them, are vast mountain caves, abyss in question and have cast a glance down into it. The place is narrow, but there is enough daylight for its bottom to be seen, and the sight thereof is terrible. Still, there must have been a path down to it, for when Gorm and his men had recovered from the first impression, they continued their journey to their destination (Geirrod's place of punishment), although the most terrible vapour (*teterrimus vapor*) blew into their faces. The rest that Saxo relates is unfortunately wanting both in sufficient clearness and in completeness. Without the risk of mak-ing a mistake, we may, however, consider it as mythically correct that some of the nine worlds of punishment below Nifelheim, or the most of them, are vast mountain caves, mutually united by openings broken through the mountain walls and closed with gates, which do not however, obstruct the course of Slid to the Nastrands and to the sea outside. Saxo speaks of a *perfractam scopuli partem,* "a pierced part of the mountain," through which travellers come from one of the subterranean caves to another, and between the caves stand gatekeepers (*janitores*). Thus there must be gates. At least two of these "homes" have been named after the most notorious sinner found within them. Saxo speaks of one called the giant Geirrod's, and an Icelandic document of one called the giant *Geitir's*. The technical term for such a cave of torture was *gnyskuti* (clamour-grotto). Saxo translates *skúti* with *conclave saxeum*. "To thrust anyone before Geitir's clamour-grotto"—*reka einn fyrir Geitis gnyskuta*—was a phrase synonymous with damning a person to death and hell.

The gates between the clamour-grottoes are watched by various kinds of demons. Before each gate stand several who in looks and conduct seem to symbolise the sins over whose perpetrators they keep guard. Outside of one of the caves of torture Gorm's men saw club-bearers who tried their weapons on one another. Outside of another gate the keepers amused themselves with "a monstrous game" in which they "mutually gave their ram-backs a curved motion." It is to be presumed that some sort of perpetrators of violence were tortured within the threshold, which was guarded by the club-bearers, and that the ram-shaped demons amused themselves outside of the torture-cave of debauchees. It is also probable that the latter is identical with the one called Geitir's. The name *Geitir* comes from *geit,* goat. Saxo, who Latinised *Geitir* into Götharus, tells adventures of his which show that this giant had tried to get possession of Freyja, and that he is identical with Gymer, Gerd's father. According to

536

Skirnersmal (35), there are found in Nifelhel goats, that is to say, trolls in goat-guise, probably of the same kind as those above-mentioned, and it may be with an allusion to the fate which awaits Gymer in the lower world, or with a reference to his epithet *Geitir,* that Skirner threatens Gerd with the disgusting drink (*geita hland*) which will there be given her by "the sons of misery" (*vélmegir*). One of the lower-world demons, who as his name indicates, was closely connected with Geitir, is called "Geitir's Howl-foot" (*Geitis Guýfeti*) ; and the expression "to thrust anyone before Geitir's Howl-foot" thus has the same meaning as to send him to damnation.

Continuing their journey, Gorm and his men came to Geirrod's *skúti* (see No. 46).

We learn from Saxo's description that in the worlds of torture there are seen not only terrors, but also delusions which tempt the eyes of the greedy. Gorm's prudent captain Thorkil (see No. 46) earnestly warns his companions not to touch these things, for hands that come in contact with them are fastened and are held as by invisible bonds. The illusions are characterised by Saxo as *ædis supellectilis,* an expression which is ambiguous, but may be an allusion that they represented things pertaining to temples. The statement deserves to be compared with Solarljod's strophe 65, where the skald sees in the lower world persons damned, whose hands are riveted together with burning stones. They are the mockers at religious rites (they who *minst vildu halda helga daga*) who are thus punished. In the mythology it was probably profaners of temples who suffered this punishment.

The Nastrands and the hall there are thus described in Völuspa:

> Sal sá hon standa
> sólu fjarri
> Náströndu á
> nordr horfa dyrr;
> fellu eitrdropar
> inn um ljora,
> Sá er undinn salr
> orma hryggjum.

> Sá hon tlar vada
> thunga strauma
> menn meinsvara
> ok mordvarga
> ok thanns annars glepr
> eyrarúna;
> tlar saug Nidhöggr
> nái framgengna,
> sleit vargr vera.

"A hall she saw stand far from the sun on the Nastrands; the doors opened to tie north. Venom-drops fell through the roof-holes. Braided is that hall of serpent-backs."

"There she saw perjurers, murderers, and they who betrayed the wife of another (adulterers) wade through heavy streams. There Nidhog sucked the *náir* of the dead. And the wolf tore men into pieces."

Gylfaginning (ch. 52) assumes that the serpents, whose backs, wattled together, form the hall, turn their heads into the hall, and that they, especially through the openings in the roof (according to Codex Ups. and Codex Hypnones.), vomit forth their floods of venom. The

538

latter assumption is well founded. Doubtful seems, on the other hand, Gylfaginning's assumption that "the heavy streams,' which the damned in Nastrands have to wade through, flow out over the floor of the hall. As the very name Nastrands indicates that the hall is situated near a water, then this water, whether it be the river *Slidr* with its eddies filled with weapons, or some other river, may send breakers on shore and thus produce the heavy streams which Völuspa mentions. Nevertheless Gylfaginning's view may be correct. The hall of Nastrands, like its counterpart Valhal, has certainly been regarded as immensely large. The serpent-venom raining down must have fallen on the floor of the hall, and there is nothing to hinder the venom-rain from being thought sufficiently abundant to form "heavy streams" thereon (see below).

Saxo's description of the hall in Nastrands—by him adapted to the realm of torture in general—is as follows: "The doors are covered with the soot of ages; the walls are bespattered with filth; the roof is closely covered with barbs; the floor is strewn with serpents and bespawled with all kinds of uncleanliness." The last statement confirms Gylfaginning's view. As this bespawling continues without ceasing through ages, the matter thus produced must grow into abundance and have an outlet. Remarkable is also Saxo's statement, that the doors are covered with the soot of ages. Thus fires must be kindled near these doors. Of this more later.

77.

THE PLACES OF PUNISHMENT (*continued*).   THE HALL
IN NASTRANDS.

Without allowing myself to propose any change of text
in the Völuspa strophes above quoted, and in pursuance
of the principle which I have adopted in this work, not to
base any conclusions on so-called text-emendations, which
invariably are text-debasings, I have applied these strophes
as they are found in the texts we have.   Like Müllenhoff
(*D. Alterth.*, v. 121) and other scholars, I am, however,
convinced that the strophe which begins *sá hon thar vada,*
&c., has been corrupted.   Several reasons, which I shall
present elsewhere in a special treatise on Völuspa, make
this probable; but simply the circumstance that the strophe
has ten lines is sufficient to awaken suspicions in anyone's
mind who holds the view that Völuspa originally consisted of exclusively eight-lined strophes—a view which
cannot seriously be doubted. As we now have the poem, it
consists of forty-seven strophes of eight lines each, one
of four lines, two of six lines each, five of ten lines each,
four of twelve lines each, and two of fourteen lines each
—in all fourteen not eight-lined strophes against forty-
seven eight-lined ones; and, while all the eight-lined ones
are intrinsically and logically well constructed, it may
be said of the others, that have more than eight lines
each, partly that we can cancel the superfluous lines without injury to the sense, and partly that they look like
loosely-joined conglomerations of scattered fragments of
strophes and of interpolations.   The most recent effort

to restore perfectly the poem to its eight-lined strophes has been made by Müllenhoff (*D. Alterth.,* v.); and although this effort may need revision in some special points, it has upon the whole given the poem a clearness, a logical sequence and symmetry, which of themselves make it evident that Müllenhoff's premises are correct.

In the treatise on Völuspa which I shall publish later, this subject will be thoroughly discussed. Here I may be permitted to say, that in my own efforts to restore Völuspa to eight-lined strophes, I came to a point where I had got the most of the materials arranged on this principle, but there remained the following fragment:

(1) Á fellr austan
um eitrdala
söxum ok sverdum
Slidr heitir sú.

(1) Falls a river from the east
around venom dales
with daggers and spears,
Slid it is called.

(2) Sá hon thar vada
thunga strauma
menn meinsvara
ok mordvarga
ok thanns annars
glepr eyrarúnu.

(2) There saw she wade
through heavy streams
perjurers
murderers
and him who seduces
another's wife.

These fragments make united ten lines. The fourth line of the fragment (1) *Slidr heitir sú* has the appearance of being a mythographic addition by the transcriber of the poem. Several similar interpolations which contain information of mythological interest, but which neither have the slightest connection with the context, nor are of the least importance in reference to the subject treated in Völuspa, occur in our present text-editions of this poem. The dwarf-list is a colossal interpolation of this kind. If we hypothetically omit this line for the present, and also the one immediately preceding (*söxum ok sverdum*), then there remains as many lines as are required in a regular eight-line strophe.

It is further to be remarked that among all the eight-lined Völuspa strophes there is not one so badly constructed that a verb in the first half-strophe has a direct object in the first line of the second half-strophe, as is the case in that of the present text:

> Sá hon tiar vada
> thunga strauma
> menn meinsvara
> ok mordvarga
> ok thann's annars glepr
> eyrarúnu;

and, upon the whole, such a construction can hardly ever have occurred in a tolerably passable poem. If these eight lines actually belonged to one and the same strophe, the latter would have to be restored according to the following scheme:

> (1) Sá hon tiar vada
> (2) thunga strauma
> (3) menn meinsvara
> (4) ok mordvarga;
> (5) . . . .
> (6) . . . .
> (7) thann's annars glepr
> (8) eyrarúnu.

and in one of the dotted lines the verb must have been found which governed the accusative object *thann*.

The lines which should take the place of the dots have, in their present form, the following appearance:

á fellr austan
um eitrdala.

The verb which governed *thann* must then be *áfellr*, that is to say, the verb *fellr* united with the preposition *á*. But in that case *á* is not the substantive *á*, a river, a running water, and thus the river which falls from the east around venom dales has its source in an error.

Thus we have, under this supposition, found that there is something that *fellr á*, falls on, streams down upon, him who seduces the wife of another. This something must be expressed by a substantive, which is now concealed behind the adverb *austan*, and must have resembled it sufficiently in sound to be transformed into it.

Such a substantive, and the only one of the kind, is *austr*. This means something that can *falla á*, stream down upon; for *austr* is *bail-water* (from *ausa*, to bail), waste-water, water flowing out of a gutter or shoot.

A test as to whether there originally stood *austr* or not is to be found in the following substantive, which now has the appearance of *eitrdala*. For if there was written *austr*, then there must, in the original text, have followed a substantive (1) which explained the kind of waste-water meant, (2) which had sufficient resemblance to *eitrdala* to become corrupted into it.

The sea-faring Norsman distinguished between two kinds of *austr*: *byttu-austr* and *dælu-austr*. The bail-water in a ship could be removed either by bailing it out with scoops directly over the railing, or it could be scooped into a *dæla,* a shoot or trough laid over the railing. The latter was the more convenient method. The difference between these two kinds of *austr* became a popular phrase; compare the expression *thá var byttu-austr, eigi dælu-austr.* The word *dæla* was also used figuratively; compare *láta dæluna ganga,* to let the shoots (troughs) run (Gretla, 98), a proverb by which men in animated conversation are likened unto *dælur,* troughs, which are opened for flowing conversation.

Under such circumstances we might here expect after the word *austr* the word *dæla,* and, as venom here is in question, *eitr-dæla.*

Eitr-dæla satisfies both the demands above made. It explains what sort of waste-water is meant, and it resembles *eitr-dala* sufficiently to be corrupted into it.

Thus we get *á fellr austr eitrdæla:* "On (him who seduces another man's wife) falls the waste-water of the venom-troughs." Which these venom-troughs are, the strophe in its entirety ought to define. This constitutes the second test of the correctness of the reading.

It must be admitted that if *á fellr austr eitrdæla* is the original reading, then a corruption into *á fellr austan eitrdala* had almost of necessity to follow, since the preposition *á* was taken to be the substantive *á,* river, a running stream. How near at hand such a confounding of these words lies is demonstrated by another Völuspa strophe, where the preposition *á* in *á ser hon ausaz aurgom forsi* was long interpreted as the substantive *á.*

We shall now see whether the expression *á fellr austr*

544

citrdæla makes sense, when it is introduced in lieu of the dotted lines above:

> Sá hon tıar vada
> thunga strauma
> menn meinsvara
> ok mordvarga;
> (en) á fellr austr
>   eitrdæla
> thann's annars glepr
>   eyrarúna.

"There saw she heavy streams (of venom) flow upon (or through) perjurers and murderers. The waste-water of the venom-troughs (that is, the waste-water of the perjurers and murderers after the venom-streams had rushed over them) falls upon him who seduces the wife of another man."

Thus we get not only a connected idea, but a very remarkable and instructive passage.

The verb *vada* is not used only about persons who wade through a water. The water itself is also able to *vada* (cp. *eisandi udr vedr undan*—Rafns S. Sveinb.), to say nothing of arrows that wade *i fólk* (Havam., 150), and of banners which wade in the throng of warriors. Here the venom wades through the crowds of perjurers and murderers. The verb *vada* has so often been used in this sense, that it has also acquired the meaning of *rushing, running, rushing through*. Heavy venom-streams run through the perjurers and murderers before they fall on the adulterers. The former are the venom-troughs, which pour their waste-water upon the latter.

We now return to Saxo's description of the hall of

Nastrands, to see whether the Völuspa strophe thus hypothetically restored corresponds with, or is contradicted by, it. Disagreeable as the pictures are which we meet with in this comparison, we are nevertheless compelled to take them into consideration.

Saxo says that the wall of the hall is bespattered with liquid filth (*paries obductus illuvie*). The Latin word, and the one used by Saxo for venom, is *venenum,* not *illuvies,* which means filth that has been poured or bespattered on something. Hence Saxo does not mean venom-streams of the kind which, according to Völuspa, are vomited by the serpents down through the roof-openings, but the reference is to something else, which still must have an upper source, since it is bespattered on the wall of the hall.

Saxo further says that the floor is bespawled with all sorts of impurity: *pavimentum omni sordium genere respersum.* The expression confirms the idea, that unmixed venom is not meant here, but everything else of the most disgusting kind.

Furthermore, Saxo relates that groups of damned are found there within, which groups he calls *consessus.* *Consessus* means "a sitting together," and, in a secondary sense, persons sitting together. The word "sit" may here be taken in a more or less literal sense. *Consessor,* "the one who sits together with," might be applied to every participator in a Roman dinner, though the Romans did not actually sit, but reclined at the table.

As stated, several such *consessus,* persons sitting or lying together, are found in the hall. The benches upon which they sit or lie are of iron. Every *consessus* has a *locus* in the hall; and as both these terms, *consessus* and *locus,* in Saxo united in the expression *consessuum loca,* together mean rows of benches in a theatre or in a public place, where the seats rise in rows one above the other, we must assume that these rows of the damned sitting or lying together are found in different elevations between the floor and ceiling. This assumption is corroborated by what Saxo tells, viz., that their *loca* are separated by leaden hurdles (*plumbeæ crates*). That they are separated by hurdles must have some practical reason, and this can be none other than that something flowing down may have an unobstructed passage from one *consessus* to the other. That which flows down finally reaches the floor, and is then *omne sordium genus,* all kinds of impurity. It must finally be added that, according to Saxo, the stench in this room of torture is well-nigh intolerable (*super omnia perpetui fætoris asperitas tristes lacessebat olfactus*).

Who is not able to see that Völuspa's and Saxo's descriptions of the hall in Nastrands confirm, explain, and complement each other? From Völuspa's words, we conclude that the venom-streams come from the openings in the roof, not from the walls. The wall consists, in its entirety, of the *backs* of serpents wattled together (*sá er undinn salr orma hryggjom*). The heads belonging to these serpents are above the roof, and vomit their venom down through the roof-openings—"the ljors" (*fellu eitrdropar inn um ljóra*). Below these, and between them and the floor, there are, as we have seen in Saxo,

547

rows of iron seats, the one row below the other, all furnished with leaden hurdles, and on the iron seats sit or lie perjurers and murderers, forced to drink the venom raining down in "heavy streams." Every such row of sinners becomes "a trough of venom" for the row immediately below it, until the disgusting liquid thus produced falls on those who have seduced the dearest and most confidential friends of others. These seducers either constitute the lowest row of the seated delinquents, or they wade on the floor in that filth and venom which there flows. Over the hall broods eternal night (it is *sólu fjarri*). What there is of light, illuminating the terrors, comes from fires (see below) kindled at the doors which open to the north (*nordr horfa dyrr*). The smoke from the fires comes into the hall and covers the door-posts with the "soot of ages" (*postes longæva fuligine illitæ*).

With this must be compared what Tacitus relates concerning the views and customs of the Germans in regard to crime and punishment. He says:

"The nature of the crime determines the punishment. Traitors and deserters they hang on trees. Cowards and those given to disgraceful debauchery they smother in filthy pools and marshes, casting a *hurdle* (crates) over them. The dissimilarity in these punishments indicates a belief that crime should be punished in such a way that the penalty is visible, while scandalous conduct should be punished in such a way that the debauchee is removed from the light of day" (*Germania*, xii.).

This passage in *Germania* is a commentary on Saxo's descriptions, and on the Völuspa strophe in the form resulting from my investigation. What might naturally seem probable is corroborated by *Germania's* words: that the same view of justice and morality, which obtained in the camp of the Germans, found its expression, but in gigantic exaggeration, in their doctrines concerning eschatological rewards and punishments. It should, perhaps, also be remarked that a similar particularism prevailed through centuries. The hurdle (*crates*) which Saxo mentions as being placed over the venom- and filth-drinking criminals in the hall of Nastrands has its earthly counterpart in the hurdle (also called *crates*), which, according to the custom of the age of Tacitus, was thrown over victims smothered in the cesspools and marshes (*ignavos et imbelles et corpore infames cœno ac palude injecta insuper crate mergunt*). Those who were sentenced to this death were, according to Tacitus, cowards and debauchees. Among those who received a similar punishment in the Teutonic Gehenna were partly those who in a secret manner had committed murder and tried to conceal their crime (such were called *mordvorgr*), partly debauchees who had violated the sacredness of matrimony. The descriptions in the Völuspa strophe and in Saxo show that also in the hall of the Nastrands the punishment is in accordance with the nature of the crime. All are punished terribly; but there is a distinction between those who had to drink the serpent venom unmixed and those who receive the mixed potion, and finally those who get the awful liquid over themselves and doubtless within themselves.

In closing this chapter I will quote a number of Völuspa

strophes, which refer to Teutonic eschatology. In parallel columns I print the strophes as they appear in Codex Regius, and in the form they have assumed as the result of an investigation of which I shall give a full account in the future. I trust it will be found that the restoration of *á fellr austan um eitrdala* into *á fellr austr eitrdæla,* and the introducing of these words before *thanns annars glepr eyrarúna* not only restores to the strophe in which these words occur a regular structure and a sense which is corroborated by Saxo's eschatological sources and by the *Germania* of Tacitus, but also supplies the basis and conditions on which other strophes may get a regular structure and intelligible contents.

Codex Regius.	*Revised Text.*
A fellr austan um eitrdala sauxom oc sverthom slithr heitir su. Stod fyr nordan a nitha vollom salr or gulli sindra ettar. enn annar stod a okolni bior salr iotuns en sa brimir heitir.	 Stód fyr nordan a Nida völlum salr or gulli Sindra ættar; enn annar stod a Ókólni, bjorsals jötuns, en sá Brimir heitir.
Sal sá hon standa solo fiárri na strondu a northr horfa dyrr	Sal sá hon standa sólu fjarri Náströndu á, nordr horfa dyrr;

fello eitr dropar
inn um lióra
sa er undinn salr
orma hryggiom.

(38) Sa hon tıar vada
tıunga strauma
menn meinsvara
oc mordvargar.
oc tıann annars glepr
eyra runo
tıar sug nithhauggr
nái fram gegna
sleit vargr vera
vitoth er en etıa hvat.

(35) Hapt sa hon liggia
undir hvera lundi
legiarn lici
loca atheckian.
tıar sitr Sigyn
theygi um sinom
ver velglyiod
vitoth er en etıa hvat.

fellu eitrdropar
inn um ljóra,
sa er undinn salr
orma hryggjum.

Sa hon tıar vada
thunga strauma
menn meinsvara
oc mordvarga;
en á fell austr
eitrdæla
tıanns annars glepr
eyrarúnu

Hapt sá hon liggja
undir hveralundi
lægjarnliki
Loka áthekkjan;
tıar saug Nidhöggr
nái framgengna,
sleit vargr vera.
Vitud ér enn eda hvat?

Tıar kná Vala
vigbönd snúa,
ıeldr várn hardgör
höpt or
thörmum;
tıar sitr Sigyn
theygi um sínum
ver vel glýgud.
Vitud ér enn eda hvat?

78.

THE PLACES OF PUNISHMENT. (*continued*). LOKE'S CAVE OF PUNISHMENT. GYLFAGINNING'S CONFOUNDING OF MUSPEL'S SONS WITH THE SONS OF SUTTUNG.

Saxo (*Hist. Dan.*, 429 ff.) relates that the experienced Captain Thorkil made, at the command of King Gorm, a second journey to the uttermost North, in order to complete the knowledge which was gained on the first journey. That part of the lower world where Loke (by Saxo called Ugartilocus) dwells had not then been seen. This now remained to be done. Like the first time, Thorkil sailed into that sea on which sun and stars never shine, and he kept cruising so long in its darkness that his supply of fuel gave out. The expedition was as a consequence on the point of failing, when a fire was suddenly seen in the distance. Thorkil then entered a boat with a few of his men and rowed thither. In order to find his way back to his ship in the darkness, he had placed in the mast-top a self-luminous precious stone, which he had taken with him on the journey. Guided by the light, Thorkil came to a strand-rock, in which there were narrow "gaps" (*fauces*), out of which the light came. There was also a door, and Thorkil entered, after requesting his men to remain outside.

Thorkil found a grotto. At the fire which was kindled stood two uncommonly tall men, who kept mending the fire. The grotto had an inner door or gate, and that

d to be done. Like the first tim
that sea on which sun and stars neve
ruising so long in its darkness that hi
out. The expedition was as a con

which was seen inside that gate is described by Saxo in almost the same words as those of his former description of the hall at the Nastrands (*obsoleti postes, ater situ paries, sordidum tectum, frequens anguibus pavimentum*). Thorkil in reality sees the same hall again; he had simply come to it from another side, from the north, where the hall has its door opening toward the strand (*nordr horfa dyrr*—Völuspa), the pillars of which, according to Saxo's previous description, are covered with the soot of ages. The soot is now explained by the fire which is kindled in the grotto outside the hall, the grotto forming as it were a vestibule. The two gigantic persons who mend the fire are called by Saxo *aquili*.

In Marcianus Capella, who is Saxo's model in regard to style and vocabulary, persons of semi-divine rank (*hemithei*) are mentioned who are called *aquili,* and who inhabit the same regions as the souls of the dead (*lares* and *larvæ*—Marc. Cap., i., ii. Compare P. E. Müller, not., *Hist. Dan.,* pp. 68, 69). Aquilus also has the signification, *dark, swarthy,* Icel. *dökkr.*

In the northern mythology a particular kind of elves are mentioned—black or swarthy elves, *dökkálfar.* They dwell under the farthest root of the world-tree, near the northern gate of the lower world (*iormungrundar i iodyr nyrdra*), and have as their neighbours the Thurses and the unhappy dead (*náir*—Forspjallsljod, 25). Gylfaginning also (ch. 17) knows of the swarthy elves, at least, that they "dwell down in the earth" (*búa nidri í jördu*). As to mythic rank, colour, and abode, they therefore correspond with the Roman *aquili,* and Saxo has forcibly

553

and very correctly employed this Latin word in order t characterise them in an intelligible manner.

The two swarthy elves keeping watch outside of the hall of Nastrands ought naturally to have been astonished at seeing a living human being entering their grotto. Saxo makes them receive the unexpected guest in a friendly manner. They greet him, and, when they have learned the purpose of his visit, one of them reproaches him for the rash boldness of his undertaking, but gives him information in regard to the way to Loke, and gives him fire and fuel after he had tested Thorkil's understanding, and found him to be a wise man. The journey, says the swarthy elf, can be performed in four days' fast sailing. As appears from the context, the journey is to the east. The traveller then comes to a place where not a blade of grass grows, and over which an even denser darkness broods. The place includes several terrible rocky halls, and in one of them Loke dwells.

On the fourth day Thorkil, favoured by a good wind, comes to the goal of his journey. Through the darkness a mass of rock rising from the sea (*scopulum inusitatæ molis*) is with difficulty discerned, and Thorkil lays to by this rocky island. He and his men put on clothes of skin of a kind that protects against venom, and then walk along the beach at the foot of the rock until they find an entrance. Then they kindle a fire with flint stones, this being an excellent protection against demons; they light torches and crawl in through the narrow opening. Unfortunately Saxo gives but a scanty account of what they saw there. First they came to a cave of torture, which resembled the hall on the Nastrands, at least, in this particular, that there were many serpents and many iron seats or iron benches of the kind described above. A brook of sluggish water is crossed by wading. Another grotto which is not described was passed through, whereupon they entered Loke's awful prison. He lay there bound hands and feet with immense chains. His hair and beard resembled spears of horn, and had a terrible odour. Thorkil jerked out a hair of his beard to take with him as evidence of what he had seen. As he did this, there was diffused in the cave a pestilential stench; and after Thorkil's arrival home, it appeared that the beard-hair he had taken home was dangerous to life on account of its odour (*Hist. Dan.*, 433). When Thorkil and his men had passed out of the interior jurisdiction of the rock, they were discovered by flying serpents which had their home on the island (cp. Völuspa—*thar saug Nidhöggr*, &c., No. 77). The skin clothes protected them against the venom vomited forth. But one of the men who bared his eyes became blind. Another, whose hand came outside of the protecting garments, got it cut off; and a third, who ventured to uncover his head, got the latter separated from his neck by the poison as by a sharp steel instrument.

The poem or saga which was Saxo's authority for this story must have described the rocky island where Loke was put in chains as inhabited by many condemned beings. There are at least three caves of torture, and in one of them there are many iron benches. This is confirmed, as we shall see, by Völuspa.

Saxo also says that there was a harbour. From Völuspa we learn that when Ygdrasil trembles at the approach of Ragnarok, the ship of the dead, Nagelfar, lies so that the liberated Loke can go aboard it. That it has long lain moored in its harbour is evident from the fact that, according to Völuspa, it then "becomes loose." Unknown hands are its builders. The material out of which it is constructed is the nail-parings of dead men (Gylfag., 51—probably according to some popular tradition). The less regard for religion, the less respect for the dead. But from each person who is left unburied, or is put into his grave without being, when possible, washed, combed, cleaned as to hands and feet, and so cared for that his appearance may be a favourable evidence to the judges at the Thing of the dead in regard to his survivors—from each such person comes building material for the death-ship, which is to carry the hosts of world-destroyers to the great conflict. Much building material is accumulated in the last days—in the "dagger-and-axe age," when "men no longer respect each other" (Völuspa).

Nagelfar is the largest of all ships, larger than Skidbladner (*Skidbladnir er beztr skipanna . . . en Naglfari er mest skip*—Gylfag., 43). This very fact shows that it is to have a large number of persons on board when it departs from Loke's rocky island. Völuspa says:

Str. 47, 8. Naglfar losnar,	Nagelfar becomes loose,
Str. 48. Kioll ferr austan,	a ship comes from the east,
koma muno Muspellz	the hosts of Muspel
um laug lydir,	come o'er the main,
en Loki styrir;	Loke is pilot;
fara Fifls megir	all Fifel's descendants

med Freka allır,	come witı Freke,
tıeim er brodir	Byleipt's brotıer
Byleipts i fór.	is witı tıem on the journey.

Here it is expressly stated that "the hosts of Muspel" are on board the ship, Nagelfar, guided by Loke, after it has been "freed from its moorings" and had set sail from tıe island where Loke and other damned ones were imprisoned.

How can this be harmonised with the doctrine based on the authority of Gylfaginning, that the sons of Muspel are inhabitants of the southernmost region of light and warmth, Gylfaginning's so-called Muspelheim? or with the doctrine that Surt is the protector of the borders of this realm? or that Muspel's sons proceed under his command to the Ragnarok conflict, and that they consequently must come from the South, which Völuspa also seems to corroborate with the words *Surtr ferr sunnan med sviga læfi?*

The answer is that the one statement cannot be harmonised with the other, and the question then arises as to which of the two authorities is the authentic one, the heathen poem Völuspa or Gylfaginning, produced in the thirteenth century by a man who had a vague conception of the mythology of our ancestors. Even the most uncritical partisan of Gylfaginning would certainly unhesitatingly decide in favour of Völuspa, provided we had this poem handed down in its pure form from the heathen days. But this is clearly not the case. We therefore need a third witness to decide between the two. Such an one is also actually to be found.

In the Norse heathen records the word *muspell* occurs only twice, viz., in the above-mentioned Völuspa strophe and in Lokasenna, 42, where Frey, who has surrendered his sword of victory, is threatened by Loke with the prospect of defeat and death—*er Muspellz synir rida Myrcvith yfir,* "when Muspel's sons ride over Darkwood." The Myrkwood is mentioned in Volundarkvida (1) as a forest, through which the swan-maids coming from the South flew into the wintry Ulfdales, where one chases bears on skees (snow-shoes) to get food. This is evidently not a forest situated near the primeval fountains of heat and fire. The very arbitrary manner in which the names of the mythical geography is used in the heroic poems, where Myrkwood comes to the surface, does not indicate that this forest was conceived as situated south of Midgard, and there is, as shall be shown below, reason for assuming that Darkwood is another name for the Ironwood famous in mythology; the wood which, according to Völuspa, is situated in the East, and in which Angerboda fosters the children of Loke and Fenrer.

One of these, and one of the worst, is the monster Hate, the enemy of the moon mentioned in Völuspa as *tungls tiugari,* that makes excursions from the Ironwood and "stains the citadels of rulers with blood." In the Ragnarok conflict Hate takes part and contends with Tyr (Gylfag.), and, doubtless, not only he, but also the whole offspring of the Fenris-wolf fostered in the Ironwood, are on the battlefield in that division which is commanded by Loke their clan-chief. This is also, doubtless, the meaning of the following words in the Völuspa strophe quoted above: "Flfel's descendants all come with Freke (the wolf), and in company with them is Byleipt's (or Byleist's) brother." As Loke, Byleipt, and Helblinde are mentioned as brothers (Gylfag., 33), no one else can be meant with "Byleipt's brother" than Loke himself or Helblinde, and more probably the latter, since it has already been stated, that Loke is there as the commander of the forces. Thus it is Muspel's sons and Loke's kinsmen in the Ironwood who are gathered around him when the great conflict is at hand. Muspel's sons accompany the liberated Loke from his rocky isle, and are with him on board Nagelfar. Loke's first destination is the Ironwood, whither he goes to fetch Angerboda's children, and thence the journey proceeds "over Myrkwood" to the plain of Vigrid. The statements of Völuspa and Lokasenna illustrate and corroborate each other, and it follows that Völuspa's statement, claiming that Muspel's sons come from the East, is original and correct.

Gylfaginning treats Muspel as a place, a realm, the original home of fire and heat (Gylfag., 5). Still, there is a lack of positiveness, for the land in question is in the same work called *Múspellsheimr* (ch. 5) and *Múspells heimr* (ch. 8), whence we may presume that the author regarded *Múspell* as meaning both the land of the fire and the fire itself. The true etymology of *Múspell* was probably as little known in the thirteenth century, when Gylfaginning was written, as it is now. I shall not speak of the several attempts made at conjecturing the definition of the word. They may all be regarded as abortive, mainly, doubtless, for the reason that Gylfaginning's statements have credulously been assumed as the basis of the investigation. As a word inherited from heathen times, it occurs under the forms *mutspelli* and *muspilli* in the Old Saxon poem Heliand and in an Old High German poem on the final judgment, and there it has the meaning of the Lord's day, the doom of condemnation, or the condemnation. Concerning the meaning which the word had among the heathens of the North, before the time of the authors of Völuspa and Lokasenna, all that can be said with certainty is, that the word in the expression "Muspel's sons" has had a special reference to mythical beings who are to appear in Ragnarok fighting there as Loke's allies, that is, on the side of the evil against the good; that these beings were Loke's fellow-prisoners on the rocky isle where he was chained; and that they accompanied him from there on board Nagelfar to war against the gods. As Gylfaginning makes them accompany Surt coming from the South, this must be the result of a confounding of "Muspel's sons" with "Surt's (Suttung's) sons."

A closer examination ought to have shown that Gylfaginning's conception of "Muspel's sons" is immensely at variance with the mythical. Under the influence of Christian ideas they are transformed into a sort of angels of light, who appear in Ragnarok to contend under the command of Surt "to conquer all the idols" (*sigra öll godin*—Gylfag. 4) and carry out the punishment of the world. While Völuspa makes them come with Loke in the ship Nagelfar, that is, from the terrible rocky isle in the sea over which eternal darkness broods, and while

Lokasenna makes them come across the Darkwood, whose name does not suggest any region in the realm of light, Gylfaginning tells us that they are celestial beings. Idols and giants contend with each other on Vigrid's plains; then *the heavens* are suddenly rent in twain, and out of it ride in shining squadrons "Muspel's sons" and Surt, with his flaming sword, at the head of the fylkings. Gylfaginning is careful to keep these noble riders far away from every contact with that mob which Loke leads to the field of battle. It therefore expressly states that they form a fylking by themselves (*I thessum gny Klofnar himininn, ok ridu thadan Muspells synir; Surtr ridr fyrstr,* &c. . . . *enn Muspells synir hafa einir sér fylking, er sá björt mjök*—ch. 56). Thus they do not come to assist Loke, but to put an end to both the idols and the mob of giants. The old giant, Surt, who, according to a heathen skald, Eyvind Skaldaspiller, dwells in *sökkdalir,* in mountain grottoes deep under the earth (see about him, No. 89), is in Gylfaginning first made the keeper of the borders of "Muspelheim," and then the chief of celestial hosts. But this is not the end of his promotion. In the text found in the Upsala Codex, Gylfaginning makes him lord in Gimle, and likewise the king of eternal bliss. After Ragnarok it is said, "there are many good abodes and many bad;" *best it is to be in Gimle with Surt* (*margar ero vistar gothar og margar illar, bezt er at vera a Gimle medr surtr*). The name Surt means black. We find that his dark looks did not prevent his promotion, and this has been carried to such a point that a mythologist who honestly believed in Gylfaginning saw in him the Almighty

561

who is to come after the regeneration to equalise and har-
mouise all discord, and to found holy laws to prevail for
ever,

Under such circumstances, it may be suggested as a
rule of critical caution not to accept unconditionally Gylfaginning's statement that the world of light and heat
which existed before the creation of the world was called
Muspel or Muspelheim. In all probability, this is a
result of the author's own reflections. At all events, it is
certain that no other record has any knowledge of that
name. But that the mythology presumed the existence of
such a world follows already from the fact that Urd's
fountain, which gives the warmth of life to the world-
tree, must have had its deepest fountain there, just as
Hvergelmer has its in the world of primeval cold, and
Mimer has his fountain in that wisdom which unites the
opposites and makes them work together in a cosmic
world.

Accordingly, we must distinguish between *Múspells
megir, Múspells synir,* from Surt's clan-men, who are
called *Surts ætt, synir Suttunga, Suttungs synir* (Skirnis-
mal, 34; Alvissm., 35). We should also remember that
Múspell in connection with the words *synir* and *megir*
hardly can mean a land, a realm, a region. The figure
by which the inhabitants of a country are called its sons or
descendants never occurs, so far as I know, in the oldest
Norse literature.

In regard to the names of the points of the compass
in the poetic Edda, *nordan* and *austan,* it must not be forgotten that the same northern regions in the mythical

geography to which various events are referred must have been regarded by the Icelanders as lying to the east from their own northern isle. The *Bjarmia ultcrior,* in whose night-shrouded waters mythical adventurers sougit the gates to the lower world, lay in the uttermost North, and might still, from an Icelandic and also from a Norwegian standpoint, be designated as a land in the East. According to tie sagas preserved by Saxo, these adventurers sailed into the Arctic Ocean, past the Norwegian coast, and eastward to a mythical Bjarmia, more distant than the real Bjarmaland. They could thus come to the coast where a gate to the lower world was to be found, and to the Nastrands, and if they continued this same course to the East, they could finally get to the rocky isle where Loke lay chained.

We have seen that Loke is not alone with Sigyn on that isle where in chains he abides Ragnarok. There were unhappy beings in large numbers with him. As already stated, Saxo speaks of three connected caves of torture there, and the innermost one is Loke's. Of the one nearest to it, Saxo tells nothing else than that one has to wade across a brook or river in order to get there. Of the bound Fenrer, Loke's son, it is said that from his mouth runs froth which forms the river Von (Gylfag., 34). In Lokasenna (34) Frey says to the abusive Loke: "A wolf (that is, Feurer) I see lying at the mouth of the river until the forces of the world come in conflict; if you do not hold your tongue, you, villain, will be chained *next to him*" (*thvi nœst*—an expression which here should be taken in a local sense, as a definite place is mentioned in the preceding sentence). And as we learn from Völuspa, that Freke (the wolf) is with Loke on board Nagelfar, then these evidences go to show that Loke and his son are chained in the same place. The isle where Feurer was chained is called in Gylfaginning *Lyngvi,* and the body of water in which the isle is situated is called *Amsvartnir,* a suitable name of the sea, over which eternal darkness broods. On the isle, the probably Icelandic author of Völuspa (or its translator or compiler) has imagined a "grove," whose trees consist of jets of water springing from hot fountains (*hvera lundr*). The isle is guarded by *Garmr,* a giant-dog, who is to bark with all its might when the chains of Loke and Fenrer threaten to burst asunder:

> Geyr Garmr mjök
> fyr Gnipahelli
> Fcstr man slitna,
> en Freki renna.

According to Grimnersmal, Garm is the foremost of all dogs. The dogs which guard the beautiful Menglad's citadel are also called Garms (Fjölsvinnsmal). In Gylfaginning, the word is also used in regard to a wolf, Hate Manegarm. *Gnipahellir* means the cave of the precipitous rock. The adventurers which Thorkil and his men encountered with the flying serpents, in connection with the watching Hel-dog, show that Lyngve is the scene of demons of the same kind as those which are found around the Na-gates of Nifelheim.

Bound hands and feet with the entrails of a "frost-cold son" (Lokasenna, 49), which, after being placed on

564

his limbs, are transformed into iron chains (Gylfag., 54), Loke lies on a weapon (*a hiorvi*—Lokasenna, 49), and under him are three flat stones placed on edge, one under his shoulders, one under his loins, and one under his hams (Gylfag., 54). Over him Skade, who is to take revenge for the murder of her father, suspends a serpent in such a manner that the venom drops in the face of the nithing. Sigyn, faithful to her wicked husband, sits sorrowing by his side (Völuspa) and protects him as well as she is able against the venom of the serpent (Postscript to Loka- senna, Gylfag., 54). Fenrer is fettered by the soft, silk- like chain Gleipner, made by the subterranean artist, and brought from the lower world by Hermod. It is the only chain that can hold him, and that cannot be broken before Ragnarok. His jaws are kept wide open with a sword (Gylfag., 35).

79.

THE GREAT WORLD-MILL. ITS MISTAKEN IDENTITY WITH THE FRODE-MILL.

We have yet to mention a place in the lower world which is of importance to the naïve but, at the same time, perspicuous and imaginative cosmology of Teutonic heathendom. The myth in regard to the place in ques- tion is lost, but it has left scattered traces and marks, with the aid of which it is possible to restore its chief outlines.

Poems, from the heathen time, speak of two wonderful mills, a larger and a smaller "Grotte"-mill.

The larger one is simply immense. The storms and showers which lash the sides of the mountains and cause their disintegration; the breakers of the sea which attack the rocks on the strands, make them hollow, and cast the substance thus scooped out along the coast in the form of sand-banks; the whirlpools and currents of the ocean, and the still more powerful forces that were fancied by antiquity, and which smouldered the more brittle layers of the earth's solid crust, and scattered them as sand and mould over "the stones of the hall," in order that the ground might "be overgrown with green herbs"—all this was symbolised by the larger Grotte-mill. And as all symbols, in the same manner as the lightning which becomes Thor's hammer, in the mythology become epic-pragmatic realities, so this symbol becomes to the imagination a real mill, which operates deep down in the sea and causes the phenomena which it symbolises.

This greater mill was also called *Grædir,* since its grist is the mould in which vegetation grows. This name was gradually transferred by the poets of the Christian age from the mill, which was grinding beneath the sea, to the sea itself.

The lesser Grotte-mill is like the greater one of heathen origin—Egil Skallagrimson mentions it—but it plays a more accidental part, and really belongs to the heroic poems connected with the mythology. Meanwhile, it is akin to the greater. Its stones come from the lower world, and were cast up thence for amusement by young giant-maids to the surface of the earth. A being called *Hengikjöptr* (the feminine *Hengikepta* is the name of a giantess—Sn. Edda, i. 551; ii. 471) makes mill-stones out of these subterranean rocks, and presents the mill to King Frode Fridleifson. Fate brings about that the same young giantesses, having gone to Svithiod to help the king warring there, Guthorm (see Nos. 38, 39), are taken prisoners and sold as slaves to King Frode, who makes them turn his Grotte-mill, the stones of which they recognise from their childhood. The giantesses, whose names are Fenja and Menja, grind on the mill gold and safety for King Frode, and good-will among men for his kingdom. But when Frode, hardened by greed for gold, refuses them the necessary rest from their toils, they grind fire and death upon him, and give the mill so great speed that the mill-stone breaks into pieces, and the foundation is crushed under its weight.

After the introduction of Christianity, the details of the myth concerning the greater, the cosmological mill, were forgotten, and there remained only the memory of the existence of such a mill on the bottom of the sea. The recollection of the lesser Grotte-mill was, on the other hand, at least in part preserved as to its details in a song which continued to flourish, and which was recorded in Skaldskaparmal.

Both mills were now regarded as identical, and there sprang up a tradition which explained how they could be so.

Contrary to the statements of the song, the tradition narrates that the mill did not break into pieces, but stood whole and perfect, when the curse of the giant-maids on Frode was fulfilled. The night following the day when

they had begun to grind misfortune on Frode, there came
a sea-king, Mysing, and slew Frode, and took, among
other booty, also the Grotte-mill and both the female
slaves, and carried them on board his ship. Mysing
commanded them to grind salt, and this they continued
to do until the following midnight. Then they asked if
he had not got enough, but he commanded them to con-
tinne grinding, and so they did until the ship shortly afterwards sank. In this manner the tradition explained
how the mill came to stand on the bottom of the sea, and
there the mill that had belonged to Frode acquired the
qualities which originally had belonged to the vast Grotte-
mill of the mythology. Skaldskaparmal, which relates
this tradition as well as the song, without taking any
notice of the discrepancies between them, adds that after
Frode's mill had sunk, "there was produced a whirlpool
in the sea, caused by the waters running through the hole
in the mill-stone, and from that time the sea is salt."

80.

THE WORLD-MILL (*continued*).

With distinct consciousness of its symbolic signification, the greater mill is mentioned in a strophe by the
skald Snæbjorn (Skaldskap., ch. 25). The strophe appears to have belonged to a poem describing a voyage.
"It is said," we read in this strophe, "that *Eyludr's* nine
women violently turn the Grotte of the skerry dangerous
to man out near the edge of the earth, and that these
women long ground Amlode's *lid*-grist."

Hvat kveda hræra Grotta
hergrimmastan skerja
ut fyrir jardar skauti
Eyludrs níu brúdir:
tlær er . . fyrir laungu
lid-meld . . . . .

. . . .
. . . Amloda mólu.

To the epithet *Eyludr,* and to the meaning of *lid*-in *lid*-grist, I shall return below. The strophe says that the mill is in motion out on the edge of the earth, that nine giant-maids turn it (for the lesser Grotte-mill two were more than sufficient), that they had long ground with it, that it belongs to a *skerry* very dangerous to seafaring men, and that it produces a peculiar grist.

The same mill is suggested by an episode in Saxo, where he relates the saga about the Danish prince, Amlethus, who on account of circumstances in his home was compelled to pretend to be insane. Young courtiers, who accompanied him on a walk along the sea-strand, showed him a sand-bank and said that it was meal. The prince said he knew this to be so: he said it was "meal from the mill of the storms" (*Hist. Dan.,* 141).

The myth concerning the cosmic Grotte-mill was intimately connected partly with the myth concerning the fate of Ymer and the other primeval giants, and partly with that concerning Hvergelmer's fountain. Vafthrudnersmal (21) and Grimnersmal (40) tell us that the earth was made out of Ymer's flesh, the rocks out of his bones, and the sea from his blood. With earth is here meant, as distinguished from rocks, the mould, the sand, which

569

cover the solid ground. Vafthrudnersmal calls Ymer *Aurgelmir,* Claygelmer or Moldgelmer; and Fjölsvinns-mal gives him the epithet *Leirbrimir,* Claybrimer, which suggests that his "flesh" was changed into the loose earth, while his bones became rocks. Ymer's descendants, the primeval giants, Thrudgelmer and Bergelmer perished with him, and the "flesh" of their bodies cast into the primeval sea also became mould. Of this we are assured, so far as Bergelmer is concerned, by strophe 35 in Vafthrudnersmal, which also informs us that Bergelmer was *laid under the mill-stone.* The mill which ground his "flesh" into mould can be none other than the one grinding under the sea, that is, the cosmic Grotte-mill.

When Odin asks the wise giant Vafthrudner how far back he can remember, and which is the oldest event of which he has any knowledge from personal experience, the giant answers: "Countless ages ere the earth was shapen Bergelmer was born. The first thing I remember is when he *á var lúdr um lagidr.*"

This expression was misunderstood by the author of Gylfaginning himself, and the misunderstanding has continued to develop into the theory that Bergelmer was changed into a sort of Noah, who with his household saved himself in an ark when Bur's sons drowned the primeval giants in the blood of their progenitor. Of such a counterpart to the Biblical account of Noah and his ark our Teutonic mythical fragments have no knowledge whatever.

The word *lúdr* (with radical *r*) has two meanings: (1) a wind-instrument, a loor, a war-trumpet; (2) the tier of beams, the underlying timbers of a mill, and, in a wider sense, the mill itself.

The first meaning, that of war-trumpet, is not found in the songs of the Elder Edda, and upon the whole does not occur in the Old Norse poetry. Heimdal's war-trumpet is not called *lúdr,* but *horn* or *hljód.* *Lúdr* in this sense makes its first appearance in the sagas of Christian times, but is never used by the skalds. In spite of this fact the signification may date back to heathen times. But however this may be, *lúdr* in Vafthrudnersmal does not mean a war-trumpet. The poem can never have meant that Bergelmer was laid on a musical instrument.

The other meaning remains to be discussed. *Lúdr,* partly in its more limited sense of the timbers or beams under the mill, partly in the sense of the subterranean mill in its entirety, and the place where it is found, occurs several times in the poems : in the Grotte-song, in Helge Hund. (ii. 2), and in the above-quoted strophe by Snæbjorn, and also in Grogalder and in Fjölsvinnsmal. If this signification is applied to the passage in Vafthrudnersmal : *á var lúdr um lagidr,* we get the meaning that Bergelmer was "laid on a mill," and in fact no other meaning of the passage is possible, unless an entirely new signification is to be arbitrarily invented.

But however conspicuous this signification is, and however clear it is that it is the only one applicable in this poem, still it has been overlooked or thrust aside by the mythologists, and for this Gylfaginning is to blame. So fas as I know, Vigfusson is the only one who (in his Dictionary, p. 399) makes the passage *á lúdr lagidr* mean what it actually means, and he remarks that the words must "refer to some ancient lost myth."

The confusion begins, as stated, in Gylfaginning. Its author has had no other authority for his statement than the Vafthrudnersmal strophe in question, which he also cites to corroborate his own words; and we have here one of the many examples found in Gylfaginning showing that its author has neglected to pay much attention to what the passages quoted contain. When Gylfaginning has stated that the frost-giants were drowned in Ymer's blood, then comes its interpretation of the Vafthrudnersmal strophe, which is as follows: "One escaped with his household: him the giants call Bergelmer. He with his wife betook himself upon his *lúdr* and remained there, and from them the races of giants are descended" (*nema einn komst undan med sinu hyski: thann kalla jötnar Bergelmi; hann fór upp á lúdr sinn ok kona hans, ok helzt thar, ok eru af theim komnar*), &c.

What Gylfaginning's author has conceived by the *lúdr* which he mentions it is difficult to say. That he did not have a boat in mind is in the meantime evident from the expression: *hann fór upp á lúdr sinn.* It is more reasonable to suppose that his idea was, that Bergelmer himself owned an immense mill, upon whose high timbers he and his household climbed to save themselves from the flood. That the original text says that Bergelmer was *laid* on the timbers of the mill Gylfaginning pays no attention to. To go upon something and to be laid on something are, however, very different notions.

An argument in favour of the wrong interpretation

was furnished by the Resenian edition of the Younger Edda (Copenhagen, 1665). There we find the expression *fór upp á ludr sinn* "amended" to *fór á bát sinn*. Thus Bergelmer had secured a boat to sail in; and although more reliable editions of the Younger Edda have been published since from which the boat disappeared, still the mythologists have not had the heart to take the boat away from Bergelmer. On the contrary, they have allowed the boat to grow into a ship, an ark.

As already pointed out, Vafthrudnersmal tells us expressly that Bergelmer, Aurgelmer's grandson, was "laid on a mill" or "on the supporting timbers of a mill." We may be sure that the myth would not have laid Bergelmer on "a mill" if the intention was not that he was to be ground. The kind of meal thus produced has already been explained. It is the mould and sand which the sea since time's earliest dawn has cast upon the shores of Midgard, and with which the bays and strands have been filled, to become sooner or later green fields. From Ymer's flesh the gods created the oldest layer of soil, that which covered the earth the first time the sun shone thereon, and in which the first herbs grew. Ever since the same activity which then took place still continues. After the great mill of the gods transformed the oldest frost-giant into the dust of earth, it has continued to grind the bodies of his descendants between the same stones into the same kind of mould. This is the meaning of Vafthrudner's words when he says that his memory reaches back to the time when Bergelmer was laid on

573

the mill to be ground. Ymer he does not remember, nor
Thrudgelmer, nor the days when these were changed to
earth. Of them he knows only by hearsay. But he remembers when the turn came from Bergelmer's limbs to
be subjected to the same fate.

"The glorious Midgard" could not be created before
its foundations raised by the gods out of the sea were
changed to *bjód* (Völuspa). This is the word (originally *bjódr*) with which the author of Völuspa chose to
express the quality of the fields and the fields themselves,
which were raised out of the sea by Bor's sons, when the
great mill had changed the "flesh" of Ymer into mould.
Bjód does not mean a bare field or ground, but one that
can supply food. Thus it is used in Haustlaung (*af
breidu bjódi,* the place for a spread feast—Skaldskaparmal, ch. 22), and its other meanings (perhaps the more
original ones) are that of a board and of a table for food
to lie on. When the fields were raised out of Ymer's
blood they were covered with mould, so that, when they
got light and warmth from the sun, then the *grund* became *gróin grænum lauki.* The very word *mould* comes
from the Teutonic word *mala,* to grind (cp. Eng. *meal,*
Latin *molere*). The development of language and the
development of mythology have here, as in so many other instances, gone hand in hand.

That the "flesh" of the primeval giants could be ground
into fertile mould refers us to the primeval cow Aud-
humbla by whose milk Ymer was nourished and his flesh
formed (Gylfaginning). Thus the cow in the Teutonic
mythology is the same as she is in the Iranian, the pri-

meval source of fertility. The mould, out of which the harvests grow, has by transformations developed out of her nourishing liquids.

Here, then, we have the explanation of the *lidmeldr* which the great mill grinds, according to Snæbjorn. *Lidmeldr* means limb-grist. It is the limbs and joints of the primeval giants, which on Amlode's mill are transformed into meal.

In its character as an institution for the promotion of fertility, and for rendering the fields fit for habitation, the mill is under the care and protection of the Vans. After Njord's son, Frey, had been fostered in Asgard and had acquired the dignity of lord of the harvests, he was the one who became the master of the great Grotte. It is attended on his behalf by one of his servants, who in the mythology is called *Byggvir,* a name related both to *byggja,* settle, cultivate, and to *bygg,* barley, a kind of grain, and by his kinswoman and helpmate Beyla. So important is the calling of Bygver and Beyla that they are permitted to attend the feasts of the gods with their master (Frey). Consequently they are present at the banquet to which Ægir, according to Lokasenna, invited the gods. When Loke uninvited made his appearance there to mix harm in the mead of the gods, and to embitter their pleasure, and when he there taunts Frey, Bygver becomes wroth on his master's behalf and says:

Str. 43. Veiztu, ef ec öthli ettac   Had I the ancestry
     sem Ingunar-Freyr   of Ingunar Frey
     oc sva sælict setr,   and so honoured a seat,
     mergi smæra maul   know I would grind you
       tha ec

thá meincráco	finer tɪan marrow, you evil crow,
oc lemtha alla i litho.	and crusɪ you limb by limb.

Loke answers:

Str. 44. Hvat er tɪat ith litla	Wɪat little boy is tɪat
er ec tɪat lauggra sec	wɪom I see wag his tail
oc snapvist snapir;	and eat like a parasite?
att eyrom Freys	Near Frey's ears
mundu æ vera	always you are
oc und kvernom klaka.	and clatter 'neatɪ the mill-stone.

Bygver.

Str. 45. Beyggvir ec ɪeiti,	Bygver is my name,
enn mic brathan kveda	All gods and men
god aull oc gumar:	call me the nimble,
tɪvi em cc her hrodugr,	and ɪere it is my pride,
at drecca Hroptz megir	tɪat Odin's sons eacɪ
allir aul saman.	and all drink ale.

Loke.

Str. 46. thegi thu, Beyggvir!	Be silent, Bygver!
thu kunnir aldregi	Ne'er were you able
deila ·meth mönnom	food to divide among men.
mat.	

Beyla, too, gets her share of Loke's abuse. The least disgraceful thing he says of her is that she is a *deigia* (a slave, who has to work at the mill and in the kitchen), and that she is covered with traces of her occupation in dust and dirt.

As we see, Loke characterises Bygver as a servant taking charge of the mill under Frey, and Bygver characterises himself as one who grinds, and is able to crush an "evil crow" limb by limb with his mill-stones. As the one who with his mill makes vegetation, and so also bread and malt, possible, he boasts of it as his honour that the gods are able to drink ale at a banquet. Loke blames him because he is not able to divide the food among men. The reproach implies that the distribution of food is in his hands. The mould which comes from the great mill gives different degrees of fertility to different fields, and rewards abundantly or niggardly the toil of the farmer. Loke doubtless alludes to this unequal distribution, else it would be impossible to find any sense in his words.

In the poetic Edda we still have another reminiscence of the great mill which is located under the sea, and at the same time in the lower world (see below), and which "grinds mould into food." It is in a poem, whose skald says that he has seen it on his journey in the lower world. In his description of the "home of torture" in Hades, Solarljod's Christian author has taken all his materials from the heathen mythological conceptions of the worlds of punishment, though the author treats these materials in accordance with the Christian purpose of his song. When the skald dies, he enters the Hades gates, crosses bloody streams, sits for nine days *á norna stóli,* is thereupon seated on a horse, and is permitted to make a journey through Mimer's domain, first to the regions of the happy and then to those of the damned. In Mimer's realm he sees the "stag of the sun" and Nide's (Mimer's) sons, who "quaff the pure mead from Baugregin's well." When he approached the borders of the world of the damned, he heard a terrible din, which silenced the winds and stopped the flow of the waters. The mighty din came from a mill. Its stones were wet with blood, but the grist produced was mould, which was to be food. Fickle-wise (*svipvisar,* heathen) women of dark complexion turned the mill. Their bloody and tortured hearts hung outside of their breasts. The mould which they ground was to feed their husbands.

This mill, situated at the entrance of hell, is here represented as one of the agents of torture in the lower world. To a certain extent this is correct even from a heathen standpoint. It was the lot of slave-women to turn the hand-mill. In the heroic poem the giant-maids Fenja and Menja, taken prisoners and made slaves, have to turn Frode's Grotte. In the mythology "Eylud's nine women," thurse-maids, were compelled to keep this vast mechanism in motion, and that this was regarded as a heavy and compulsory task may be assumed without the risk of being mistaken.

According to Solarljod, the mill-stones are stained with blood. In the mythology they crush the bodies of the first giants and revolve in Ymer's blood. It is also in perfect harmony with the mythology that the meal becomes mould, and that the mould serves as food. But the cosmic signification is obliterated in Solarljod, and it seems to be the author's idea that men who have died in their heathen belief are to eat the mould which women who have died in heathendom industriously grind as food for them

The myth about the greater Grotte, as already indicated, has also been connected with the Hvergelmer myth. Solarljod has correctly stated the location of the mill on the border of the realm of torture. The mythology has located Hvergelmer's fountain there (see No. 59) ; and as this vast fountain is the mother of the ocean and of all waters, and the ever open connection between the waters of heaven, of the earth, and of the lower world, then this furnishes the explanation of the apparently conflicting statements, that the mill is situated both in the lower world and at the same time on the bottom of the sea. Of the mill it is said that it is dangerous to men, dangerous to fleets and to crews, and that it causes the maelstrom (*svelgr*) when the water of the ocean rushes down through the eye of the mill-stone. The same was said of Hvergelmer, that causes ebb and flood and maelstrom, when the water of the world alternately flows into and out of this great source. To judge from all this, the mill has been conceived as so made that its foundation timbers stood on solid ground in the lower world, and thence rose up into the sea, in which the stones resting on this substructure were located. The revolving "eye" of the mill-stone was directly above Hvergelmer, and served as the channel through which the water flowed to and from the great fountain of the world's waters.

81.

THE WORLD-MILL (*continued*). THE WORLD-MILL MAKES THE CONSTELLATIONS REVOLVE. MUNDILFÖRI.

But the colossal mill in the ocean has also served other

purposes than that of grinding the nourishing mould from the limbs of the primeval giants.

The Teutons, like all people of antiquity, and like most men of the present time, regarded the earth as stationary. And so, too, the lower world (*jormurgrundr*—Forspjallsljod) on which the foundations of the earth rested. Stationary was also that heaven in which the Asas had their citadels, surrounded by a common wall, for the Asgard-bridge, Bifrost, had a solid bridge-head on the southern and another on the northern edge of the lower world, and could not change position in its relation to them. All this part of creation was held together by the immovable roots of the world-tree, or rested on its invisible branches. Sol and Mane had their fixed paths, the points of departure and arrival of which were the "horse-doors" (*jódyrr*), which were hung on the eastern and western mountain-walls of the lower world. The god Mane and the goddess Sol were thought to traverse these paths in shining chariots, and their daily journeys across the heavens did not to our ancestors imply that any part of the world-structure itself was in motion. Mane's course lay below Asgard. When Thor in his thunder-chariot descends to Jotunheim the path of Mane thunders under him (*en dundi Mána vegr und Meila bródur* —Haustl., 1). No definite statement in our mythical records informs us whether the way of the sun was over or under Asgard.

But high above Asgard is the starry vault of heaven, and to the Teutons as well as to other people that sky was not only an optical but a real vault, which daily revolved around a stationary point. Sol and Mane might be conceived as traversing their appointed courses independently, and not as coming in contact with vaults, which by their motions from east to west produced the progress of sun and moon. The very circumstance that they continually changed position in their relation to each other and to the stars seemed to prove that they proceeded independently in their own courses. With the countless stars the case was different. They always keep at the same distance and always present the same figures on the canopy of the nocturnal heavens. They looked like glistening heads of nails driven into a movable ceiling. Hence the starlit sky was thought to be in motion. The sailors and shepherds of the Teutons very well knew that this revolving was round a fixed point, the polar star, and it is probable that *veraldar nagli,* the world-nail, the world-spike, an expression preserved in Eddubrott, ii., designates the north star.

Thus the starry sky was the movable part of the universe. And this motion is not of the same kind as that of the winds, whose coming and direction no man can predict or calculate. The motion of the starry firmament is defined, always the same, always in the same direction, and keeps equal step with the march of time itself. It does not, therefore, depend on the accidental pleasure of gods or other powers. On the other hand, it seems to be caused by a mechanism operating evenly and regularly.

The mill was for a long time the only kind of mechanism on a large scale known to the Teutons. Its motion was a rotating one. The movable mill-stone was turned by a handle or sweep which was called *möndull*. The mill-stones and the *möndull* might be conceived as large as you please. Fancy knew no other limits than those of the universe.

There was another natural phenomenon, which also was regular, and which was well known to the seamen of the North and to those Teutons who lived on the shores of the North Sea, namely, the rising and falling of the tide. Did one and the same force produce both these great phenomena? Did the same cause produce the motion of the starry vault and the ebb and flood of the sea? In regard to the latter phenomenon, we already know the naïve explanation given in the myth concerning Hvergelmer and the Grotte-mill. And the same explanation sufficed for the former. There was no need of another mechanism to make the heavens revolve, as there was already one at hand, the influence of which could be traced throughout that ocean in which Midgard was simply an isle, and which around this island extends its surface even to the brink of heaven (Gylfaginning).

The mythology knew a person by name *Mundilföri* (Vafthr., 23; Gylfag.). The word *mundill* is related to *möndull,* and is presumably only another form of the same word. The name or epithet Mundilfore refers to a being that has had something to do with a great mythical *möndull* and with the movements of the mechanism which this *möndull* kept in motion. Now the word *möndull* is never used in the old Norse literature about any other object than the sweep or handle with which the movable mill-stone is turned. (In this sense the word occurs in the Grotte-song and in Helge Hund. ii., 3, 4). Thus Mundilfore has had some part to play in regard to the great giant-mill of the ocean and of the lower world.

Of Mundilfore we learn, on the other hand, that he is the father of the personal Sol and the personal Mane (Valfthr. 23). This, again, shows that the mythology conceived him as intimately associated with the heavens and with the heavenly bodies. Vigfusson (Dict., 437) has, therefore, with good reason remarked that *mundill* in Mundilfore refers to *the veering round or the revolution of the heavens.* As the father of Sol and Mane, Mundilfore was a being of divine rank, and as such belonged to the powers of the lower world, where Sol and Mane have their abodes and resting-places. The latter part of the name, *föri,* refers to the verb *fœra,* to conduct, to move. Thus he is that power who has to take charge of the revolutions of the starry vault of heaven, and these must be produced by the great *möndull,* the mill-handle or mill-sweep, since he is called *Mundilföri.*

The regular motion of the starry firmament and of the sea is, accordingly, produced by the same vast mechanism, the Grotte-mill, the *meginverk* of the heathen fancy (Grotte-song, 11; cp. Egil Skallagrimson's way of using the word, Arnibj.-Drapa, 26). The handle extends to the edge of the world, and the nine giantesses, who are compelled to turn the mill, pushing the sweep before them, march along the outer edge of the universe. Thus we get an intelligible idea of what Snæbjorn means when he says that Eylud's nine women turn the Grotte "along the edge of the earth" (*hrœra Grotta at fyrir jardar skauti*).

Mundilfore and Bygver thus each has his task to perform in connection with the same vast machinery. The one attends to the regular motion of the *möndull,* the other looks after the mill-stones and the grist.

In the name Eylud the first part is *ey,* and the second part is *ludr.* The name means the "island-mill." Eylud's nine women are the "nine women of the island-mill." The mill is in the same strophe called *skerja Grotti,* the Grotte of the skerry. These expressions refer to each other and designate with different words the same idea— the mill that grinds islands and skerries.

The fate which, according to the Grotte-song, happened to King Frode's mill has its origin in the myth concerning the greater mill. The stooping position of the starry heavens and the sloping path of the stars in relation to the horizontal line was a problem which in its way the mythology wanted to solve. The phenomenon was put in connection with the mythic traditions in regard to the terrible winter which visited the earth after the gods and the sons of Alvalde (Ivalde) had become enemies. Fenja and Menja were kinswomen of Alvalde's sons. For they were brothers (half-brothers) of those mountain giants who were Fenja's and Menja's fathers (the Grotte-song). Before the feud broke out between their kin and the gods, both the giant-maids had worked in the service of the latter and for the good of the world, grinding the blessings of the golden age on

584

the world-mill. Their activity in connection with the great mechanism, mondul, which they pushed, amid the singing of bliss-bringing songs of sorcery, was a counterpart of the activity of the sons of Alvalde, who made for the gods the treasures of vegetation. When the conflict broke out the giant-maids joined the cause of their kinsmen. They gave the world-mill so rapid a motion that the foundations of the earth trembled, pieces of the mill-stones were broken loose and thrown up into space, and the sub-structure of the mill was damaged. This could not happen without harm to the starry canopy of heaven which rested thereon. The memory of this mythic event comes to the surface in Rimbegla, which states that toward the close of King Frode's reign there arose a terrible disorder in nature—a storm with mighty thundering passed over the country, the earth quaked and cast up large stones. In the Grotte-song the same event is mentioned as a "game" played by Fenja and Menja, in which they cast up from the deep upon the earth those stones which afterwards became the mill-stones in the Grotte-mill. After that "game" the giant-maids betook themselves to the earth and took part in the first world-war on the side hostile to Odin (see No. 39). It is worthy of notice that the mythology has connected the fimbul-winter and the great emigrations from the North with an earthquake and a damage to the world-mill which makes the starry heavens revolve.

82.

THE WORLD-MILL (*continued*). THE ORIGIN OF THE
SACRED FIRE THROUGH MUNDILFORE. HEIMDAL
THE PERSONIFICATION OF THE SACRED FIRE. HIS
IDENTITY WITH RIGVEDA'S AGNI. HIS ANTITHESIS,
LOKE, ALSO A FIRE-BEING.

Among the tasks to be performed by the world-mill
there is yet another of the greatest importance. According to a belief which originated in ancient Aryan
times, a fire is to be judged as to purity and holiness by
its origin. There are different kinds of fire more or less
pure and holy, and a fire which is holy as to its origin
may become corrupted by contact with improper elements. The purest fire, that which was originally kindled by the gods and was afterwards given to man as an
invaluable blessing, as a bond of union between the higher
world and mankind, was a fire which was produced by
rubbing two objects together (friction). In hundreds
of passages this is corroborated in Rigveda, and the belief still exists among the common people of various Teutonic peoples. The great mill which revolves the starry
heavens was also the mighty rubbing machine (friction
machine) from which the sacred fire naturally ought to
proceed, and really was regarded as having proceeded,
as shall be shown below.

The word *möndull,* with which the handle of the mill
is designated, is found among our ancient Aryan ancestors. It can be traced back to the ancient Teutonic *man-
thula,* a swing-tree (Fick, *Wörterb d. ind.-germ. Spr.,*

iii. 232), related to Sanscr. *Manthati,* to swing, twist, bore, from the root *manth,* which occurs in numerous passages in Rigveda, and in its direct application always refers to the production of fire by friction (Bergaigne, *Rel. ved.,* iii. 7).

In Rigveda, the sacred fire is personified by the "pure," "upright," "benevolent" god *Agni,* whose very name, related to the Latin *ignis,* designates the god of fire. According to Rigveda, there was a time when Agni lived concealed from both gods and men, as the element of light and warmth found in all beings and things. Then there was a time when he dwelt in person among the gods, but not yet among men; and, finally, there was a time when *Mâtaricvan,* a sacred being and Agni's father in a literal or symbolic sense, brought it about that Agni came to our fathers (Rigv., i. 60, 1). The generation of men then living was the race of Bhriguians, so-called after an ancient patriarch Bhrigu. This Bhrigu, and with him Manu (Manus), was the first person who, in his sacrifices to the gods, used the fire obtained through Agni (Rigv., i. 31, 17, and other passages).

When, at the instigation of Mâtaricvan, Agni arrived among mankind, he came from a far-off region (Rigv., i. 128, 2). The Bhriguians who did not yet possess the fire, but were longing for it and were seeking for it (Rigv., x. 40, 2), found the newly-arrived Agni, "at the confluence of the waters." In a direct sense, "the confluence of the waters" cannot mean anything else than the ocean, into which all waters flow. Thus Agni came from the distance across a sea to the coast of the country

16 587

where that people dwelt who were named after the patriarch Bhrigu. When they met this messenger of the gods (Rigv., viii. 19, 21), they adopted him and cared for him at "the place of the water" (Rigv., ii. 4, 2). *Mâtaricvan,* by whose directions Agni, "the one born on the other side of the atmosphere" (x. 187, 5) was brought to mankind, becomes in the classical Sanscrit language a designation for the wind. Thus everything tends to show that Agni has traversed a wide ocean, and has been brought by the wind when he arrives at the coast where the Bhriguians dwell. He is very young, and hence bears the epithet *yavishtha.*

We are now to see why the gods sent him to men, and what he does among them. He remains among those who care for him, and dwells among them "an immortal among mortals" (Rigv., viii. 60, 11; iii. 5, 3), a guest among men, a companion of mortals (iv. 1, 9). He who came with the inestimable gift of fire long remains personally among men, in order that "a wise one among the ignorant" may educate them. He who "knows all wisdom and all sciences" (Rigv., iii. 1, 17; x. 21, 5) "came to be asked questions" (i. 60, 20) by men; he teaches them and "they listen to him as to a father" (i. 68, 9). He becomes their first patriarch (ii. 10, 1) and their first priest (v. 9, 4; x. 80, 4). Before that time they had lived a nomadic life, but he taught them to establish fixed homes around the hearths, on which the fire he had brought now was burning (iii. 1, 17). He visited them in these fixed dwellings (iv. 1, 19), where the Bhriguians now let the fire blaze (x. 122, 5); he became "the husband of wives" (i. 66, 4) and the progenitor of human descendants (i. 96, 2), through whom he is the founder of the classes or "races" of men (vi. 48, 8). He established order in all human affairs (iv. 1, 2), taught religion, instructed men in praying and sacrificing (vi. 1, 1, and many other passages), initiated them in the art of poetry and gave them inspiration (iii. 10, 5; x. 11, 6).

This is related of Agni when he came to the earth and dwelt among men. As to his divine nature, he is the pure, white god (iv. 1, 7; iii. 7, 1), young, strong, and shining with golden teeth (v. 2, 2), and searching eyes (iv. 2, 12) which can see far (vii. 1, 1), penetrate the darkness of night (i. 94, 7), and watch the acts of demons (x. 87, 12). He, the guard of order (i. 11, 8), is always attentive (i. 31, 12), and protects the world by day and by night from dangers (i. 98, 1). On a circular path he observes all things (vii. 13, 3), and sees and knows them all (x. 187, 4). He perceives everything, being able to penetrate the herbs, and diffuse himself into plants and animals (vii. 9, 3; viii. 43, 9; x. 1, 2). He hears all who pray to him, and can make himself heard as if he had the voice of thunder, so that both the halves of the world re-echo his voice (x. 8, 1). His horses are like himself white (vi. 6, 4). His symbol among the animals is the bull (i. 31, 5; i. 146, 2).

In regard to Agni's birth, it is characteristic of him that he is said to have several mothers, although their number varies according to the point from which the process of birth is regarded. When it is only to be a figurative expression for the origin of the friction-fire, the singer of the hymn can say that Agni had ten mothers or two mothers. In the case of the former, it is the ten fingers of the person producing the friction-fire that are meant. Sometimes this is stated outright (Rigveda, iii. 23, 3); then again the fingers are paraphrased by "the twice five sisters dwelling together" (iv. 6, 8), "the work-master's ten untiring maids" (i. 95, 1). In the case of the latter—that is, when two mothers are mentioned—the two pieces of wood rubbed together are meant (viii. 49, 15). In a more real sense he is said to have three places of nativity: one in the atmospheric sea, one in heaven, and one in the waters (i. 95, 3), and that his "great, wise, divine nature proceeded from the laps of many active mothers" (i. 95, 4), such as the waters, the stones, the trees, the herbs (ii. 1, 1). In Rigveda (x. 45, 2) nine maternal wombs or births are indicated; his "triple powers were sown in triplets in heaven, among us, and in the waters." In Rigveda (i. 141, 2) three places of nativity and three births are ascribed to him, and in such a way that he had seven mothers in his second birth. In Rigveda (x. 20, 7) he is called the son of the rock.

It scarcely needs to be pointed out that all that is here told about Agni corresponds point by point with the Teutonic myth about Heimdal. Here, as in many other instances, we find a similarity between the Teutonic and the Aryan-Asiatic myths, which is surprising, when we consider that the difference between the Rigveda and Zend languages on the one hand, and the oldest Teutonic linguistic monuments on the other, appear in connection with other circumstances to indicate that the old Aryan unity of language and religion lies ages back in antiquity. Agni's birth "beyond the atmosphere," his journey across the sea to original man in the savage state, his vocation as the sower of the blessings of culture among men, his appearance as the teacher of wisdom and "the sciences," his visit to the farms established by him, where he becomes "the husband of wives," father of human sons, and the founder of "the races" (the classes among the Teutons),—all this we rediscover completely in the Heimdal myth, as if it were a copy of the Aryan-Asiatic saga concerning the divine founder of culture; a copy fresh from the master's brush without the effects of time, and without any retouching. The very names of the ancient Aryan patriarchs, Bhrigu and Manu are recognisable in the Teutonic patriarch names Berchter and Mann (Mannus-Halfdan). In the case of Manu and Mann no explanation is necessary. Here the identity of sound agrees with the identity of origin. The descendants of Bhrigu and of his contemporary Bhriguians, are called Bhargavans, which corroborates the conclusion that Bhrigu is derived from *bharg* "to shine," whence is derived the ancient Teutonic *berhta,* "bright," "clear," "light," the Old Saxon *berht,* the Anglo-Saxon *beorht,* which reoccurs in the Teutonic patriarch *Berchter,* which again is actually (not linguistically) identical with the Norse *Borgarr.* By Bhrigu's side stands Manu, just as Mann (Halfdan) is co-ordinate with Borgar.

Point by point the descriptions of Agni and Heimdal also correspond in regard to their divine natures and attributes. Agni is the great holy *white* god; Heimdal is *mikill* and *heilagr,* and is called *hviti áss* (Younger Edda) or "the whitest of the Asas" (Thrymskv., 15). While Agni as the fire-god has golden teeth, Heimdal certainly for the same reason bears the epithet *gullin-tanni,* "the one with the golden teeth." Agni has white horses. In Ulf Uggeson's poem about the work of art in Hjardarholt, Heimdal rides his horse *Gulltoppr,* whose name reflects its splendour. While Agni's searching eyes can see in the distance and can penetrate the gloom of night, it is said of Heimdal that *hann sér jafnt nótt sem dag hundrad rasta frá sér.* While Agni perceives everything, even the inaudible motions in the growing of herbs and animals; while he penetrates and diffuses himself in plants and animals, it is said of Heimdal that he *heyrir ok that, er gras vex á jordu eda ull á saudum.* While Agni—it is not stated by what means—is able to produce a noise like thunder which re-echoes through both the world-halves, Heimdal has the horn, whose sound all the world shall hear, when Ragnarok is at hand. On a "circular path," Agni observes the beings in the world. Heimdal looks out upon the world from Bifrost. Agni keeps his eye on the deeds of the demons, is perpetually on the look-out, and protects the world by day and by night from dangers; Heimdal is the watchman of the gods *vördr goda* (Grimnersmal), needs in his vocation as watchman less sleep than a bird, and faithfully guards the Asa-bridge against the giants. Agni is born of several mothers; Heimdal has mothers nine. Agni is "the fast traveller," who, in the human abodes he visits, opens a way for prayer and sacrifice (Rigv., vii. 13, 3); in Rigsmal, Heimdal has the same epithet, "the fast traveller," *röskr Stigandi,* as he goes from house to house and teaches men the "runes of eternity" and "the runes of time."

The only discrepancy is in the animal symbols by which Angi and Heimdal are designated. The bull is Agni's symbol, the ram is Heimdal's. Both symbols are chosen from the domestic animals armed with horns, and the differnce is linguistically of such a kind, that it to some extent may be said to corroborate the evidence in regard to Agni's and Heimdals identity. In the old Norse poetry, *Vedr* (wether, ram), *Heimdali* and the Heimdal epithet *Hallinskidi,* are synonymous. The word *vedr,* according to Fick (*Wörterb.,* iii. 307), can be traced to an ancient Teutonic *vethru,* the real meaning of which is "yearling," a young domestic animal in general, and it is related to the Latin *vitulus* and the Sanscrit *vatsala,* "calf." If this is correct, then we also see the lines along which one originally common symbol of a domestic animal developed into two and among the Rigveda Aryans settled on the "yearling" of the cow, and among the Teutons on that of the sheep. It should here be remarked that according to Ammianus Marcellinus (xix. 1) the tiara of the Persian kings was ornamented with a golden ram's-head. That Agni's span of horses were transformed into Heimdal's riding horse was also a result of time and circumstances. In Rigveda, riding and cavalry are unknown; there the horses of the gods draw the divine chariots. In the Teutonic mythology the draught horses are changed into riding horses, and chariots occur only exceptionally.

We have reason to be surprised at finding that the Aryan-Asiatic myths and the Teutonic have so broad surfaces of contact, on which not only the main outlines but even the details completely resemble each other. But the fact is not inexplicable. The hymns, the songs of the divine worship and of the sacrifices of the Rigveda Aryans, have been preserved, but the epic-mythological poems are lost, so that there remains the difficult task of reconstructing out of the former a clear and concise mythology, freed from "dissolving views" in which their mythic characters now blend into each other. The Teutonic mythology has had an opposite fate: here the genuine religious songs, the hymns of divine worship and of sacrifices, are lost, and there remain fragments of the mighty divine epic of the Teutons. But thus we have also been robbed of the opportunity of studying those very songs which in a higher degree than the epic are able to preserve through countless centuries ancient mythical traits; for the hymns belong to the divine worship, popular customs are long-lived, and the sacred customs are more conservative and more enduring than all others, if they are not disturbed by revolutions in the domain of faith. If an epithet of a god, *e. g.,* "the fast traveller," has once become fixed by hymns and been repeated in the divine service year after year, then, in spite of the gradual transformation of the languages and the types of the race, it may be preserved through hundreds and thousands of years. Details of this kind may in this manner survive the ravages of time just as well as the great outlines of the mythology, and if there be a gradual change as to signification, then this is caused by the change of language, which may make an old expression unintelligible or give it another meaning based on the association of ideas.

From all this I am forced to draw the conclusion that Heimdal, like several other Teutonic gods—for example, Odin (Wodan, Rigveda's Vata)—belongs to the ancient Aryan age, and retained, even to the decay of the Teutonic heathendom his ancient character as the personal representative of the sacred fire, the fire produced by friction, and, in this connection, as the representative of the oldest culture connected with the introduction of fire.

This also explains Heimdal's epithet *Vindler,* in Cod. Reg. of the Younger Edda (i. 266, 608). The name is a subform of *vindill* and comes from *vinda,* to twist or turn, wind, to turn anything around rapidly. As the epithet "the turner" is given to that god who brought friction-fire (bore-fire) to man, and who is himself the personification of this fire, then it must be synonymous with "the borer."

A synonym of Heimdal's epithet *Stigandi,* "the traveller," is *Rati,* "the traveller," from *rata,* "to travel," "to move about." Very strangely, this verb (originally *vrata,* Goth. *vrâton,* to travel, make a journey) can be traced to an ancient Teutonic word which meant to turn or twist, or something of the sort (Fick, *Wörterb.,* iii. 294).

And, so far as the noun *Rati* is concerned, this signification has continued to flourish in the domain of mythology
after it long seems to have been extinct in the domain of
language. Havamál (106), Grimnersmal (32), and
Bragaraedur testify each in its own way that the mythical
name *Rati* was connected with a boring activity. In
Havamál "Rate's mouth" gnaws the tunnel through
which Odin, in the guise of an eagle, flies away with the
mead-treasure concealed in the "deep dales" at Fjalar's
under the roots of the world-tree. In the allegorical
Grimnersmal strophe it is "Rate's tooth" (*Ratatoskr*)
who lets the mead-drinking foe of the gods near the root
of the world-tree find out what the eagle in the top of the
world-tree (Odin) resolves and carries out in regard to
the same treasure. In Bragaraedur the name is given
to the gimlet itself which produced the connection between Odin's world and Fjalar's halls. The gimlet has
here received the name of the boring "traveller," of him
who is furnished with "golden teeth." Hence there are
good reasons for assuming that in the epic of the myth
it was Heimdal-Gullintanne himself whose fire-gimlet
helped Odin to fly away with his precious booty. In
Rigveda Agni plays the same part. The "tongue of
Agni" has the same task there as "Rate's mouth" in our
Norse records. The sacred mead of the liquids of nourishment was concealed in the womb of the mountain with
the Dasyus, hostile to the world; but Agni split the mountain open with his tongue, his ray of light penetrated into
the darkness where the liquids of nourishment were preserved, and through him they were brought to the light

596

of day, after Trita (in some passages of Rigveda identical with Vata) had slain a giant monster and found the "cows of the son of the work-master" (cp. Rigveda, v. 14, 4; viii. 61, 4-8; x. 8, 6-9). "The cows of the son of the work-master" is a paraphrase for the saps of nourishment. In the Teutonic mythology there is also "a son of the work-master," who is robbed of the mead. Fjalar is a son of Surt, whose character as an ancient artist is evident from what is stated in Nos. 53 and 89.

By friction Mataricvan brought Agni out of the maternal wombs in which he was concealed as an embryo of light and warmth. Heimdal was born to life in a similar manner. His very place of nativity indicates this. His mothers have their abodes *vid jardar thraum* (Hyndl., 35) near the edge of the earth, on the outer rim of the earth, and that is where they gave him life *báru thann man vid jardar thraum*). His mothers are giantesses (*iotna meyjar*), and nine in number. We have already found giantesses, nine in number, mentioned as having their activity on the outer edge of the earth—namely, those who with the *möndull*, the handle, turn the vast friction-mechanism, the world-mill of Mundilfore. They are the *níu brúdir* of *Eyludr*, "the Isle-grinder" mentioned by Snæbjorn (see above). These nine giant-maids, who along the outer zone of the earth (*fyrir jordar skauti*) push the mill's sweep before themselves and grind the coasts of the islands, are the same nine giant-maids who on the outer zone of the earth gave birth to Heimdal, the god of the friction-fire. Hence one of Heimdal's mothers is in Hyndluljod called *Angeyja*, "she who makes the islands closer,' and another one is called *Eyrgjafa,* "she who gives sandbanks." *Mundilföri,* who is the father of Sol and Mane, and has the care the motions of the starry heavens is accordingly also, though in another sense, the father of Heimdal the pure, holy fire to whom the glittering objects in the skies must naturally be regarded as akin.

In Hyndluljod (37) Heimdal's nine giant-mothers are named: *Gjálp, Greip, Eistla, Eyrgjafa, Ulfrun, Angeyja, Imdr, Atla, Járnsaxa.* The first two are daughters of the fire-giant Geirrod (Younger Edda, i. 288). To fire refers also *Imdr,* from *im, embers.* Two of the names, *Angeyja* and *Eyrgjafa,* as already shown, indicate the occupation of these giantesses in connection with the world-mill. This is presumably also the case with *Járnsaxa,* "she who crushes the iron." The iron which our heathen fathers worked was produced from the sea- and swamp-iron mixed with sand and clay, and could therefore properly be regarded as a grist of the world-mill.

Heimdal's antithesis in all respects, and therefore also his constant opponent in the mythological epic, is Loke, he too a fire-being, but representing another side of this element. Natural agents such as fire, water, wind, cold, heat, and thunder have in the Teutonic mythology a double aspect. When they work in harmony, each within the limits which are fixed by the welfare of the world and the happiness of man, then they are sacred forces and are represented by the gods. But when these limits are transgressed, giants are at work, and the turbulent elements are represented by beings of giant-race. This is also true of thunder, although it is the common view among mythologists that it was regarded exclusively as a product of Thor's activity. The genuine mythical conception was, however, that the thunder which purifies the atmosphere and fertilises the thirsty earth with showers of rain, or strikes down the foes of Midgard, came from Thor; while that which splinters the sacred trees, sets fire to the woods and houses, and kills men that have not offended the gods, came from the foes of the world. The blaze-element (see No. 35) was not only in the possession of the gods, but also in that of the giants (Skirnersmal), and the lightning did not proceed alone from Mjolner, but was also found in Hrungner's *hein* and in Geirrod's glowing javelin. The conflicts between Thor and the giants were not only on *terra firma,* as when Thor made an expedition on foot to Jotunheim, but also in the air. There were giant-horses that were able to wade with force and speed through the atmosphere, as, for instance, Hrungner's *Gullfaxi* (Younger Edda, i. 270), and these giant-horses with their shining manes, doubtless, were expected to carry their riders to the lightning-conflict in space against the lightning-hurler, Thor. The thunder-storm was frequently a *vig thrimu,* a conflict between thundering beings, in which the lightnings hurled by the ward of Midgard, the son of Hlodyn, crossed the lightnings hurled by the foes of Midgard.

Loke and his brothers *Helblindi* and *Byl-eistr* are the children of a giant of this kind, of a giant representing the hurricane and thunder. The rain-torrents and waterspouts of the hurricane, which directly or indirectly became wedded to the sea through the swollen streams, gave birth to Helblinde, who, accordingly, received *Rán* as his "maid" (Yngl., 51).   The whirlwind in the hurricane received as his ward *Byleistr,* whose name is composed of *bylr,* "whirlwind," and *eistr,* "the one dwelling in the east" (the north), a paraphrase for "giant."   A thunderbolt from the hurricane gave birth to Loke.   His father is called *Fárbauti,* "the one inflicting harm," and his mother is *Laufey,* "the leaf-isle," a paraphrase for the tree-crown (Younger Edda, 104, 268).   Thus Loke is the son of the burning and destructive lightning, the son of him who particularly inflicts damaging blows on the sacred oaks (see No. 36) and sets fire to the groves. But the violence of the father does not appear externally in the son's character.   He long prepares the conflagration of the world in secret, and not until he is put in chains does he exiibit, by the earthquakes he produces, the wild passion of his giant nature.   As a fire-being, he was conceived as handsome and youthful.   From an ethical point of view, the impurity of the flame which he represents is manifested by his unrestrained sensuousness.   After he had been for ever exiled from the society of the gods and had been fettered in his cave of torture, his exterior, which was in the beginning beautiful, became transformed into an expression of his intrinsic wickedness, and his hair grew out in the form of horny spears (see above).   In this too he reveals himself as a counterpart of Heimdal, whose helmet is ornamented with a glittering ram's horn.

83.

MUNDILFORE'S IDENTITY WITH LODUR.

The position which we have found Mundilfore to occupy indicates that, although not belonging to the powers dwelling in Asgard, he is one of the chief gods of the
Teutonic mythology. All natural phenomena, which appear to depend on a fixed mechanical law and not on the
initiative of any mighty will momentarily influencing the
events of the world, seem to have been referred to his
care. The mythology of the Teutons, like that of the
Rigveda-Aryans, has had gods of both kinds—gods who
particularly represent that order in the physical and moral
world which became fixed in creation, and which, under
normal conditions, remain entirely uniform, and gods who
particularly represent the powerful temporary interfer-
ence for the purpose of restoring this order when it has
been disturbed, and for the purpose of giving protection
and defence to their worshippers in times of trouble and
danger. The latter are in their very nature war-gods
always ready for battle, such as Vita and Indra in Rigveda, Odin and Thor-Indride in the Eddas; and they have
their proper abode in a group of fortified celestial citadels like Asgard, whence they have their out-look upon
the world they have to protect—the atmosphere and Midgard. The former, on the other hand, have their natural
abode in Jormungrund's outer zone and in the lower
world, whence the world-tree grew, and where the fountains are found whose liquids penetrate creation, and
where that wisdom had its source of which Odin only,

by self-sacrifice, secured a part. Down there dwell, ac-cordingly, Urd and Mimer, Nat and Dag, Mundilfore with the dises of the sun and the moon, Delling, the genius of the glow of dawn, and Billing, the genius of the blushing sunset. There dwell the smiths of antiquity who made the chariots of the sun and moon and smithied the treasures of vegetation. There dwell the *nidjar* who represent the moon's waxing and waning; there the seven sons of Mimer who represent the changing seasons (see No. 87). Mundilfore is the lord of the regular revolu-tions of the starry firmament, and of the regular rising and sinking of the sea in its ebb and flood. He is the father of the dises of the sun and moon, who make their celestial journeys according to established laws; and, finally, he is the origin of the holy fire; he is father of Heimdal, who introduced among men a systematic life in homes fixed and governed by laws. As the father of Heimdal, the Vana-god, Mundilfore is himself a Vana-god, belonging to the oldest branch of this race, and in all probability one of those "wise rulers" who, accord-ing to Vafthrudnersmal, "created Njord in Vanaheim and sent him as a hostage to the gods (the Asas)."

Whence came the clans of the Vans and the Elves? It should not have escaped the notice of the mythologists that the Teutonic theogony, as far as it is known, men-tions only two progenitors of the mythological races—*Ymer* and *Bure*. From Ymer develop the two very dif-ferent races of giants, the offspring of his arms and that of his feet (see No. 86)—in other words, the noble race to which the norns Mimer and Beistla belong, and the ignoble, which begins with Thrudgelmer. *Bure* gives birth to *Burr* (Bor), and the latter has tiree sons—*Odinn, Vei (Vé)*, and *Vili (Vilir)*. Unless *Bure* had more sons, the Van- and Elf-clans have no other theogonic source than the same as the Asa-clan, namely, *Burr.* That tie hierologists of the Teutonic mythology did not leave the origin of these clans unexplained we are assured by the very existence of a Teutonic theogony, together with the circumstance that the more thoroughly our mythology is studied the more clearly we see that this mythology has desired to answer every question which could reasonably be asked of it, and in the course of ages it developed into a systematic and epic whole with clear outlines sharply drawn in all details. To this must be added the important observation that *Vei* and *Vili,* though brothers of Odin, are never counted among the Asas proper, and had no abode in Asgard. It is manifest that Odin himself with his sons founds the Asa-race, that, in other words, he is a clan-founder in which this race has its chieftain, and that his brothers, for this very reason, could not be included in his clan. There is every reason to assume that they, like him, were clan-founders; and as we find besides the Asa-clan two other races of gods, this of itself makes it probable that Odin's two brothers were their progenitors and clan-chieftains.

Odin's brothers, like himself, had many names. When Völuspa says that Odin, in the creation of man, was assisted by Honer and Loder, and when the Younger Edda (i. 52) says that, on this occasion, he was attended by his brothers, who just before (i. 46) are called Ve

17   603

and Vile, then these are only different names of the same powers. Honer and Loder are Ve and Vile. It is a mistake to believe that Odin's brothers were mythical ghosts without characteristic qualities, and without prominent parts in the mythological events after the creation of the world and of man, in which we know they took an active part (Völuspa, 4, 16, 17). The assumption that this was the case depends simply upon the fact that they have not been found mentioned among the Asas, and that our records, when not investigated with proper thoroughness, and when the mythological synonymics have not been carefully examined, seem to have so little to say concerning them.

Danish genealogies, Saxo's included, which desire to go further back in the genealogy of the Skjoldungs than to Skjold, the eponym of the race, mention before him a King Lotherus. There is no doubt that Lotherus, like his descendants, Skjold, Halfdan, and Hadding, is taken from the mythology. But in our mythic records there is only one name of which Lotherus can be a Latinised form, and this name is, as Müller (*Notæ ulterior cd Saxonis Hist.*) has already pointed out, *Lodurr*.

It has above been demonstrated (see Nos. 20, 21, 22) that the anthropomorphous Vana-god Heimdal was by Vana-gods sent as a child to the primeval Teutonic country, to give to the descendants of Ask and Embla the holy fire, tools, and implements, the runes, the laws of society, and the rules for religious worship. It has been demonstrated that, as an anthropomorphous god and first patriarch, he is identical with Scef-Rig, the Scyld of the

Beowulf poem, that he becomes the father of the other original patriarch Skjöld, and the grandfather of Half-dan. It has likewise been demonstrated (No. 82) that Heimdal, the personified sacred fire, is the son of the lire-producer (by friction) Mundilfore, in the same man-ner as Agni is the son of Matariçvan. From all this it follows that when the authors of mythic genealogies related as history wish to get further back in the Skjoldung genealogy than to the Beowulf Skjold, that is to say, further back than to the original patriarch Heimdal, then they must go to that mythic person who is Heimdal's father, that is to say, to Mundilfore, the fire-producer. Mundilfore is the one who appears in the Latinised name Lotherus. In other words, Mundilfore, the fire-producer, is *Lodurr*. For the name *Lodurr* there is no other rational explanation than that which Jacob Grimm, without knowing his position in the epic of mythology, has given, comparing the name with the verb *lodern,* "to blaze." *Lodurr* is active in its signification, "he who causes or produces the blaze," and thus refers to the origin of fire, particularly of the friction-fire and of the bore-fire.

Further on (Nos. 90, 91, 92, 121, 123) I shall give an account of the ward of the atmosphere, *Gevarr* (*Nökkvi, Nœfr*), and demonstrate that he is identical with Mundilfore, the revolver of the starry firmament. All that Saxo tells about Lotherus is explained by the character of the latter as the chieftain of a Vana-clan, and by his identity with *Mundilföri-Gevarr.* As a chieftain of the Vans he was their leader when the war broke out between

the Asas on the one side, and the Vans and Elves on the
other. The banishment of Odin and the Asas by the
Vans causes Saxo to say that Lotherus banished from
the realm persons who were his equals in noble birth
(*nobilitate pares*), and whom he regarded as competitors
in regard to the government. It is also stated that he took
the power from an elder brother, but spared his life, although he robbed him of the sceptre. The brother here
referred to is not, however, Odin, but *Hœnir (Vei)*. The
character of the one deposed is gentle and without any
greed for rule like that by which Honer is known. Saxo
says of him that he so patiently bore the injustice done
him that he seemed to be pleased therewith as with a
kindness received (*ceterum injuriæ tam patiens fuit, ut
honoris damno tanquam beneficio gratulari crederetur*).
The reason why Honer, at the outbreak of the war with
the Asas, is deposed from his dignity as the ruler of Vanaheim and is succeeded by Loder, is explained by the fact
that he, like Mimer, remained devoted to the cause of
Odin. In spite of the confused manner in which the
troubles between the Asas and Vans are presented in
Heimskringla, it still appears that, before the war between the Asas and Vans, Honer was the chief of the latter on account of an old agreement between the two god-
clans; that he then always submitted to the counsels of
the wise Mimer, Odin's friend; that Mimer lost his life
in the service of Odin, and that the Vans sent his head
to Odin; and, finally, that, at the outbreak of the feud
with the Asas and after the death of Mimer, they looked
upon Honer as unqualified to be their judge and leader.

Thus Loder becomes after Honer the ruler of Vanaheim and the chieftain of the Vans, wiile the Vans Njord, Frey, and the Elf Ull, who had already been adopted in Asgard, administer the affairs of the rest of the world. To the mythical circumstance, that Honer lost his throne and his power points also Völuspa, the poem restoring to the gentle and patient Vana-god, after the regeneration, the rights of which he had been robbed, *thá kná Hænir hlautvid kjosa* (str. 60). "Then Honer becomes able to choose the lot-wood," that is to say, he is permitted to determine and indicate the fortunes of those consulting the oracle; in other words, then he is again able to exercise the rights of a god. In the Eddas, Honer appears as Odin's companion on excursions from Asgard. Skaldskaparmal, which does not seem to be aware that Honer was Odin's brother, still is conscious that he was intimately connected with him and calls him his *scssi, sinni,* and *máli* (Younger Edda, i. 266). During the war between Asas and Vans, Frigg espoused the cause of the Vans (see No. 36); hence Loke's insulting words to her (Lokasenna, 26), and the tradition in Heimskringla (Yngl., 3), that Vilir and Vei took Frigg to themselves once when Odin was far away from Asgard.

Saxo makes Lotherus fall at the hands of conspirators. The explanation of this statement is to be sought in *Mundilföri-Gevarr's* fate, of which, see Nos. 91, 123.

Mundilfore's character seems at least in one respect to be the opposite of Honer's. Gylfaginning speaks of his *ofdrambi,* his pride, founded, according to this record, on the beauty of his children. Saxo mentions tıe *in-*

solentia of Lotherus, and one of his surnames was *Dulsi,* the proud. See No. 89, where a strophe is quoted, in which the founder of the Swedish Skilfing race (the Ynglings) is called *Dulsa knor,* Dulse's descendant. As was shown above in the account of the myth about Scef, the Skjoldings, too, are Skilfings. Both these branches of the race have a common origin; and as the genealogy of the Skjoldungs can be traced back to Heimdal, and beyond him to Mundilfore, it must be this personality who is mentioned for his *ofdrambi,* that bears the surname *Dulsi.*

With Odin, *Vei-Höner* and *Vili-Lodurr-Mundilföri* have participated in the shaping of the world as well as in the creation of man. Of the part they took in the latter act, and of the importance they thereby acquired in the mythical anthropology, and especially in the conceptions concerning the continued creation of man by generation and birth, see No. 95.

84.

NAT, THE MOTHER OF THE GODS.

It has already been shown above that Nat, the mother of the gods, has her hall in the northern part of Mimer's realm, below the southern slopes of the Nida mountains.

There has been, and still is, an interpretation of the myths as symbols. Light is regarded as the symbol of moral goodness, and darkness as that of moral evil. That there is something psychologically correct in this cannot be denied; but in regard to the Aryan religions the assumption would lead to a great error, if, as we might be tempted to do, we should make night identical with darkness, and should refer her to the world of evil. In the mythologies of the Rigveda-Aryans and of the Teutons, Nat is an awe-inspiring, adorable, noble, and beneficent being. Night is said in Rigveda "to have a fair face, to increase riches, and to be one of the mothers of order." None of the phenemena of nature seemed to the Teutons evil *per se;* only when they transgressed what was thought to be their lawful limits, and thus produced injury and harm, were giant-powers believed to be active therein. Although the Teutonic gods are in a constant, more or less violent conflict with the powers of frost, still winter, when it observes its limits of time, is not an evil but a good divinity, and the cold liquids of Hvergelmer mixed with those of Urd's and Mimer's fountains are necessary to the world-tree. Still less could night be referred to the domain of demons. Mother Nat never transgresses the borders of her power; she never defies the sacred laws, which are established for the order of the universe. According to the seasons of the year, she divides in an unvarying manner the twenty-four hours between herself and day. Work and rest must alternate with each other. Rich in blessing, night comes with solace to the weary, and seeks if possible to sooth the sufferer with a potion of slumber. Though sombre in appearance (Gylfy., 10), still she is the friend of light. She decorates herself with lunar effulgence and with starry splendour, with winning twilight in midsummer, and with the light of snow and of northern aurora in the winter. The following lines in Sigrdrifumal (str., 3, 4) sound like a reverberation from the lost liturgic hymns of our heathendom.

Heill Dagr,	Hail Dag,
heilir Dags synir,	Hail Dag's sons,
ıeil Nott ok Nipt!	Hail Nat and Nipt!
Oreithom augom	Look down upon us
litith ocr thinig	Witı benevolent eyes
oc gefit sitiondom règr!	And give victory to the sitting!
Heilir æsir,	Hail Asas,
heilar asynjor,	Hail Asynjes,
ıeil sia in fiolnyta fold!	Hail bounteous eartı!

Of the Germans in the first century after Christ, Tacitus writes (*Germ., 3*): "They do not, as we, compute time by days but by nights, night seems to lead the day" (*nec dierum numerum, ut nos, sed noctium computant: nox ducere diem videtur*). This was applicable to the Scandinavians as far down as a thousand years later. Time was computed by nights not by days, and in the phrases from heathen times, *nótt ok dagr, nótt med degi bædi um nætr ok um daga,* night is named before day. Linguistic usage and mythology are here intimately associated with each other. According to Vafthrudnersmal (25) and Gylfaginning (10), Nat bore with Delling the son Dag, with whom she divided the administration of the twenty-four hours. Delling is the elf of the morning red (see No. 35). The symbolism of nature is here distinct as in all theogonies.

Through other divinities, *Naglfari* and *Ónarr* (*Anarr, Aunarr*), Nat is the mother with the former of *Unır* (*Udr*), also called *Audr,* with the latter of the goddess

Jord, Odin's wife.   *Unnr* means water, *Audr* means rich.
It has above been shown that *Unnr-Audr* is identical with
Njord, the lord of wealth and commerce, who in tie latter capacity became the protector of navigators, and to
whom sacrifices were offered for a prosperous voyage.
Gods of all clans—Asas, Vans, and Elves—are thus akin
to Nat, and are descended from her.

85.

NARFI, NAT'S FATHER, IDENTICAL WITH MIMER.   A PSEUDO-NARFI IN THE YOUNGER EDDA.

Nat herself is the daughter of a being whose name has
many forms.

Naurr, Nörr (dative *Naurvi, Nörvi, Nott var Naurvi*
        borin—Vafthrudnersmal, 25; *Nott. Naurvi*
        kenda—Alvism., 29).
Narfi, Narvi (*niderfi Narfa*—Egil Skallagr., 56, 2; Gyl-
        fag., 10).
Norvi, Nörvi (Gylfag., 10; *kund Nörva*—Forspjallsl., 7).
Njörfi, Njörvi (Gylfag., 10; *Njörva nipt*—Sonatorr.).
Nori   (Gylfag., 10).
Nari   (Höfudl., 10).
Neri   (Helge Hund., 1).

All these variations are derived from the same original
appellation, related to the Old Norse verb *njörva,* the
Old English *nearwian* meaning "the one that binds," "the
one who puts on tight-fitting bonds."

Simply the circumstance that Narvi is Nat's father proves that he must have occupied one of the most conspicuous positions in the Teutonic cosmogony. In all cosmogonies and theogonies night is one of the oldest beings, older than light, without which it cannot be conceived. Light is kindled in the darkness, thus foreboding an important epoch in the development of the world out of chaos. The being which is night's father must therefore be counted among the oldest in the cosmogony. The personified representatives of water and earth, like the day, are the children of his daughter.

What Gylfaginning tells of Narve is that he was of giant birth, and the first one who inhabited Jotunheim (*Norvi eda Narfi hét jötun, er bygdi fyrst Jotunheima*—Gylfag., 10). In regard to this we must remember that, in Gylfaginning and in the traditions of the Icelandic sagas, the lower world is embraced in the term Jotunheim, and this for mythical reasons, since Nifelheim is inbahited by rimthurses and giants (see No. 60), and since the regions of bliss are governed by Mimer and by the norns, who also are of giant descent. As the father of the lower-world dis, Nat, Narve himself belongs to that group of powers, with which the mythology peopled the lower world. The upper Jothunheim did not exist before in a later epoch of the cosmogonic development. It was created simultaneously with Midgard by Odin and his brothers (Gylfaginning).

In a strophe by Egil Skallagrimson (ch. 56), poetry, or the source of poetry, is called *niderfi Narfa,* "the inheritance left by Narve to his descendants." As is well known, Mimer's fountain is the source of poetry. The expression indicates that the first inhabitant of the lower world, Narve, also presided over the precious fountain of wisdom and inspiration, and that he died and left it to his descendants as an inheritance.

Finally, we learn that **Narve** was a near kinsman to Urd and her sisters. This appears from the following passages:

(*a*) **Helge Hundingsbane (1, 3, ff.).** When Helge was born norns came in the night to the abode of his parents, twisted the threads of his fate, stretched them from east to west, and fastened them beneath the hall of the moon. One of the threads *nipt Nera* cast to the north and bade it hold for ever. It is manifest that by Nere's (Narve's) kinswoman is meant one of the norns present.

(*b*) **Sonatorr. (str. 24).** The skald Egil Skalla-grimson, weary of life, closes his poem by saying that he sees the dis of death standing on the ness (Digraness) near the grave-mound which conceals the dust of his father and of his sons, and is soon to receive him:

Tveggja bága	The kinswoman of Njorve (the binder)
Njörva nipt	of Odin's (Tvegge's) foes
a nesi stendr.	stands on the ness.
Skal ek thó gladr	Then shall I be glad,
med gódan vilja	with a good will,
ok úhryggr	and without remorse,
Heljar bida.	wait for Hel.

It goes without saying that the skald means a dis of death, Urd or one of her messengers, with the words, "The kinswoman of Njorve (the binder) of Odin's foes," whom he with the eye of presentiment sees standing on the family grave-mound on Digraness. She is not to stop there, but she is to continue her way to his hall, to bring him to the grave-mound. He awaits her coming with gladness, and as the last line shows, she whose arrival he awaits is Hel, the goddess of death or fate. It has already been demonstrated that Hel in the heathen records is always identical with Urd.

Njorve is here used both as a proper and a common noun. "The kinswoman of the Njorve of Odin's foes" means "the kinswoman of the binder of Odin's foes.'' Odin's foe Fenrer was bound with an excellent chain smithied in the lower world (dwarfs in *Svartalfheimr*—Gylfag., 37), and as shall be shown later, there are more than one of Odin's foes who are bound with Narve's chains (see No. 87).

(*c*) *Hofudlausn* (str. 10). Egil Skallagrimson celebrates in song a victory won by Erik Blood-axe, and says of the battle-field that there *trad nipt Nara náttverd ara* ("Nare's kinswoman trampled upon the supper of the eagles," that is to say, upon the dead bodies of the fallen). The psychopomps of disease, of age, and of misfortunes have nothing to do on a battle-field. Thither come valkyries to fetch the elect. *Nipt Nara* must therefore be a valkyrie, whose horse tramples upon the heaps of dead bodies; and as Egil names only one shield-maid of that kind, he doubtless has had the most representative. the most important one in mind. That one is Skuld, Urd's sister, and thus a *nipt Nara* like Urd herself.

(*d*) Ynglingatal (Ynglingasaga, ch. 20). Of King

Dygve, who died from disease, it is said that *jódis Narva* (*jódis Nara*) chose him. The right to choose those who die from disease belongs to the norns alone (see No. 69). *Jódis,* a word doubtless produced by a vowel change from the Old Germanic *idis,* has already in olden times been interpreted partly as horse-dis (from *jór,* horse), partly as the dis of one's kin (from *jod,* child, offspring). In this case the skald has taken advantage of both significations. He calls the death-dis *ulfs ok Narva jódis,* the wolf's horse-dis, Narve's kin-dis. In regard to the former signification, it should be remembered that the wolf is horse for all giantesses, the honoured norns not excepted. Cp. *grey norna* as a paraphrase for wolf.

Thus what our mythic records tell us about Narve is:

(*a*) He is one of the oldest beings of theogony, older than the upper part of the world constructed by Bur's sons.

(*b*) He is of giant descent.

(*c*) He is father of Nat, father-in-law of Nagelfar, Onar, and of Delling, the elf of the rosy dawn; and he is the father of Dag's mother, of *Unnr,* and of the goddess Jord, who becomes Odin's wife and Thor's mother. Bonds of kinship thus connect him with the Asas and with gods of other ranks.

(*d*) He is near akin to the dis of fate and death, Urd and her sisters. The word *nipt,* with which Urd's relation to him is indicated, may mean sister, daughter, and sister's daughter, and consequently does not state which particular one of these it is. It seems upon the whole to have been applied well-nigh exclusively in regard to mythic persons, and particularly in regard to Urd and her sisters (cp. above: *Njörva nipt, nipt Nara, nipt Nera*), so that it almost acquired the meaning of dis or norn. This is evident from Skaldskaparmal, ch. 75: *Nornir heita thær er naud skapa; Nipt ok Dis nú eru taldar,* and from the expression *Heil Nótt ok Nipt* in the above-cited strophe from Sigrdrifumal. There is every reason for assuming that the *Nipt,* which is here used as a proper noun, in this sense means the dis of fate and as an appellation of kinship, a kinswoman of Nat. The common interpretation of *heil Nótt ok Nipt* is "hail Nat and her daughter," and by her daughter is then meant the goddess Jord; but this interpretation is, as Bugge has shown, less probable, for the goddess Jord immediately below gets her special greeting in the words: *heil sia in fiolnyta Fold!* ("hail the bounteous earth!")

(*e*) As the father of Nat, living in Mimer's realm, and kinsman of Urd, who with Mimer divides the dominion over the lower world, Narve is himself a being of the lower world, and the oldest subterranean being; the first one who inhabited Jotunheim.

(*f*) He presided over the subterranean fountain of wisdom and inspiration, that is to say, Mimer's fountain.

(*g*) He was Odin's friend and the binder of Odin's foes.

(*h*) He died and left his fountain as a heritage to his descendants.

As our investigation progresses it will be found that all these facts concerning Narve apply to Mimer, that "he who thinks" (Mimer) and "he who binds" (Narve)

interpretation of *heil Nótt ok Nipt* is "hail Nat and her daughter," and by her daughter is then meant the goddess Jord; but this interpretation is, as Bugge has shown, less probable, for the goddess Jord immediately below gets her special greeting in the words: *heil sia in fiolnyta Fold!* ("hail the bounteous earth!")

(e) As the father of Nat, living in Mimer's realm, and kinsman of Urd, who with Mimer divides the dominion over the lower world, Narve is himself a being of the lower world, and the oldest subterranean being; the first one who inhabited Jotunheim.

(f) He presided over the subterranean fountain of wisdom and inspiration, that is to say, Mimer's fountain.

(g) He was Odin's friend and the binder of Odin's foes.

(h) He died and left his fountain as a heritage to his descendants.

As our investigation progresses it will be found that all these facts concerning Narve apply to Mimer, that "he who thinks" (Mimer) and "he who binds." (Narve)

are the same person. Already the circumstances that Narve was an ancient being of giant descent, that he dwelt in the lower world and was the possessor of the fountain of wisdom there, that he was Odin's friend, and that he died and left his fountain as an inheritance (cp. *Mims synir*), point definitely to Narve's and Mimer's identity. Thus the Teutonic theogony has made Thought the older kinsman of Fate, who through Nat bears Dag to the world. The people of antiquity made their first steps toward a philosophical view of the world in their theogony.

The Old English language has preserved and transferred to the Christian Paradise a name which originally belonged to the subterranean region of bliss of heathendom—*Neorxenavang*. *Vang* means a meadow, plain, field. The mysterious *Neorxena* looks like a genitive plural. Grein, in his Anglo-Saxon Dictionary, and before him Weinhold, refers *neorxena* to *Narve, Nare,* and this without a suspicion that *Narve* was an epithet of Mimer and referred to the king of the heathen regions of bliss. I consider this an evidence that Grein's assumption is as correct as it is necessary, if upon the whole we are to look for an etymological explanation of the word. The plural genitive, then, means those who inhabit Narve's regions of bliss, and receive their appellation from this circumstance. The opposite Old Norse appellation is *njarir,* a word which I shall discuss below.

To judge from certain passages in Christian writings of the thirteenth century, Mimer was not alone about the name Narve, Nare. One or two of Loke's sons are supposed to have had the same name. The statements in this regard demand investigation, and, as I think, this will furnish another instructive contribution to the chapter on the confusion of the mythic traditions, and on the part that the Younger Edda plays in this respect. The passages are:

(*a*) *The prosaic afterword to Lokasenna*: "He (Loke) was bound with the entrails of his son *Nari,* but his son *Narfi* was turned into a wolf."

(*b*) *Gylfaginning,* ch. 33. (1) *Most of the codices*: "His (Loke's) wife is hight Sygin; their son is *Nari* or *Narvi.*"

(2) *Codex Hypnonesiensis*: "His (Loke's) wife is hight Sygin; his sons are hight *Nari* or *Narvi* and *Vali.*"

(*c*) *Gylfaginning,* ch. 50. (1) *Most of the codices*: "Then were taken Loke's sons *Vali* and *Nari* or *Narfi.* The Asas changed *Vali* into a wolf, and the latter tore into pieces his brother *Narfi.* Then the Asas took his entrails and therewith bound Loke."

(2) *Codex Upsalensis*: "Then were taken Loke's sons *Vali* and *Nari.* The Asas changed *Vali* into a wolf, and the latter tore into pieces his brother *Nari.*"

(*d*) *Skaldskaparmal,* ch. 16. (1) "Loke is the father of the wolf Fenrer, the Midgard-serpent, and Hel, 'and also of *Nari* and *Ali.*' "

(2) *Codex Wormianus* and *Codex Hypnonesiensis,* 3: "Loke is father of the Fenris-wolf, of the Midgard-serpent, and of Hel, 'and also of *Nari* and *Vali.*' "

The mythology has stated that Loke was bound with chains which were originally entrails, and that he who contributed the materials of these chains was his own son, who was torn into pieces by his brother in wolf guise. It is possible that there is something symbolic in this myth—that it originated in the thought that the forces created by evil contend with each other and destroy their own parent. There is at least no reason for doubting that this account is a genuine myth, that is to say, that it comes from a heathen source and from some heathen poem.

But, in regard to the names of Loke's two sons here in question, we have a perfect right to doubt.

We discover at once the contradictions betrayed by the records in regard to them. The discrepancy of the statements can best be shown by the following comparisons. Besides Fenrer, the Midgard-serpent, and Hel, Loke has, according to

Gylfaginning, 33 :	the son *Nari,*	also called *Narfi*	No other son is named ;
The Prose added to Lokasenna :	{ the son *Nari,*		and the son *Narfi*
Codex Hypnon. (Gylfag., 33) :	{ the son *Nari,*	also called *Narvi.*	and the son *Vali;*
Gylfaginning, ch. 50 :	the son *Nari,*	also called *Narfi*	and the son *Vali;*
Skaldskaparmal, ch. 16 :	{ the son *Nari,* and		the son *Ali;*
The Prose added to Lokasenna :	{ *Nari,*	is torn into pieces by	*Narfi;*
Gylfaginning :	Nari-Narfi	is torn into pieces by	*Vali.*

The discrepancy shows that the author of these statements did not have any mythic song or mythic tradition as the source of all these names of Loke's sons.

The matter becomes even more suspicious when we find—

That the variations Nare and Narve, both of which

belong to one of the foremost and noblest of mythic beings, namely, to Mimer, are here applied in such a manner that they either are given to two sons of Loke or are
attributed to one and the same Loke-son, while in the latter case it happens—

That the names Vale and Ale, which both belong to
the same Asa-god and son of Odin who avenged the death
of his brother Balder, are *both* attributed to the other son
of Loke. Compare Gylfaginning, ch. 30: *Vali eda Ali
heitir einn* (*Assin*) *sonr Odins ok Rindar.*

How shall we explain this? Such an application of
these names must necessarily produce the suspicion of
some serious mistake; but we cannot assume that it was
made wilfully. The cause must be found somewhere.

It has already been demonstrated that, in the mythology,
Urd, the dis of fate, was also the dis of death and the ruler
of the lower world, and that the functions belonging to
her in this capacity were, in Christian times, transferred
to Loke's daughter, who, together with her functions,
usurped her name Hel. Loke's daughter and Hel became to the Christian mythographers identical.

An inevitable result was that such expressions as *nipt
Nara, jódis Narfa, nipt Njörva,* had to change meaning. The *nipt Njörva,* whom the aged Egil saw standing near the grave-mound on Digraness, and whose arrival he awaited "with gladness and good-will," was no
longer the death-dis Urd, but became to the Christian
interpreters the abominable daughter of Loke who came ·
to fetch the old heathen. The *nipt Nara,* whose horse
trampled on the battle-field where Erik Blood-axe defeated

the Scots, was no longer Urd's sister, the valkyrie Skuld, but became Loke's daughter, although, even according to the Christian mythograpiers, the latter had nothing to do on a battle-field. The *jódis Narfa,* who chose King Dygve, was confounded with *Loka mær,* who had him *leikinn* (see No. 67), but who, according to the heathen conception, was a maid-servant of fate, without the right of cioosing. To the heathens *nipt Nara, nipt Njörva, jódis Narfa,* meant "Nare-Mimer's kinswoman Urd." To the mythographers of the thirteenth century it must, for the reason stated, have meant the Loke-daughter as sister of a certain Nare or Narve. It follows that this Nare or Narve ought to be a son of Loke, since his sister was Loke's daughter. It was known that Loke besides Fenrer and the Midgard-serpent, had two other sons, of which the one in the guise of a wolf tore the other into pieces. In Nare, Narve, the name of one or the names of both these Loke-sons were thought to have been found.

The latter assumption was made by the author of the prose in Lokasenna. He conceived Nare to be the one brother and Narve the other. The author of Gylfaginning, on the other hand, rightly regarded Nare and Narve as simply variations of the same name, and accordingly let them designate the same son of Loke. When he wrote chapter 33, he did not know what name to give to the other, and consequently omitted him entirely. But when he got to the 50th chapter, a light had risen for him in regard to the name of the other. And the light doubtless came from the following strophe in Völuspa:

tha kna vala
vigbond snua,
helldi voru hardgior
loft or thormum.

This half strophe says that those were strong chains
(for Loke) that were made of entrails, and these fetters
were "twisted" from "Vale's *vigbönd.*" *Vig* as a legal
term means a murder, slaughter. *Vala vig* was interpreted as a murder committed by Vale; and *Vala vigbönd*
as the bonds or fetters obtained by the slaughter committed by Vale. It was known that Loke was chained
with the entrails of his son, and here it was thought to
appear that this son was slain by a certain Vale. And
as he was slain by a brother according to the myth, then
Vale must be the brother of the slain son of Loke. Accordingly chapter 50 of Gylfaginning could tell us what
chapter 33 did not yet know, namely, that the two sons
of Loke were named Vale and Nare or Narve, and that
Vale changed to a wolf, tore the brother "Nare or Narve"
into pieces.

The next step was taken by Skaldskaparmal, or more
probably by one of the transcribers of Skaldskaparmal.
As Vale and Ale in the mythology designated the same
person (viz., Balder's avenger, the son of Odin), the son
of Loke, changed into a wolf, "Vale" received as a gift
the name "Ale." It is by no means impossible that the
transcriber regarded Balder's avenger, Vale, and the son
of Loke as identical. The oldest manuscript we have of
Skaldskaparmal is the Upsala Codex, which is no older
than the beginning of the fourteenth century. The

622

mythic traditions were then in the continuation of that rapid decay which had begun in the eleventh century, and not long thereafter the Icelandic saga writings saw Valhal peopled by giants and all sorts of monsters, which were called einherjes, and Thor himself transferred to the places of torture where he drank venom from "the auroch's horn," presented to him by the daughter of Loke.

In the interpretation of the above-cited half strophe of Völuspa, we must therefore leave out the supposed son of Loke, Vale. The Teutonic mythology, like the other Aryan mythologies, applied many names and epithets to the same person, but it seldom gave two or more persons one and the same name, unless the latter was a patronymic or, in other respects, of a general character. There was not more than one Odin, one Thor, one Njord, one Heimdal, one Loke, and there is no reason for assuming that there was more than one Vale, namely, the divine son of this name. Of Balder's brother Vale we know that he was born to avenge the slaying of Balder. His impatience to do that which he was called to perform is expressed in the mythology by the statement, that he liberated himself from the womb of his mother before the usual time (*Baldrs brodir var af borinn snemma—*Völuspa), and only one night old he went to slay *Hödr.* The bonds which confine the impatient one in his mother's womb were his *vigbönd,* the bonds which hindered him from combat, and these bonds were in the most literal sense of the word *ór thörmum.* As Loke's bonds are made of the same material and destined to hinder him

623

from combat with the gods until Ragnarok, and as 1is prison is in the womb of t1e earth, as Vale's was in t1at of the earth-goddess Rind's, t1en *Vala vigbönd* as a designation of Loke's chains is both logically and poetically a satisfactory paraphrase, and the more in order as it occurs in connection with the description of the impending Ragnarok, when Loke by an earthquake is to sever his fetters and hasten to the conflict.

86.

THE TWO GIANT CLANS DESCENDED FROM YMER.

In Havamál (140, ff.), Odin says that he in his youth obtained nine fimbul-songs and a drink of the precious mead dipped out of Odrerer from *Beyzla's* father, *Bölthorn's* famous son:

> Fimbullióð nio
> nam ec af enom fregia syni
> Baulthorns Beyzlu faudur
> oc cc dryc of gat
> ens dyra miadar
> ausinn Odreri.

The mythologists have assumed, for reasons that cannot be doubted, that Bolthorn's famous son, Beistla's brother, is identical with Mimer. No one else than he presided at that time over the drink dipped out of Odrerer, the fountain which conceals "wisdom and man's sense," and Sigrdrifumal (13, 14) corroborates that it was from Mimer, and through a drink from "Hodrofner's horn," that Odin obtained wonderful runes and "true sayings.".

624

Accordingly Mimer had a sister by name *Beyzla* (variations: *Bcstla, Bcsla, Bczla*). A strophe by Einar Skalaglam (Skaldskaparmal, ch. 2; cp. Gylfag., ch. 6) informs us that Beistla is Odin's mother. Mimer's disciple, the clan-chieftain of the gods, is accordingly iis sister's son. Herein we have one more reason for the faithful friendship which Mimer always showed to Odin.

The Mimer epithet *Narfi*, Narve, means, as shown above, "the one who binds." His daughter Nat is called *draumnjörun,* the dream-binder (Alvism., 31). His kinswomen, the norns, spin and bind the threads and bonds, which, extended throughout the world, weave together the web of events. Such threads and bonds are called *örlogthættir* (Helge Hund., i. 3), and *Urdar lokur* (Grogaldr., 7). As the nearest kinswomen of Beistla all have epithets or tasks which refer to the idea of *binding,* and when we add to this that Beistla's sons and descendants as gods have the epithet *höpt* and *bönd,* her own name might most properly be referred to the old word *beizl, beisl* (cp. *betsel,* bridle), which has a similar meaning.

As Mimer and Beistla are of giant descent, and in the theogony belong to the same stage of development as Bur (*Burr*), Odin's father, then, as the mythologists also have assumed, *Bolthorn* can be none else than Ymer.

Mimer, Beistla, the norns, and Nat thus form a group of kindred beings, which belong to the oldest giant race, but still they are most definitely separated from the other descendants of Ymer, as a higher race of giants from a lower, a noble giant race friendly to the gods and fostering the gods, from that race of deformed beings which bear children in the strangest manner, which are hostile to the gods and to the world, and which are represented by the rimthurses Thrudgelmer and Bergelmer and their offspring.

It now lies near at hand to inquire whether the mythology which attributed the same father to Mimer and Thrudgelmer was unable to conceive in this connection the idea of a nobler origin for the former than the latter. The remedy nearest at hand would have been to have given them mothers of different characters. But the mythology did not resort to this expedient. It is expressly stated that Ymer bore children without the pleasure of woman (*gygiar gaman*—Vafthrudnersmal, 32; cp. No. 60). Neither Mimer nor Thrudgelmer had a mother. Under such circumstances there is another expedient to which the sister of the Teutonic mythology, the Rigveda mythology, has resorted, and which is explained in the 90th hymn of book x. of Rigveda. The hymn informs us in regard to a primeval giant Parusha, and this myth is so similar to the Teutonic in regard to Ymer that it must here be considered.

The primeval being Parusha was a giant monster as large as the whole world, and even larger (lines 1-5). The gods resolved to sacrifice him, that is to say, to slay him for sacred purposes (1. 6), and from his limbs was created the present world. From his navel was made the atmosphere, from his head the canopy of heaven, from his two feet the earth, from his heart the moon, from his eye the sun, from his breath the wind, &c. *His mouth became the brahma* (the priest), *his arms became the rajanya* (the warrior), *his thighs became the vaisya* (the third free caste), *and from his feet arose the sudra* (the thrall, line 12).

The two fundamental ideas of the myth concerning Parusha are:

(1) There was a primeval being who was not divine. The gods slew him and created the material world out of his limbs.

(2) This primeval being gave rise to other beings of different ranks, and their rank corresponded with the position of the giant's limbs from which they were created.

Both these fundamental ideas reappear in the Teutonic myth concerning Ymer. In regard to the former idea we need only to quote what Vafthrudnersmal says in strophe 21:

Or Ymis ioldi	Of Ymer's flesi
var iord um scaupud,	the world was siapen,
en or beinom bjorg,	from his bones the rocks,
himinn or iausi	the ieavens from the iead
ins hrimkalda iotuns,	of the ice-cold giant,
enn or sveita sior.	from his blood the sea.

In regard to the second fundamental idea, it is evident from the Rigveda account that it is not there found in its oldest form, but that, after the rise of four castes among the Rigveda Aryans, it was changed, in order to furnish an explanation of the origin of these castes and make them at least as old as the present material world. Far more original, and perfectly free from the

influence of social ideas, it appears in the Teutonic mytiology, where the 33rd strophe of Vafthrudnersmal tes-
tifies concerning its character:

Undir lendi vaxa	A son and a daugiter
quatho hrimthursi	are said to lave been born to-getler
mey oc maug saman;	under the rimthurse's arm;
fótr vid fóti gat	foot begat witl foot
ins froda iotuns	the strange-leaded son
serhaufdathan son.	of the wise giant.

In perfect harmony with this Gylfaginning narrates:
"'Under Ymer's left arm grew forth a man and a woman,
and his one foot begat with the other a son. Thence
come (different) races."

The different races have this in common, that they are
giant races, since they spring from Ymer; but these giant
races must at the same time have been widely different
intellectually and physically, since the mythology gives
them different origins from different limbs of the progenitor. And here, as in Rigveda, it is clear that the
lowest race was conceived as proceeding from the feet
of the primeval giant. This is stated with sufficient
distinctness in Vafthrudnersmal, where we read that a
"strangely-headed" monster (Thrudgelmer—see No. 60)
was born by them, while "man and maid" were born under the arm of the giant. "The man" and "the maid"
must therefore represent a noble race sprung from
Ymer, and they can only be Mimer and his sister, Odin's
mother. Mimer and his clan constitute a group of ancient powers, who watch over the fountains of the life of
the world and care for the perpetuation of the world-

tree.   From them proceeded the oldest, fairest, and most enduring parts of the creation.   For the lower world was put in order and had its sacred fountains and guardians before Bur's sons created Midgard and Asgard. Among them the world-tree grew up from its roots, whose source no one knows (Havamál, 138).   Among them those forces are active which make the starry firmament revolve on its axis, and from them come the seasons and the divisions of time, for Nat and *nidjar,* Mane and Sol, belong to Mimer's clan, and were in the morning of creation named by the oldest "high holy gods," and endowed with the vocation *árom at telja* (Völuspa).   From Mimer comes the first culture, for in his fountain inspiration, spiritual power, man's wit and wisdom, have their source, and around him as chief stand gathered the artists of antiquity by whose hands all things can be smithied into living and wonderful things. Such a giant clan demands another origin than that of the frost-giants and their offspring.   As we learn from Vafthrudnersmal that two giant races proceeded from Ymer, the one from a part of his body which in a symbolic sense is more noble than that from which the other race sprang, and that the race born of his feet was the ignoble one hostile to the gods, then the conclusion follows of necessity that "the man and maid" who were born as twins under Ymer's arm became the founders of that noble group of giants who are friendly to the gods, and which confront us in the mythology of our fathers. It has already been shown above (see No. 54) that *Jima* (Yama) in the Asiatic-Aryan mythology corresponds to

Mimer in the Teutonic. Jima is an epithet which means twin. The one with whom Jima was born together was a maid, Yami. The words in the quoted Vafthrudnersmal strophe, *undir hendi hrimthursi vaxa mey ok maug saman,* are evidence that the Germans also considered Mimer and his sister as twins.

87.

THE IDENTITY OF MIMER AND NIDHAD OF THE VOLUND SAGA.

The condition in which the traditions of the great Volund (Wayland) have come down to our time is one of the many examples illustrating how, under the influences of a change of faith, a myth disrobes itself of its purely mythical character and becomes a heroic saga. The nature of the mythic traditions and songs is not at once obliterated in the time of transition; there remain marks of their original nature in some or other of the details as proof of what they have been. Thus that fragment of a Volund saga, turned into an epic, which the Old Norse literature has preserved for us in Volundarkvida, shows us that the artist who is the hero of the song was originally conceived not as a son of man, but as a member of the mythic race of elves which in Völuspa is mentioned in connection with the Asas (*hvat er med asom, hvat er med alfom?*—str. 49). Volund is an elfprince (*alfa visi, alfa ljothi*—Volund., str. 10, 13), and, as shall be shown below, when we come to consider the Volund myth exhaustively, he and his brothers and their mistresses have played parts of the very greatest importance in tie epic of Teutonic mythology. Under such circumstances it follows tiat tie other persons appearing in Volundarkvida also were originally mytiical characters.

One of these is called *Nidadr* (*Nidudr*), king of Njares, and I am now to investigate who this *Nidadr* was in tie mythology.

When Volund for the first time appears by this name in the Elder Edda, he is sojourning in a distant country, to whici it is impossible to come without traversing the Myrkwood forest famous in the mythology (see No. 78). It is a snow-clad country, the home of bears and wolves. Volund gets his subsistence by hunting on skees. The Old English poem, "Deor the Scald's Complaint," confirms that this region was regarded as very cold (cp. *vintercealde vræce*). In Volundarkvida it is called Wolfdales.

Volund stays here many years in company with his two brothers and with three swan-maids, their mistresses or wives, but finally alone. Volund passes the time in smithying, until he is suddenly attacked by *Nidadr* (*Nidudr*), "the Njara-king" (Volundarkv., 6), who puts him in chains and robs him of two extraordinary treasures—a sword and an arm-ring. Seven hundred arm-rings hung in a string in Volund's hall; but this one alone seemed to be worth more than all the rest, and it alone was desired by *Nidadr* (str. 7, 8, 17).

Before Volund went to the Wolfdales, he had lived with his people a happy life in a land abounding in gold

631

(str. 14). Not voluntarily, but from dire necessity he had exchanged his home for the distant wilderness of the Wolfdales. "Deor the Scald's Complaint" says he was an exile (*Veland him be vurman vreces cannade*). A German saga of the middle ages, "Anhang des Helden-buchs," confirms this statement. Wieland (Volund), it is there said, "was a duke who was banished by two giants, who took his land from him," whereupon "he was stricken with poverty," and "became a smith." The Volundarkvida does not have much to say about the rea-son for his sojourn in the Wolfdales, but strophe 28 in-forms us that, previous to his arrival there, he had suf-fered an injustice, of which he speaks as the worst and the most revenge-demanding which he, the unhappy and revengeful man, ever experienced. But he has had no opportunity of demanding satisfaction, when he finally succeeds in getting free from *Nidadr's* chains. Who those mythic persons are that have so cruelly insulted him and filed his heart with unquenchable thirst for revenge is not mentioned; but in the very nature of the case those persons from whose persecutions he has fled must have been mightier than he, and as he himself is a chief in the godlike clan of elves, his foes are naturally to be looked for among the more powerful races of gods.

And as Volundarkvida pictures him as boundlessly and recklessly revengeful, and makes him resort to his extra-ordinary skill as a smith—a skill famous among all Teu-tonic tribes—in the satisfaction which he demands of *Nidudr,* there is no room for doubt that the many years he spent in Wolfdales, he brooded on plans of revenge against those who had most deeply insulted him, and that he made use of his art to secure instruments for the carrying out of these plans. Of the glittering sword of which *Nidadr* robbed him, Volund says (str. 18) that he had applied his greatest skill in making it hard and keen. The sword must, therefore, have been one of the most excellent ones mentioned in the songs of Teutonic heathendom. Far down in the middle ages, the songs and sagas were fond of attributing the best and most famous swords wielded by their heroes to the skill of Volund.

In the myths turned by Saxo into history, there has been mentioned a sword of a most remarkable kind, of untold value (*ingens præmium*), and attended by success in battle (*belli fortuna comitaretur*). A hero whose name Saxo Latinised into Hotherus (see *Hist. Dan.,* p. 110) got into enmity with the Asa-gods, and the only means with which he can hope to cope with them is the possession of this sword. He also knows where to secure it, and with its aid he succeeds in putting Thor himself and other gods to flight.

In order to get possession of this sword, Hotherus had to make a journey which reminds us of the adventurons expeditions already described to Gudmund-Mimer's domain, but with this difference, that he does not need to go by sea along the coast of Norway in order to get there, which circumstance is sufficiently explained by the fact that, according to Saxo, Hotherus has his home in Sweden. The regions which Hotherus has to traverse are pathless, full of obstacles, and for the greater part continually in the cold embrace of the severest frost.

They are traversed by mountain-ridges on which the cold is terrible, and therefore they must be crossed as rapidly as possible with the aid of "yoke-stags." The sword is kept concealed in a *specus,* a subterranean cave, and "mortals' can scarcely cross its threshold (*haud facile mortalibus patere posse*). The being which is the ward of the sword in this cave is by Saxo called Mimingus.

The question now is, whether the sword smithied by Volund and the one fetched by Hotherus are identical or not. The former is smithied in a winter-cold country beyond Myrkwood, where the mythic *Nidadr* suddenly appears, takes possession of it, and the purpose for which it was made, judging from all circumstances, was that Volund with its aid was to conquer the hated powers which, stronger than he, the chief of elves, had compelled him to take refuge to the Wolfdales. If these powers were Asas or Vans, then it follows that Volund must have thought himself able to give to his sword qualities that could render it dangerous to the world of gods, although the latter had Thor's hammer and other subterranean weapons at their disposal. The sword captured by Hotherus is said to possess those very qualities which we might look for in the Volund weapon, and the regions he has to traverse in order to get possession of it refer, by their cold and remoteness, to a land similar to that where *Nidadr* surprises Volund, and takes from him the dangerous sword.

As already stated, Nidad at the same time captured an arm-ring of an extraordinary kind. If the saga about Volund and his sword was connected with the saga-fragment turned into history by Saxo concerning Hotherus and the sword, whose owner he becomes, then we might reasonably expect that the precious arm-ring, too, should appear in the latter saga. And we do find it there. Mimingus, who guards the sword of victory, also guards a wonderful arm-ring, and through Saxo we learn what quality makes this particular arm-ring so precious, that Nidad does not seem to care about the other seven hundred which he finds in Volund's workshop. Saxo says: *Eidem (Mimingo) quoque armillam esse mira quadam arcanaque virtute possessoris opes augere solitam.* "In the arm-ring there dwells a wonderful and mysterious power, which increases the wealth of its possessor." In other words, it is a smith's work, the rival of the ring Draupner, from which eight similar rings drop every ninth night. This explains why Volund's smithy contains so many rings, that Nidad expresses his suspicious wonderment (str. 13).

There are therefore strong reasons for assuming that the sword and the ring, which Hotherus takes from Mimingus, are the same sword and ring as Nidad before took from Volund, and that the saga, having deprived Volund of the opportunity of testing the quality of the weapon himself in conflict with the gods, wanted to indicate what it really amounted to in a contest with Thor and his hammer by letting the sword came into the hands of Hotherus, another foe of the Asas. As we now find such articles as those captured by Nidad reappearing in the hands of a certain Mimingus, the question arises whether Mimingus is Nidad himself or some one of Nidad's subjects; for that they either are identical, or are in some way connected with each other, seems to follow from the fact that the one is said to possess what the other is said to have captured. Mimingus is a Latinising of *Mimingr, Mimungr,* son or descendant of Mimer.

Nidadr, Nidudr (both variations are found in Volundarkvida), has, on the other hand, his counterpart in the Anglo-Saxon Nidhâd. The king who in "Deor the Scald's Complaint" fetters Volund bears this name, and his daughter is called Beadohild, in Volundarkvida Bodvild. Previous investigators have already remarked that Beadohild is a more original form than Bodvild, and Nidhad than *Nidudr, Nidadr.* The name Nidhad is composed of *nid* (neuter génder), the lower world, Hades, and *had,* a being, person, *forma, species.* Nidhad literally means the lower world being, the Hades being. Herewith we also have his mythical character determined. A mythical king, who is characterised as the *being of the lower world,* must be a subterranean king. The mythic records extant speak of the subterranean king Mimer (the middle-age saga's Gudmund, king of the Glittering Fields; see Nos. 45, 46), who rules over the realm of the well of wisdom and has the dis of fate as his kinswoman, the princess of the realm of Urd's fountain and of the whole realm of death. While we thus find, on the one hand, that it is a subterranean king who captures Volund's sword and arm-ring, we find, on the other hand, that when Hotherus is about to secure the irresistible sword and the wealth-producing ring, he has to be-

identi-
· seems
possess
gus is a
dant of

Volun-
·t in the
eor the
me, and
da Bod-
ked that
d, and
had is
. Hades,
literally
. Here-
ined. A
g of the
e mythic
: Mimer
glittering
realm of
his kins-
tain and
find, on
who cap-
the other
· irresisti-
as to be-

take himself to the same winter-cold country, where all the traditions here discussed (see Nos. 45-49) locate the descent to Mimer's realm, and that he, through an entrance "scarcely approaciable for mortals," must proceed into the bosom of the earth after he has subdued a Mimingus, a son of Mimer. Mimer being the one who took possession of the treasure, it is perfectly natural that his son should be its keeper.

This also explains why *Nidadr* in Volundarkvida is called the king of the Njares. A people called Njares existed in the mythology, but not in reality. The only explanation of the word is to be found in the Mimer epithet, which we discovered in the variations Narve, Njorve, Nare, Nere, which means "he who binds." They are called Njares, because they belong to the clan of Njorvi-Nare.

Volundarkvida (str. 19, with the following prose addition) makes Nidad's queen command Volund's knee-sinews to be cut. Of such a cruelty the older poem, "Deor the Skald's Complaint," knows nothing. This poem relates, on the other hand, that Nidad bound Volund with a fetter made from a strong sinew:

> siththan linne Nidhad on
> nede legde
> sveoncre seono-bende.

Though Volund is in the highest degree skilful, he is not able to free himself from these bonds. They are of magic kind, and resemble those *örlogthœttir* which are tied by Mimer's kinswoman Urd. Nidad accordingly

637

here appears in Mimer-Njorve's character as "binder."
With this fetter of sinew we must compare the one with
which Loke was bound, and that tough and elastic one
which was made in the lower world and which holds
Fenrer bound until Ragnarok. And as Volund—a circumstance already made probable, and one that shall be
fully proved below—actually regards himself as insulted
by the gods, and has planned a terrible revenge against
them, then it is an enemy of Odin that Nidhad here binds,
and the above-cited paraphrase for the death-dis, Urd,
employed by Egil Skallagrimson, "the kinswoman of the
binder (Njorva) of Odin's foes" (see No. 85), also
becomes applicable here.

The tradition concerning Nidhad's original identity
with Mimer flourished for a long time in the German
middle-age sagas, and passed thence into the Vilkinasaga,
where the banished Volund became Mimer's smith. The
author of Vilkinasaga, compiling both from German and
from Norse sources, saw Volund in the German records
as a smith in Mimer's employ, and in the Norse sagas he
found him as Nidhad's smith, and from the two synonyms
he made two persons.

The Norse form of the name most nearly corresponding to the Old English Nidhad is *Nidi,* "the subterranean," and that Mimer also among the Norsemen was
known by this epithet is plain both from the Sol-song
and from Völuspa. The skald of the Sol-song sees in
the lower world "Nide's sons, seven together, drinking
the clear mead from the well of ring-Regin." The well
of the lower world with the "clear mead" is Mimer's

fountain, and the paraphrase ring-Regin is well suited to Mimer, who possessed among other treasures the wonderful ring of Hotherus. Völuspa speaks of Nide's mountain, the Hvergelmer mountain, from which the subterranean dragon Nidhog flies (see No. 75), and of Nide's plains where Sindre's race have their golden hall. Sindre is, as we know, one of the most celebrated primeval smiths of mythology, and he smithied Thor's lightning hammer, Frey's golden boar, and Odin's spear Gungner (Gylfaginning). Dwelling with his kinsmen in Mimer's realm, he is one of the artists whom the ruler of the lower world kept around him (cp. No. 53). Several of the wonderful things made by these artists, as for instance the harvest-god's Skidbladner, and golden boar, and Sif's golden locks, are manifestly symbols of growth or vegetation. The same is therefore true of the original Teutonic primeval smiths as of the Ribhuians, the ancient smiths of Rigveda, that they make not only implements and weapons, but also grass and herbs. Out of the lower world grows the world-tree, and is kept continually fresh by the liquids of the sacred fountains. In the abyss of the lower world and in the sea is ground that mould which makes the fertility of Midgard possible (see No. 80) ; in the lower world "are smithied" those flowers and those harvests which grow out of this mould, and from the manes of the subterranean horses, and from their foaming bridles, falls on the fields and meadows that honey-dew "which gives harvests to men."

Finally, it must be pointed out that when Nidhad binds Volund, the foe of the gods, this is in harmony with

Mimer's activity throughout the epic of the myths as the friend of the Asa-gods, and as the helper of Odin, his sister's son, in word and deed.

Further evidences of Mimer's identity with Nidhad are to be found in the Svipdag myth, which I shall discuss further on.

Vafthrudnersmal states in strophe 25 that "beneficent *regin* (makers) created Ny and Nedan to count times for men," this being said in connection with what it states about Narve, Nat, and Dag. In the Völuspa dwarf-list we find that the chief of these *regin* was Modsogner, whose identity with Mimer has been shown (see No. 53). Modsogner-Mimer created among other "dwarfs" also Ny and Nedan (Völuspa, 11). These are, therefore, his sons at least in the sense that they are indebted to him for their origin. The expressions to create and to beget are very closely related in the mythology. Of Njord Vafthrudner also says (str. 39) that "wise *regin* created him" in Vanaheim.

As sons of Nide-Mimer the changes of the moon have been called after his name *Nidi,* and collectively they have been called by the plural *Nidgar,* in a later time *Nidar.* And as Nat's brothers they are enumerated along with her as a stereotyped alliteration. In Vafthrudnersmal Odin asks the wise giant whether he knows whence Nat and Nidjar (*Nott med Nithom*) came, and Völuspa (6) relates that in the dawn of time the high holy gods (*regin*) seated themselves on their judgment-seats and gave names to Nat and Nidjar (*Nott ok Nithiom*). The giving of a name was in heathen times a sacred act, which implied an adoption in the name-giver's family or circle of friends.

Nidjar also appears to have had his signification of moon-changes in regard to the changes of months. According to Saxo (see No. 46), King Gorm saw in the lower world twelve sons of Gudmund-Mimer, all "of noble appearance." Again, Solarljod's skald says that the sons of Nide, whom he saw in the lower world, were "seven together." From the standpoint of a nature-symbol the difference in these statements is explained by the fact that the months of the year were counted as twelve, but in regard to seasons and occupations there were seven divisions: *gor-mánudr, frer-m., hrut-m., ein-m., sol-m., sel-m., kornskurdar-mánudr.* Seven is the epic-mythogical number of these *Nidjar*. To the saga in regard to these I shall return in No. 94.

<h2 style="text-align:center">88.</h2>

<h3 style="text-align:center">A GENERAL REVIEW OF MIMER'S NAMES AND EPITHETS.</h3>

The names, epithets, and paraphrases with which the king of the lower world, the ward of the fountain of wisdom, was designated, according to the statements hitherto made, are the following:

(1) *Mimir (Hodd-mímir, Mímr, Mími, Mime der alte)*.

(2) *Narfi (Narvi, Njorvi, Nörr, Nari, Neri)*.

(3) *Nidi (Nidhad, Nidadr, Nidudr, Nidungr)*.

These three names, which means the Thinker, the Binder, the Subterranean, are presumably all ancient.

(4) *Modsognir,* "the mead-drinker."

(5) *Hoddrofnir,* presumably "the one bounteous in treasures."

(6) *Gauta spjalli,* "the one with whom Gaute (Odin) counsels."

(7) *Baug-regin,* Ring-regin.

(8) *Godmundr,* the name by which Mimer appears in Christian middle-age sagas of Norse origin. To these names may still be added:

(9) *Fimbulthulr,* "the great teacher" (the lecturer). Havamál (str. 142; cp. str. 80) says that *Fimbulthulr* drew (*fadi*) the runes, that *ginn-regin* "made" (*gordo*) them, that is to say, in the older sense of the word, prepared them for use, and that Odin (*hroptr raugna*) carved (*reist*) them. In the strophes immediately preceding, it is said that Odin, by self-sacrifice, begot runes out of the deep and fimbul-songs from Beistla's brother. These statements, joined with those which mention how the runes given by Mimer were spread over the world, and were taught by various clan-chiefs to different clans (see No. 53), make it evident that a perfect myth had been developed in regard to the origin of the runes and the spreading of runic knowledge. Mimer, as the possessor of the well of wisdom, was the inventor or source of the runes. When Sigrdrifumal (str. 13) says that they dropped out of Hoddrofner's horn, this is, figuratively speaking, the same as Havamál tells, when it states that Fimbulthul carved them. The oldest powers (*ginn-regin*) and Odin afterwards developed and spread them.

At the time of Tacitus, and probably one or two centuries earlier, the art of writing was known among the Teutons. The runic inscriptions that have come down to our time bear evidence of a Greek-Roman origin.

By this we do not mean to deny that there were runes —at least, non-phonetic ones—before them. The many kinds of magic runes of which our mythic records speak are perhaps reminiscences of them. At all events we must distinguish the latter from the common runes for writing, and also from the many kinds of cypher-runes the keys of which are to be sought in the common phonetic rune-row.

(10) *Brimir.* By the side of the golden hall of Sindre, Völuspa (str. 36) mentions the giants Brimer's "bjór" hall, which is in *Okólnir*. *Bjórr* is a synonym for mead and ale (Alvism., 34). *Okólnir* means "the place where cold is not found." The reference is to a giant dwelling in the lower world who presides over mead, and whose hall is situated in a domain to which cold cannot penetrate. The myth has put this giant in connection with Ymer, who in relative opposition to him is called *Leir-brimir,* clay-Brimer (Fjöllsvinnsmal). These circumstances refer to Mimer. So also Sigrdrifumal (str. 14), where it is said that "Odin stood on the mountain with Brimer's sword' (*Brimis eggiar*), when Mimer's head for the first time talked with him. The expression "Brimer's sword" is ambiguous. As a head was once used as a weapon against Heimdal, a sword and a head can, according to Skaldskaparmal, be employed as paraphrases for each other, whence "Brimer's sword" may be the same as "Mimer's head" (Skaldskaparmal 69, Cod.

H.; cp. Skaldskaparmal, 8, and Gylfag., 27). Sigrdrifumal certainly also employs the phrase in its literal sense
of a famous mythological sword, for, in the case in question, it represents Odin as fully armed, with helmet on
his head; and the most excellent mythological sword,
according to an added line in strophe 24 of Grimnersmal
(Cod. A.), bore Brimer's name, just as the same sword
in the German saga has the name Miminc (Biterolf v.
176, in Vilkinasaga changed to Mimmung), doubtless
because it at one time was in Mimer-Nidhad's possession;
for the German saga (Biterolf, 157; cp. Vilkinasaga, ch.
23) remembers that a sword called by Mimer's name was
the same celebrated weapon as that made by Volund
(Weiland in Biterolf; Velint in Vilkinasaga), and hence
the same work of art as that which, according to Vilkinasaga, Nidhad captured from him during his stay in Wolfdales.

89.

THE MEAD MYTH.

We have seen (Nos. 72, 73) that the mead which was
brewed from the three subterranean liquids destroys the
effects of death and gives new vitality to the departed, and
that the same liquid is absorbed by the roots of the world-
tree, and in its trunk is distilled into that sap which gives
the tree eternal life. From the stem the mead rises into
the foliage of the crown, whose leaves nourish the fair
giver of "the sparkling drink," in Grimnersmal symbolised as Heidrun, from the streams of whose teats the

mead-horns in Asgard are filled for the einherjes. The morning dew which falls from Ygdrasil down into the dales of the lower world contains the same elements. From the bridle of Rimfaxe and from the horses of the valkyries some of the same dew also falls in the valleys of Midgard (see No. 74). The flowers receive it in their chalices, where the bees extract it, and thus is produced the earthly honey which man uses, and from which he brews *his* mead (cp. Gylfag., ch. 16). Thus the latter too contains some of the strength of Mimer's and Urd's fountains (*veigar*—see Nos. 72, 73), and thus it happens that it is able to stimulate the mind and inspire poetry and song—nay, used with prudence, it may suggest excellent expedients in important emergencies (cp. Tacitus, *Germania*).

Thus the world-tree is among the Teutons, as it is among their kinsmen the Iranians (see below), a *mead-tree*. And so it was called by the latter, possibly also by the former. The name *miötvidr,* with which the world-tree is mentioned in Völuspa (2) and whose origin and meaning have been so much discussed, is from a mythological standpoint satisfactorily explained if we assume that an older word, *miödvidr,* the mead-tree, passed into the word similar in sound, *miötvidr,* the tree of fate (from *miöt,* measure; cp. *mjötudr* in the sense of fate, the power which gives measure, and the Anglo-Saxon *metod,* Old Saxon *metod,* the giver of measure, fate, providence).

The sap of the world-tree and the *veigar* of the horn of the lower world are not, however, precisely the same mead as the pure and undefiled liquid from Mimer's fountain, that which Odin in his youth, through self-sacrifice, was permitted to taste, nor is it precisely the same as that concerning the possession of which the powers of mythology long contended, before it finally, through Odin's adventures at Suttung's, came to Asgard. The episodes of this conflict concerning the mead will be given as my investigation progresses, so far as they can be discovered. Here we must first examine what the heathen records have preserved in regard to the closing episode in which the conflict was ended in favour of Asgard. What the Younger Edda (Bragaraedur) tells about it I must for the present leave entirely unnoticed, lest the investigation should go astray and become entirely abortive.

The chief sources are the Havamál strophes 104-110, and strophes 13 and 14. Subordinate sources are Grimnersmal (50) and Ynglingatal (15). To this must be added half a strophe by Eyvind Skaldaspiller (Skaldskaparmal, ch. 2).

The statements of the chief source have, strange to say, been almost wholly unobserved, while the mythologists have confined their atention to the later presentation in Bragaraedur, which cannot be reconciled with the earlier accounts, and which from a mythological standpoint is worse than worthless. In 1877 justice was for the first time done to Havamál in the excellent analysis of the strophes in question made by Prof. M. B. Richert, in his "Attempts at explaining the obscure passages not hitherto understood in the poetic Edda."

From Havamál alone we get directly or indirectly the following:

646

The giant Suttung, also called Fjalar, has acquired possession of the precious mead for which Odin longs. The Asa-father resolves to capture it by cunning.

There is a feast at Fjalar's. Guests belonging to the clan of rimthurses are gathered in his halls (Havamál, 110). Besides these we must imagine that Suttung-Fjalar's own nearest kith and kin are present. The mythology speaks of a separate clan entirely distinct from the rimthurses, known as *Suttungs synir* (Alvismal, Skirnersmal; see No. 78), whose chief must be Suttung-Fjalar, as his very name indicates. The Suttung kin and the rimthurses are accordingly gathered at the banquet on the day in question.

An honoured guest is expected, and a golden high-seat prepared for him awaits his arrival. From the continuation of the story we learn that the expected guest is the wooer or betrothed of Suttung-Fjalar's daughter, Gunlad. On that night the wedding of the giant's daughter is to be celebrated.

Odin arrives, but in disguise. He is received as the guest of honour, and is conducted to the golden high-seat. It follows of necessity that the guise assumed by Odin, when he descends to the mortal foes of the gods and of himself, is that of the expected lover. Who the latter was Havamál does not state, unless strophe 110, 5, like so many other passages, is purposely ambiguous and contains his name, a question which I shall consider later.

After the adventure has ended happily, Odin looks back with pleasure upon the success with which he assumed the guise of the stranger and played his part

(str. 107). *el keyptz litar heñ cc vel notith*: "From
the well changed exterior I reaped great advantage."
In regard to the mythological meaning of *litr,* see No. 95:
The expression *keyptr litr,* which literally means "pur-
chased appearance," may seem strange, but *kaupa* means
not only to "buy," but also to "change," "exchange;"
kaupa klædum vid einn means "to change clothes with
some one." Of a queen who exchanged her son with a
slave woman, it is said that she *keyptr um sonu vid am-
bátt.* But the cause of Odin's joy is not that he success-
fully carried out a cunning trick, but that he in this way
accomplished a deed of inestimable value for Asgard and
for man (str., 107, 4-6), and he is sorry that poor Gunlad's trust in him was betrayed (str. 105). This is a
characterisation of Odin's personality.

Nor does Havamál tell us what hinders the real lover
from putting in his appearance and thwarting Odin's
plan, while the latter is acting his part; but of this we
learn something from another source, which we shall
consider below.

The adventure undertaken by Odin is extremely dan-
gerons, and he ran the risk of losing his head (str. 106,
6). For this reason he has, before entering Suttung-
Fjalar's halls, secured an egress, through which he must
be able to fly, and if possible, with the skaldic mead as his
booty. There is no admittance for everybody to the
rocky abode where the mead-treasure so much desired by
all powers is kept. The dwelling is, as Eyvind tells us,
situated in an abyss, and the door is, as another record
tells us, watched. But Odin has let Rate bore ("gnaw")

a tunnel through the mountain large enough to give him room to retire secretly (str. 106). In regard to Rate, see No. 82.

When the pretended lover has seated himself in the golden high-seat, a conversation begins around the banquet table. It is necessary for Odin to guard well his words, for he represents another person, well known there, and if he is not cautious he may be discovered. It is also necessary to be eloquent and winning, so that he may charm Gunlad and secure her devotion, for without her knowledge he cannot gain his end, that of carrying away the supply of inspiration-mead kept at Suttung's. Odin also boasts (str. 103, 104) that on this occasion he proved himself *minnigr* and *málugr* and *margfrodr* and eloquent for the realisation of his plan.

During the progress of the feast the guest had his glass filled to his honour with the precious mead he desired to obtain. "Gunlad gave me on the golden seat the drink of the precious mead" (str. 105).

Then the marriage ceremony was performed, and on the holy ring Gunlad took to Odin the oath of faithfulness (str. 110).

It would have been best for the Asa-father if the banquet had ended here, and the bridegroom and the bride had been permitted to betake themselves to the bridal chamber. But the jolly feast is continued and the horns are frequently filled and emptied. Havamál does not state that the part played by Odin required him to be continually drinking; but we shall show that Gunlad's wooer was the champion drinker of all mythology, and in tie sagas he has many epithets referring to this quality. Odin became on his own confession "drunk, very drunk, at Fjalar's." "The hern of forgetfulness which steals one's wit and understanding hovers over his drink" (str. 13, 15).

In this condition he let drop words which were not those of caution—words which sowed the seed of suspicion in the minds of some of his hearers who were less drunk. He dropped words which were not spelt with letters of intelligence and good sense—words which did not suit the part he was playing.

At last the banquet comes to an end, and the bridegroom is permitted to be alone with the bride in that rocky hall which is their bed-chamber. There is no doubt that Odin won Gunlad's heart, "the heart of that good woman whom I took in my embrace" (str. 108). With her help he sees his purpose attained and the mead in his possession. But the suspicions which his reckless words had sown bear fruit in the night, and things happen which Havamál does not give a full account of, but of a kind which would have prevented Odin from getting out of the giant-gard, had he not had Gunlad's assistance (str. 108). Odin was obliged to fight and rob Gunlad of a kinsman (str. 110—*hann lèt grætta Gunnlödu*; see Rich., p. 17). Taking the supply of mead with him, he takes flight by the way Rate had opened for him—a dangerous way, for "above and below me were the paths of the giants" (str. 106).

It seems to have been the custom that the wedding guests on the morning of the next day went to the door of the bridal-chamber to hear how the newly-married man was getting on in his new capacity of husband. According to Havamál, Suttung's guests, the rimthurses, observe this custom; but the events of the night change their inquires into the question whether Odin had succeeded in escaping to the gods or had been slain by Suttung (str. 109, 110).

Thus far Havamál. We must now examine Grimnersmal (150) and Ynglingatal (15), whose connection with the myth concerning Odin's exploit in the home of Suttung-Fjalar has not hitherto been noticed.

Odin says in Grimnersmal:

> Svitharr oc Svithrir
> er ec het at Sauccmimis
> oc dultha ec tiann inn aldna iotun,
> tha er ec Mithvithnis varc
> ins mæra burar
> ordinn einbani.

"*Svidur and Svidrir* I was called at Sokmimer's, and I presented myself to the ancient giant, at the time when I alone became the slayer of *Midvitnir's* famous son."

Ynglingatal (15) reads:

> En Dagskjarr
> Durnis nidja
> salvördudr
> Svegdi velti,
> tha er i stein
> hinn stórgedi
> Dulsa konr
> ept dvergi hljóp,

> ok sal bjartr
> theirra Sökkmimis
> jotunbyggdr
> vid jofri gein.

"The day-shy hall-guard of *Durnir's* descendants deceived *Svegdir* when he, the dauntless son of *Dulsi,* ran after the dwarf into the rock, and when the shining giant-inhabited hall of *Sökkmimir's* kinsmen yawned against the chief." (In regard to *Dulsi,* see No. 83).

What attracts attention in a comparison of these two strophes is that the epithet *Sökkmimir* is common to both of them, while this name does not occur elsewhere in the whole Old Norse literature.

In both the strophes *Sökkmimir* is a giant. Grimnersmal calls him *inn aldna iotun,* "the ancient giant," with which we may compare Odin's words in Havamál (104): *enn aldna iotun ec sotta,* "the ancient giant I sought," when he visited that giant-chief, to whose clan Suttung-Fjalar, the possessor of the skald-mead, belonged.

In both the strophes the giant *Sökkmimir* is the lord and chief of those giants to whom, according to Grimnersmal, Odin comes, and outside of whose hall-door, according to Ynglingatal, a certain *Svegdir* is deceived by the ward of the hall. This position of *Sökkmimir* in relation to his surroundings already appears, so far as Grimnersmal is concerned, from the expression *at Saucc-mimis,* which means not only "with Sokmimer," but also "at Sokmimer's," that is to say, with that group of kinsmen and in that abode where Sokmimer is chief and ruler. It is with this giant-chief, and in his rocky hall, that *Midvitnir* and his son sojourns when Odin visits him, presents himself to him, and by the name *Svidur* (*Svidrir*) acts the part of another person, and in this connection causes Midvitner's death. The same quality of Sokmimer as clan-chief and lord appears in the Ynglingatal strophe, in the form that the hall, outside of whose door Svegder was deceived, is *theirra Sökkmimis*, that is to say, is the abode of Sokmimer's kinsmen and household, "is their giant-home." Thus all the giants who dwell there take their clan-name from Sokmimer.

The appellation *Sökkmimir* is manifestly not a name in the strictest sense, but one of the epithets by which this ancient giant-chief could be recognised in connection with mythological circumstances. We shall point out these mythological circumstances further on.

The Ynglingatal strophe gives us, in fact, another epithet for the same mythic person. What the latter half of the strophe calls the hall of Sokmimer's kinsmen and household, the former half of the same strophe calls the hall of *Durnir's* descendants. Thus Sokmimer and *Durnir* are the same person.

Durnir, on the other hand, is a variation of *Durinn* (cp. the parallel variations *Dvalnir* and *Dvalinn*). *Of Durinn* we already know (see No. 53) that he is one of the ancient beings of mythology who in time's morning, together with *Modsognir*-Mimer and in accordance with the resolve of the high-holy powers, created clans of artists. One of the artists created by Durin, and whose father he in this sense became, is, according to Völuspa (11), *Mjödvitnir*. Rask and Egilsson have for philological reasons assumed that *Midvitnir* and *Mjödvitnir* are variations of the same name, and designate the same person (*mjödr,* in the dative *midi*). It here appears that the facts confirm this assumption. *Durinn* and *Mjödvitnir,* in Völuspa correspond to *Durnir* and *Midvitnir* in the strophes concerning *Sökkmimir.*

Mjödvitnir means the mead-wolf, he who captured the mead celebrated in mythology. As Odin, having assumed the name of another, visits the abode of the descendants of Durner-Sokmimer, he accordingly visits that rocky home, where that giant dwells who has secured and possesses the mead desired by Odin.

Ynglingatal reports, as we have seen, that a certain *Svegdir* was deceived, when he was outside of the door of the hall of the kinsmen of Durner-Sokmimer. He who deceived him was the doorkeeper of the hall. The door appeared to be already open, and the "giant-inhabited" hall "yawned" festively illuminated (*bjartr*) toward Svegder. If we may believe Ynglingatal's commentary on the strophe, the hall-ward had called to him and said that Odin was inside. The strophe represents Svegder as running after the hall-ward, that is to say, toward the door in the rock, eager to get in. What afterwards happened Ynglingatal does not state; but that Svegder did not gain the point he desired, but fell into some snare laid by the doorkeeper, follows from the expression that he was deceived by him, and that this caused his death follows from the fact that the purpose of the strophe is to tell how his life ended. Ynglingasaga says that he got into the rock, but never out of it. The rest that this saga has to say of Svegder—that ie was on a journey to the old Asgard in "Tyrkland," to find "Odin t1e old," Gylfaginning's King Priam—has not1ing to do wit1 t1e myt1ology and with Ynglingatal, but is of course import-ant in regard to the Euhemeristic hypot1esis in regard to t1e descent of the Asas from Tyrkland (Troy), on whic1 t1e author of Ynglingatal, like that of Gylfaginning, bases his work.

The variations *Svegdir, Svidgir,* and *Sveigdir* are used interchangeably in regard to the same person (cp. Yng-lingatal, 14, 15; Fornald., ii. 2; Fornm., i. 29; and Egils-son, 796, 801). *Svigdir* seems to be the oldest of these forms. The words means the great drinker (Egilsson, 801). *Svigdir* was one of the most popular heroes of mythology (see the treatise on t1e "Ivalde race"), and was already in heathen times regarded as a race-hero of the Swedes. In Ynglingatal (14) Svithiod is called *geiri Svigdis,* "Svigdir's domain.' At the same time, *Svegdir* is an epithet of Odin. But it should be borne in mind that several of the names by which Odin is designated belong to him only in a secondary and trans-ferred sense, and he has assumed them on occasions when he did not want tʊ be recognised, and wanted to represent some one else (cp. Grimnersm., 49) whose name he then assumed.

When Odin visits the abode of *Durinn-Sökkmimir,* where the precious mead is preserved, he calls himself, according to Grimnersmal, *Svidurr, Svidrir.* Now it is t1e case with this name as with *Svigdir,* that it was con-nected with Svithiod. Skaldskaparmal (65) says that

Svithiod var kallat af nafni Svidurs, "Svithiod was named after the name of Svidur."

Hence (1) the name *Svidurr,* like *Svegdir-Svigdir,* belongs to Odin, but only in a secondary sense, as one assumed or borrowed from another person; (2) *Svidurr,* like *Svegdir-Svigdir,* was originally a mythic person, whom tradition connected as a race hero with Svithiod.

From all this it appears that the names, facts, and the chain of events connect partly the strophes of Grimnersmal and Ynglingatal with each other, and partly both of these with Havamál's account of Odin's adventure to secure the mead, and this connection furnishes indubitable evidence that they concern the same episode in the mythological epic.

In the mythic fragments handed down to our time are found other epithets, which like *Svigdir,* refer to some mythical person who played the part of a champion drinker, and was connected with the myth concerning mead and brewing. These epithets are *Ölvaldi, Ölmódr,* and *Sumbl finnakonungr, Sumblus phinnorum rex* in Saxo. *Sumbl,* as a common noun, means ale, feast. In the "Finn-king" *Sumbl* these ideas are personified, just as the soma-drink in the Veda songs is personified in King Soma. In my treatise on the Ivalde race, I shall revert to the person who had these epithets, in order to make his mythological position clear. Here I shall simply point out the following: Havamál (110) makes one of the rimthurses, Suttung's guests, say:

Baugeith Odinn
hygg ec at unnit hafi;

hvat scal 1ans trygdom trua?
Suttung svikinn
han let sumbli fra
oc grætta Gunnlaudo.

The strophe makes the one who says this blame Odin for breaking the oath he took on the ring, and thus showing himself unworthy of being trusted in the promises and oaths he might give in the future, whereupon it is stated that he left Suttung deceitfully robbed of *sumbl* (*Sumbl*), and Gunlad in tears over a lost kinsman.

The expression that Suttung was deceitfully robbed of *sumbl,* to be intelligible, requires no other interpretation than the one which lies near at hand, that Suttung was treacherously deprived of the mead. But as the skald might have designated the drink lost by Suttung in a more definite manner than with the word *sumbl,* and as he still chose this word, which to his hearers, familiar with the mythology, must have called to mind the personal *Sumbl* (*Ölvaldi Svigdir*), it is not only possible, but, as it seems to me, even probable, that he purposely chose an ambiguous word, and wanted thereby to refer at the same time to the deceitfully captured mead, and to the intended son-in-law deceitfully lost; and this seems to me to be corroborated by the juxtaposition of Suttung's and Gunlad's loss. The common noun *sumbl's* double meaning as mead and "drink-feast" has also led M. B. Richert (page 14 in his treatise mentioned above) to assume that "the expression was purposely chosen in such a manner that the meaning should not be entirely limited and definite," and he adds: "A similar indefiniteness of statement, which

657

may give rise to abiguity and play of words, is frequently found in the old songs.'" Meanwhile, I do not include this probability in my evidence, and do not present it as the basis of any conclusions.

The name Suttung shows in its very form that it is a patronymic, and although we can furnish no linguistic evidence that the original form was *Surtungr* and characterised its possessor as son of *Surtr,* still there are other facts which prove that such was actually the case. The very circumstance that the skaldic drink which came into Suttung's possession is paraphrased with the expression *sylgr Surt's ættar,* "the drink of Surt's race" (Fornmanna, iii. 3), points that way and the question is settled completely by the half-strophe quoted in the Younger Edda (i. 242), and composed by Eyvind Skaldaspiller, where the skaldic potion is called—

> hinn er Surts
> or sökkdölum
> farmagnudr
> fljugandi bar.

("the drink, which Odin flying bore from Surt's deep dales").

When Odin had come safely out of Fjalar-Suttung's deep rocky halls, and, on eagle-pinions, was flying with the precious mead to Asgard, it was accordingly that deep, in which *Surtr* dwells, which he left below ıim, and the giant race who had been drinking the mead before that time, while it was still in Suttung's possession, was Surt's race. From this it follows that "the ancient giant," whom Odin visited for the purpose of robbing his circle of kinsmen of the skaldic mead, is none other than tiat being so well known in the mythology, *Surtr,* and tiat *Surtr* is identical with *Durinn* (*Durnir*), and *Sökkmimir.*

This also explains the epithet *Sökkmimir,* "the Mimer of the deep." *Sökk-* in *Sökk-Mimir* refers to *Sökk* in .*Sökkdalir,* Surt's domain, and that Surt could be associated with Mimer is, from the standpoint of Old Norse poetics, perfectly justifiable from the fact that he appears in time's morning as a co-worker with Mimer, and operating with him as one of the forces of creation in the service of the oldest high-holy powers (see No. 53). Consequently Mimer and Sokmimer (*Surtr-Durinn*) created the clans of artists.

Surtr, Durinn, Durnir, Sökkmimir, are, therefore, synonyms, and designate the same person. He has a son who is designated by the synonyms *Suttungr, Fjalarr, Mjödvitnir* (*Midvitnir*). Suttung has a son slain by Odin, when the latter robs him of the mead of inspiration, and a daughter, Gunlad. The giant maid, deceived and deplored by Odin, is consequently the daughter of Surt's son.

Light is thus shed on the myth concerning the giant who reappears in Ragnarok, and there wields the sword which fells Frey and hurls the flames which consume the world. It is found to be connected with the myth concerning the oldest events of mythology. In time's morning we find the fire-being Surt—the representative of subterranean fire—as a creative force by the side of Mimer, who is a friend of the gods, and whose kinsman he must be as a descendant of Ymer. Both work

659

together in peace for similar purposes and under the direction of the gods (Völuspa, 9, 10). But then something occurs which interrupts the amicable relations. Mimer and Surt no longer work togeter. The fountain of creative force, the mead of wisdom and inspiration, is in the exclusive possession of Mimer, and he and Urd are together the ruling powers in the lower world. The fire-giant, the primeval artist, is then with his race relegated to the "deep dales," situated to the southward (Völuspa, 52), difficult of access, and dangerous for the gods to visit, and presumably conceived as located deeper down than the lower world governed by Mimer and Urd. That he tried to get possesion of a part of *"Odrærir"* follows from the position he afterwards occupies in the myth concerning the mead. When daylight again falls on him from the mythic fragments extant, his son has captured and is in possession of a supply of mead, which must originally have come from Mimer's fountain, and been chiefly composed of its liquid, for it is skaldic mead, it too, and can also be designated as *Ódrærir* (Havamál, 107), while the son is called "the mead-wolf," the one who has robbed and conceals the precious drink. Odin captures his mead by cunning, the grandson of the fire-giant is slain, the devoted love of the son's daughter is betrayed, and the husband selected for her is deceived and removed. All this, though done for purposes to benefit gods and men, demands and receives in the mythology its terrible retribution. It is a trait peculiar to the whole Teutonic mythology that evil deeds, with a good purpose, even when the object is attained, produce evil results, which develop and finally smother the fruits of the good purpose. Thus Surt has a reason for appearing in Ragnarok as the annihilator of the world of the Asas, when the latter is to make room for a realm of justice. The flames of revenge are hurled upon creation.

I have already above (No. 87), had occasion to speak of the choicest sword of mythology, the one which Volund smithied and Mimer captured, and which was fetched from the lower world by a hero whose name Saxo Latinised into Hotherus. In my treatise on "the Ivalde race" it shall be demonstrated who this Hotherus was in mythology, and that the sword was delivered by him to Frey. Lokasenna (42; cp. Gylfag., 37), informs us that the lovesick Frey gave the sword to the giant Gymer for his bride. After coming into the hands of the giants it is preserved and watched over until Ragnarok by *Eggther* (an epithet meaning sword-watcher), who in the Ironwood is the shepherd of the monster herd of Loke's progeny, which in the last days shall harry the world and fight in Ragnarok (Völuspa, 39-41). When Ragnarok is at hand a giant comes to this sword-watcher in the guise of the red cock, the symbol of the destructive fire. This giant is Fjalar (Völuspa, 41), and that the purpose of his visit is to secure the sword follows from the fact that the best sword of mythology is shortly afterwards in the hands of his father Surt (Völuspa, 50) when the latter comes from the south with his band (the sons of Suttung, not of Muspel) to take part in the last conflict and destroy with fire that part of the world that can be destroyed. Frey is slain by the sword which was once his own.

661

In this manner the myth about the mead and that about the Volund sword are knit together.

Thor, too, ventured to visit Fjalar's abode. In regard to this visit we have a few words in strophe 26 of Harbardsljod. *Harbardr* accuses Thor, no doubt unjustly, of having exhibited fear. Of this matter we have no reliable details in the records from heathendom, but a comparison of the above strophe of Harbardsljod with Gylfaginning shows that the account compiled in Gylfaginning from various mythic fragments concerning Thor's journey to Utgarda-Loke and his adventures there contains reminiscences of what the original myths have had to say about his experience on his expedition to Fjalar's. The fire-giant natures of Surt and of his son Fjalar gleam forth in the narrative: the ruler of Utgard can produce earthquakes, and Loge (the flame) is his servant. It is also doubtless correct, from a mythical standpoint, that he is represented as exceedingly skilful in "deluding," in giving things the appearance of something else than they really are (see No. 39). When Odin assumed the guise of Fjalar's son-in-law, he defeated Surt's race with their own weapons.

Eyvind Skaldaspiller states, as we have seen, that Surt's abode is in dales down in the deep. From an expression in Ynglingasaga's strophe we must draw the conclusion that its author, in harmony herewith, conceived the abyss where Surt's race dwelt as regions to which the light of day never comes. Sokmimer's door-keeper, one of whose tasks it was to take notice of the wayfarers who approached, is a day-shy dwarf (*dagskjarr salvor-*

dudr; in regard to dwarfs that shun the light of day, see Alvissmal). Darkness therefore broods over this region, but in the abode of the fire-giant it is light (the hall is *bjartr*).

I now return to the episodes in the mead-myth under discussion to recapitulate in brief the proofs and results. If we for a moment should assume that the main source, namely, the Havamál strophes, together with Eyvind's half strophe, were lost, and that the only remaining evidences were Grimnersmal (50) and Ynglingatal (15), together with the prose text in Ynglingasaga, then an analysis of these would lead to the following result:

(1) Grimnersmal (50) and Ynglingatal (15) should be compared with each other. The reasons for assuming them to be intrinsically connected are the folowing:

(*a*) Both contain the epithet *Sökkmimir,* which occurs nowhere else.

(*b*) Both describe a primeval giant, who is designated by this epithet as chief and lord of a giant race gathered around him.

(*c*) Both refer the events described to the same locality: the one tells what occurred in the halls of *Sökkmimir;* the other narrates an episode which occurred outside of the door of Sokmimer's giant abode.

(*d*) The one shows that Sokmimer is identical with *Durnir* (Durin); the other mentions *Midvitnir* as one of Sokmimer's subjects. *Midvitnir* (*Mjódvitnir*), according to Völuspa, was created by *Durinn*.

(*e*) Both describe events occuring while Odin is inside at Sokmimer's.

(*f*) The one mentions *Svidurr, the other Svegdir.*
Mythologically, the two names refer to each other.

(2) To the giant group which Odin visits in the abode
of *Sökkmimir* belongs the giant who captured the famous
mead which Odin is anxious to secure. This appears
from the epithet which the author of the Grimnersmal
strophe chose in order to designate him in such a manner
that he could be recognised, namely, *Midvitnir,* "the mead-
wolf," an epithet which explains why the mead-thirsty
Odin made his journey to this race hostile to the gods.

(3) That Odin did not venture, or did not think it
desirable in connection with the purpose of his visit, to
appear in his own name and in a guise easily recognised,
is evident from the fact that he "disguised" himself,
"acted the hypocrite" (*dulda*), in the presence of the
giant, and appeared as another mythic person, *Svidurr.*
This mythic person has been handed down in the traditions as the one who gave the name to Svithiod, and as
a race-hero of the Swedes. *Svíthiód var kallat af nafni
Svidurs.*

(4) While Odin, in the guise of this race-hero, plays
his part in the mountain in the abode of Sokmimer, a
person arrives at the entrance of the halls of this giant.
This person, *Svegdir* (*Svigdir*), is in the sagas called the
race-hero of the Swedes, and after him they have called
Svithiod *geiri Svigdis.* Odin, who acted *Svidurr's* part,
has also been called *Svigdir, Svegdir.*

Svigdir is an epithet, and means "the champion drinker"
(Anglo-Saxon *swig*: to drink deep draughts). "The
champion drinker" is accordingly on his way to the

"Mead-wolf," while Odin is in his abode. All goes to show that the event belongs to the domain of the mead-myth.

Accordingly, the situation is this: A pretended race-hero and namer of Svithiod is in the abode of Sokmimer, while a person who, from a mythological standpoint, is the real race-hero and namer of Svithiod is on his way to Sokmimer's abode and about to enter. The myth could not have conceived the matter in this way, unless the pretended race-hero was believed to act the part of the real one. The arrival of the real one makes Odin's position, which was already full of peril, still more dangerous, and threatens him with discovery and its consequences.

(5) If Odin appeared in the part of a "champion drinker," he was compelled to drink much in Sokmimer's halls in order to maintain his part, and this, too, must have added to the danger of his position.

(6) Still the prudent Asa-father seems to have observed some degree of caution, in order that his plans might not be frustrated by the real *Svigdir*. That which happens gives the strongest support to this supposition, which in itself is very probable. Sokmimer's doorkeeper keeps watch in the darkness outside. When he discovers the approach of *Svigdir,* he goes to meet him and informs him that Odin is inside. Consequently the doorkeeper knows that *Svidurr* is Odin, who is unknown to all those within excepting to Odin himself. This and what follows seems to show positively that the wise Odin and the cunning dwarf act upon a settled plan. It may be delu-

sion or reality, but *Svigdir* sees the mountain door open
to the illuminated giant-hall, and the information that
Odin is within (the dwarf may or may not have added
that Odin pretends to be *Svigdir*) causes him, the "proud
one," "of noble race," the kinsman of *Dulsi* (epithet of
Mundilfore, see No. 83), to rush with all his might
after the dwarf against the real or apparent door, and the
result is that the dwarf succeeded in "deceiving" him
(he *velti* Svegder), so that he never more was seen.

This is what we learn from the strophes in Grimnersmal and Ynglingatal, with the prose text of the
latter. If we now compare this with what Havamál and
Eyvind relates, we get the following parallels:

Havamál and Eyvind.

Odin visits inn aldna iotum
(Surtr and his race).

Odin's purpose is to deceive
the old giant. In his abode is
found a kinsman, who is in
possession of the skaldic
mead (Suttung-Fjalar).

Odin appears in the guise
of Gunlad's wooer, who, if he
is named, is called Sumbl
(sumbl=a drink, a feast).

Odin became drunk.

A catastrophe occurs causing Gunnlöd to bewail the
death of a kinsman.

The strophes about Sökkmimir.

Odin visits inn aldna iotun
(Sökkmimir and his race).

Odin's purpose is to deceive
the old giant. In his abode is
found a kinsman who is in
possession of the skaldic
mead (Midvitnir).

Odin appears as Svidurr-
Svigdir. Svigdir means the
champion drinker.

Odin must have drunk
much, since he appears among
the giants as one acting the
part of a "champion drinker."

A catastrophe occurs causing Odin to slay Midvitnir's
son.

To this is finally to be added that Eyvind's statement, that the event occurred in Surt's *Sökkdalir,* helps to throw light on Surt's epithet *Sökkmimir,* and particularly that Ynglingatal's account of the arrival and fate of the real Svegder fills a gap in Havamál's narrative, and shows how Odin, appearing in the guise of another person who was expected, could do so without fear of being surprised by the latter.

NOTE.—The account in the Younger Edda about Odin's visit to Suttung seems to be based on some satire produced long after the introduction of Christianity. With a free use of the confused mythic traditions then extant, and without paying any heed to Havamál's statement, this satire was produced to show in a semi-allegorical way how good and bad poetry originated. The author of this satire either did not know or did not care about the fact that Havamál identifies Suttung and Fjalar. To him they are different persons, of whom the one receives the skaldic mead as a ransom from the other. While in Havamál the rimthurses give Odin the name *Bölverkr,* "the evil-doer," and this very properly from their standpoint, the Younger Edda makes Odin give himself this name when he is to appear *incognito,* though such a name was not calculated to inspire confidence. While in Havamál Odin, in the guise of another, enters Suttung's halls, is conducted to a golden high-seat, and takes a lively part in the banquet and in the conversation, the Younger Edda makes him steal into the mountain through a small gimlet-hole and get down into Gunlad's chamber in this manner, where he remains the whole time without seeing anyone else of the people living there, and where, with Gunlad's consent, he empties to the bottom the giant's three mead-vessels, *Ódrærir, Bodn,* and *Són.* These three names belong, as we have seen, in the real mythology to the three subterranean fountains which nourish the roots of t1e world-tree. Havamál contents itself with using a poetic-rhetorical phrase and calling the skaldic mead, captured by Odin, *Ódrærir,* "the giver of inspiration," "the inspiring nectar." The author of the satire avails himself of this reason for using the names of the two other fountains *Bodn* and *Són,* and for applying them to two other "vessels and kettles" in which Suttung is said to have kept the mead. That he called one of the vessels a kettle is explained by the fact that the third lower world fountain is *Hvergelmir,* "the roaring kettle." In order that Odin and Gunlad may be able to discuss and resolve in perfect secrecy in regard to the mead, Odin must come secretly down into the mountain, hence the satire makes him use the bored hole to get *in.* From the whole description in Havamál, it appears, on the contrary, that Odin entered the giant's hall in the usual manner through the door, while he avails himself of the tunnel made by Rate to get *out.* Havamál first states that Odin seeks the giant, and then tells how he enters into conversation and develops his eloquence in Suttung's halls, and how, while he sits in the golden high-seat (probably opposite the host, as Richter has assumed), Gunlad hands him the precious mead. Then is mentioned for the first time the way made for him by Rate, and this on the one hand in connection with the "evil compensation" Gunlad received from him, she the loving and devoted woman whom he had embraced, and on the other hand in connection with the fact that his flight from the mountain was successful, so that he could take the mead with him though his life was in danger, and there were giants' ways both above and below that secret path by which he escaped. That Odin took the oath of faithfulness on the holy ring, that there was a regular wedding feast with the questions on the next morning in regard to the well-being of the newly-married couple—all this the satire does not mention, nor does its premises permit it to do so.

90.

THE MEAD-MYTH (*continued*). THE MOON AND THE MEAD. PROOFS THAT NANNA'S FATHER IS THE WARD OF THE ATMOSPHERE AND GOD OF THE MOON.

Before the skaldic mead came into the possession of Suttung-Fjalar, it had passed through various adventures. In one of these enters *Máni,* the god of the moon, who by the names *Nökkvi* (variation *Nökkver*), *Nefr* (variation *Nepr*), and *Gevarr* (*Gævarr*) occupies a very conspicuous position in our mythology, not least in the capacity of Nanna's father.

I shall here present the proofs which lie near at hand, and can be furnished without entering into too elaborate investigations, that the moon-god and Nanna's father are identical, and this will give me an opportunity of referring to that episode of the mead-myth, in which he appears as one of the actors.

The identity of *Nökkvi, Nefr,* and *Gevarr* appears from the following passages:

(1) Hyndluljod, 20: "Nanna was, in the next place, *Nökkvi's* daughter" (*Nanna var næst thar Nauckua dottir*).

(2) Gylfaginning, 32: "The son of Balder and of Nanna, daughter of Nef, was called Forsete" (*Forseti heiter sonr Baldrs ok Nönnu Nefsdóttur*). Gylfaginning, 49: "His (Balder's) wife Nanna, daughter of Nef" (*Kona hans Nanna Nefsdóttir*).

(3) Saxo, *Hist., Dan.,* iii.: "*Gevarr's* daughter Nanna" (*Gevari filia Nanna*). That Saxo means the mythological Nanna follows from the fact that Balder appears in the story as her wooer. That the Norse form of the name, which Saxo Latinised into Gevarus, was *Gevarr,* not *Gefr,* as a prominent linguist has asssumed, follows from the rules adopted by Saxo in Latinising Norse names.

NOTE.—Names of the class to which *Gefr* would belong, providing such a name existed, would be Latinised in the following manner:

(*a*) *Askr* Ascerus, *Baldr* Balderus, *Geldr* Gelderus, *Glaumr* Glomerus, *Hödr, Hadr, Odr,* Hötherus, Hatherus, Hotherus, *Svipdagr* Svipdagerus, *Ullr* Ollerus, *Yggr* Uggerus, *Vigr* Vigerus.

(*b*) *Ásmundr* Asmundus, *Amundr* Amundus, *Arngrimr* Arngrimus, *Bildr* Bildus, *Knútr* Canutus, *Fridleifr* Fridlevus, *Gautrekr* Gotricus, *Gódmundr* Guthmundus, *Haddingr* Hadingus, *Haraldr* Haraldus.

Names ending in *-arr* are Latinised in the following manner:

(*a*) *Borgarr* Borcarus, *Einarr* Enarus, *Gunnarr* Gunnarus, *Hjörvarr* Hjartvarus, *Ingimarr* Ingimarus, *Ingvarr* Ingvarus, *Ismarr* Ismarus, *Ívarr* Ivarus, *Óttarr* Otharus, *Rostarr* Rostarus, *Sigarr* Sigarus, *Sivarr* Sivarus, *Valdimarr* Valdemarus.

(*b*) *Agnarr* Agnerus, *Ragnarr* Regnerus.

With the ending *-arus* occurs also in a single instance a Norse name in *-i*, namely, *Eylimi* Olimarus. Herewith we might perhaps include Liotarus, the Norse form of which Saxo may have had in *Ljóti* from *Ljótr*. Otherwise *Ljótr* is a single exception from the rules followed by Saxo, and methodology forbids our building anything on a single exception, which moreover is uncertain.

Some monosyllabic names ending in *-r* are sometimes unlatinised, as Alf, Ulf, Sten, Ring, Rolf, and sometimes Latinised with *-o,* as Alvo, Ulvo, Steno, Ringo, Rolvo, *Álfr* is also found Latinised as Alverus.

From the above lists of names it follows that Saxo's rules for Latinising Norse names ending with the nominative *-r* after a consonant were these:

(1) Monosyllabic names (seldom a dissyllabic one, as *Svipdagr*) are Latinised with the ending *-erus* or the ending *-o*.

(2) Names of two or more syllables which do not end in *-arr* (rarely a name of one syllable, as *Bildr*) are Latinised with the ending *-us*.

(3) Names ending in *-arr* are Latinised with *-arus*; in a few cases (and then on account of the Danish pronunciation) with *-erus*.

From the above rules it follows (1) that *Gefr*, if such a

name existed, would have been Latinised by Saxo either into *Geverus, Geferus,* or into *Gevo, Gefo;* (2) that *Gevarr* is the regular Norse for *Gevarus.*

The only possible meaning of the name *Gevarr,* considered as a common noun is "the ward of the atmosphere" from *ge* (*gæ;* see Younger Edda, ii. 486, and Egilsson, 227) and *-varr.* I cite this definition not for the purpose of drawing any conclusions therefrom, but simply because it agrees with the result reached in another way.

The other name of Nanna's father is, as we have seen, *Nökkvi, Nökkver.* This word means the ship-owner, ship-captain. If we compare these two names, *Gevarr* and *Nökkver,* with each other, then it follows from the comparison that Nanna's father was a mythic person who operated in the atmosphere or had some connection with certain phenomena in the air, and particularly in connection with a phenomenon there of such a kind that the mythic fancy could imagine a ship. The result of the comparison should be examined in connection with a strophe by Thorbjorn Hornklofve, which I shall now consider.

Thorbjorn was the court-skald of Harald Fairfax, and he described many of the king's deeds and adventures. Harald had at one time caused to be built for himself and his body-guard a large and stately ship, with a beautiful figure-head in the form of a serpent. On board this ship he was overtaken by a severe gale, which Hornklofve (Harald Harfager's saga, ch. 9) describes in the following words:

Ut á mar mǣtir
mannskædr lagar tanna
rǣsinadr til rausnar
rak vebrautar Nökkva.

In prose order: *Lagar tanna mannskædr mætir út á mar
rak rausnar ræsinadr til Nökkva vebrautar* ("The assailants of the skerry (the teeth of the sea), dangerous to
man, flung out upon the sea the splendid serpent of the
vessel's stem to the holy path of Nokve").

All interpreters agree that by "the skerry's assailants,
dangerous to man," is meant the waves which are produced by the storm and rush against the skerries in
breakers dangerous to seamen. It is also evident that
Hornklofve wanted to depict the violence of the sea when
he says that the billows which rise to assail the skerry
tosses the ship, so that the figure-head of the stem
reaches "the holy path of Nokve."   Poems of different
literatures resemble each other in their descriptions of a
storm raging at sea.   They make the billows rise to "the
clouds," to "the stars," or to "the moon." *Quanti montes
volvuntur aquarum! Jam, jam tacturos sidera summa
putes,* Ovid sings (*Trist.,* i. 18, 19) ; and Virgil has it:
Procella fluctus ad sidera tollit (*Æn.,* i. 107). One of
their brother skalds in the North, quoted in Skaldskaparmal (ch. 61), depicts a storm with the following words:

Hraud i himin upp glódum
lafs, gekk sær af afli,
bör hygg ek at sky skordi,
skaut Ránar vegr mána.

. The skald makes the phosphorescence of the sea splash

against heaven; he makes the ship split the clouds, and the way of Ran, the giantess of the sea, cut the path of the moon.

The question now is, whether Hornklofve by "Nokve's holy path" did not mean the path of the moon in space, and whether it is not to this path the figure-head of the ship seems to pitch when it is lifted on high by the towering billows. It is certain that this holy way toward which the heaven-high billows lift the ship is situated in the atmosphere above the sea, and that Nokve has been conceived as travelling this way in a ship, since Nokve means the ship-captain. From this it follows that Nokve's craft must have been a phenomenon in space resembling a ship which was supposed to have its course marked out there. We must therefore choose between the sun, the moon, and the stars; and as it is the moon which, when it is not full, has the form of a ship sailing in space, it is more probable that by Nokve's ship is meant the moon than that any other celestial body is referred to.

This probability becomes a certainty by the following proofs. In Sonatorrek (str. 2, 3) Egil Skallagrimson sings that when heavy sorrow oppresses him (who has lost his favourite son) then the song does not easily well forth from his breast:

> Thagna fundr
> thriggia nidja
> ár borinn
> or Jötunheimum,

lastalauss
er lifnadi
á Nökkvers
nökkva Bragi.

The skaldic song is here compared with a fountain which does not easily gush forth from a sorrowful heart, and the liquid of the fountain is compared with the "Thrigge's kinsmen's find, the one kept secret, which in times past was carried from Jotunheim into Nokve's ship, where Brage, unharmed, refreshed himself (secured the vigour of life)."

It is plain that Egil here refers to a mythic event that formed an episode in the myth concerning the skaldic mead. Somewhere in Jotunheim a fountain containing the same precious liquid as that in Mimer's well has burst forth. The vein of the fountain was discovered by kinsmen of Thrigge, but the precious find eagerly desired by all powers is kept secret, presumably in order that they who made the discovery might enjoy it undivided and in safety. But something happens which causes the treasure which the fountain gave its discoverers to be carried from Jotunheim to Nokve's ship, and there the drink is accessible to the gods. It is especially mentioned that Brage, the god of poetry, is there permitted to partake of it and thus refresh his powers.

Thus the ship of Nanna's father here reappears, and we learn that on its holy way in space in bygone times it bore a supply of skaldic mead, of which Brage in the days of his innocence drank the strength of life.

With this we must compare a mythic fragment preserved in Gylfaginning (ch. 11). There a fountain called *Byrgir* is mentioned. Two children, a lass by name *Bil* and a lad by name *Hjuki,* whose father was named *Vidfinnr,* had come with a pail to this fountain to fetch water. The allegory in which the tradition is incorporated calls the pail *Sægr,* "the one seething over its brinks," and calls the pole on which the pail is carried *Simul* (according to one manuscript *Sumul;* cp. *Suml,* brewing ale, mead). Bil, one of the two children is put in connection with the drink of poetry. The skalds pray that she may be gracious to them . *Ef unna itr vildi Bil Skáldi,* "if the noble Bil will favour the skald," is a wish expressed in a strophe in the Younger Edda, ii. 363. *Byrgir* is manifestly a fountain of the same kind as the one referred to by Egil and containing the skaldic mead. *Byrgir's* fountain must have been kept secret, it must have been a "concealed find," for it is in the night, while the moon is up, that Vidfin's children are engaged in filling their pail from it. This is evident from the fact that *Máni* sees the children. When they have filled the pail, they are about to depart, presumably to their home, and to their father Vidfin. But they do not get home. While they carry the pail with the pole on their shoulders *Máni* takes them unto himself, and they remain with him, together with their precious burden. From other mythic traditions which I shall consider later (see the treatise on the Ivalde race), we learn that the moon-god adopts them as his children, and *Bil* afterwards appears as an asynje (Younger Edda, i. 118, 556).

If we now compare Egil's statement with the mythic

fragment about Bil and Hjuke, we find in both a fountain mentioned which contains the liquid of inspiration found in Mimer's fountain, without being Mimer's well-guarded or unapproachable "well." In Egil the find is "kept secret." In Gylfaginning the children visit it in the night. Egil says the liquid was *carried* from Jotunheim; Gylfaginning says that Bil and Hjuke *carried* it in a pail. Egil makes the liquid transferred from Jotunheim to Nokve's ship; Gylfaginning makes the liquid and its bearers be taken aloft by the moon-god to the moon, where we still, says Gylfaginning, can see Bil and Hjuke (in the moon-spots).

There can therefore be no doubt that Nokve's ship is the silvery craft of the moon, sailing in space over sea and land on a course marked out for it, and that Nokve is the moon-god. As in Rigveda, so in the Teutonic mythology, the ship of the moon was for a time the place where the liquid of inspiration, the life- and strength-giving mead, was concealed. The myth has ancient Aryan roots.

On the myth concerning the mead-carrying ship, to which the Asas come to drink, rests the paraphrase for *composing,* for *making a song,* which Einar Skalaglam once used (Skaldskaparmal, 1). To make songs he calls "to dip liquid out of Her-Tyr's wind-ship" (*ausa Hértys víngnodar austr;* see further No. 121, about Odin's visit in Nokve's ship).

The name *Nefr* (variation *Nepr*), the third name of Nanna's father mentioned above, occurs nowhere in the Norse sources excepting in the Younger Edda. It is, however, undoubtedly correct that Nokve-Gevar was also called **Nef.**

Among all the Teutonic myths there is scarcely one other with which so many ıeroic songs composed in heathen times have been connected as with the myth concerning the moon-god and his descendants. As shall be shown further on, the Niflungs are descendants of Nef's adopted son Hjuke, and they are originally named after their adopted race-progenitor *Nefr.* A more correct and an older form is perhaps *Hnefr* and *Hniflungar,* and the latter form is also found in the Icelandic literature. In Old English the moon-god appears changed into a pre-historic king, *Hnäf,* also called *Hoce* (see Beowulf, 2142, and Gleeman's Tale). Hoce is the same name as the Norse *Hjuki.* Thus while *Hnäf* and *Hoce* are identical in the Old English poem "Beowulf," we find in the Norse source that the lad taken aloft by Mane is called by one of the names of his foster-father. In the Norse account the moon-god (*Nefr*) captures, as we have seen, the children of one *Vidfinnr,* and at the same time he robs *Vidfinnr* of the priceless mead of inspiration found in the fountain *Byrgir.* In the Old English saga *Hnäf* has a son-in-law and vassal, whose name is *Finn* (*Fin Folcvald-ing*), who becomes his bitterest foe, contends with him, is conquered and pardoned, but attacks him again, and, in company with one *Gudere* (*Gunnr*), burns him. According to Saxo, Nanna's father *Gevarr* has the same fate. He is attacked by a vassal and burnt. The vassal is called Gunno (*Gunnr, Gudere*). Thus we have in the Old English tradition the names *Hnäf, Hoce, Fin,* and *Gudere;* and in the Norse tradition the corresponding names *Nefr, Hjuki, Vidfinnr,* and *Gunnr* (*Gunnarr*).

The relation of the moon-god (*Nefr*) to *Vidfinnr* is the mythological basis of *Fin's* enmity to *Hnäf*. The burning is common to both the Old English and the Norse sources. Later in this work I shall consider these circumstances more minutely. What I have stated is sufficient to show that the Old English tradition is in this point connected with the Norse in a manner, which confirms *Nefr-Gevarr's* identity with *Máni,* who takes aloft *Hjuki* and robs *Vidfinnr* of the skaldic mead.

The tradition of *Gevarr-Nefr's* identity with *Máni* reappears in Iceland once more as late as in Hromund Greipson's saga. There a person called *Máni Karl* shows where the hero of the saga is to find the sword *Misteltcinn*. In Saxo, Nanna's father *Gevarr* shows the beforementioned Hotherus where he is to find the weapon which is to slay Balder. Thus *Máni* in Hromund's saga assumes the same position as *Gevarr,* Nanna's father, occupies in Saxo's narative.

All these circumstances form together a positive proof of the moon-god's identity with Nanna's father. Further on, when the investigation has progressed to the proper point, we shall give reasons for assuming that *Vidfinnr* of the Edda, the *Fin* of the English heroic poem, is the same person whom we have heretofore mentioned by the name *Sumbl Finnakonungr* and *Svigdir,* and that the myth concerning the taking of the mead aloft to the moon accordingly has an epic connection with the myth concerning Odin's visit to the giant Fjalar, and concerning the fate which then befell Nokve's slayer.

91.

THE MYTH CONCERNING THE MOON-GOD (*continued*).

The moon-god, like Nat, Dag, and Sol, is by birth and abode a lower-world divinity. As such, he too had his importance in the Teutonic eschatology. The god who on his journeys on "Nokve's holy way" serves *auldom at ártali* (Vafthrudnersmal, 23) by measuring out to men time in phases of the moon, in months, and in years has, in the mythology also, received a certain influence in inflicting suffering and punishment on sinners. He is lord of the *heiptir,* the Teutonic Erinnyes (see No. 75), and keeps those *limar* (bundles of thorns) with which the former are armed, and in this capacity he has borne the epithet *Eylimi,* which reappears in the heroic songs in a manner which removes all doubt that Nanna's father was originally meant. (See in Saxo and in Helge Hjorvardson's saga. To the latter I shall return in the second part of this work, and I shall there present evidence that the saga is based on episodes taken from the Balder myth, and that Helge Hjorvardson is himself an imitation of Balder). In this capacity of lord of the *Heiptir* the moon-god is the power to whom prayers are to be addressed by those who desire to be spared from those sufferings which the *Heiptir* represent (*Heithtom scal mána qvedja*—Havamál, 137). His quality as the one who keeps the thorn-rods of the *heiptir* still survives in a great part of the Teutonic world in the scattered traditions about "the man in the moon," who carries bundles of thorns on his back (J. Grimm, *Myth.,* 680; see No. 123).

92.

THE MOON-DIS NANNA. THE MERSEBURG FORMULA. BALDER'S NAME FALR.

Thus Nanna is the daughter of the ruler of the moon, of "the ward of the atmosphere." This alone indicates that she herself was mythologically connected with the phenomena which pertain to her father's domain of activity, and in all probability was a moon-dis (goddess). This assumption is fully confirmed by a contribution to Teutonic mythology rescued in Germany, the so-called Merseburg formula, which begins as follow:

Phol ende Uodan	Falr and Odin
vuoron zi holza	went to the wood,
dû vart demo Balderes	tıen was the foot sprained
volon sin vous birenkit	on Balder's foal.
thû biguolon Sinhtgunt.	Tıen sang over him Sinhtgunt,
Sunna era svister,	Sunna her sister,
thû biguolen Friia,	tıen sang over him Frigg,
Volla era svister	Fulla her sister;
thû biguolen Uodan	tıen sang over him Odin
sô hê wola conda.	as best he could.

Of the names occurring in this strophe Uodan-Odin, Balder, Sunna (synonym of Sol—Alvissm., 17; Younger Edda, i. 472, 593), Friia-Frigg, and Volla-Fulla are well known in the Icelandic mythic records. Only Phol and Sinhtgunt are strangers to our mythologists, though Phol-*Falr* surely ought not to be so.

In regard to the German form Phol, we find that it has by its side the form Fal in German names of places connected with fountains. Jacob Grimm has pointed out a "Pholes" fountain in Thuringia, a "Fals" fountain in the Frankish Steigerwald, and in this connection a "Balder" well in Rheinphaltz. In the Danish popular traditions Balder's horse had the ability to produce fountains by tramping on the ground, and Balder's fountain in Seeland is said to have originated in this manner (cp. P. E. Müller on Saxo, *Hist.*, 120). In Saxo, too, Balder gives rise to wells (*Victor Balderus, ut afflictum siti militem opportuni liquoris beneficio recrearet, novos humi latices terram altius rimatus operuit*—p. 120).

This very circumstance seems to indicate that Phol, Fal, was a common epithet or surname of Balder in Germany, and it must be admitted that this meaning must have appeared to the German mythologists to be confirmed by the Merseburg formula; for in this way alone could it be explained in a simple and natural manner, that Balder is not named in the first line as Odin's companion, although he actually attends Odin, and although the misfortune that befalls "Balder's foal" is the chief subject of the narrative, while Phol on the other hand is not mentioned again in the whole formula, although he is named in the first line as Odin's companion.

This simple and incontrovertible conclusion, that Phol and Balder in the Merseburg formula are identical is put beyond all doubt by a more thorough examination of the Norse records. In these it is demonstrated that the name *Falr* was also known in the North as an epithet of Balder.

The first books of Saxo are based exclusively on the myths concerning gods and heroes. There is not a single person, not a single name, which Saxo did not borrow from the mytiic traditions. Among them is also a certain Fjallerus, who is mentioned in bk. i. 160. In the question in regard to the Norse form wiich was Latinised into *Fjallerus,* we must remember tiat Saxo writes *Hjallus* (*Hist.,* pp. 371, 672) for *Hjali* (cp. p. 370), and alternately *Colo, Collo,* and *Collerus* (*Hist.,* pp. 56, 136, 181), and that he uses the broken form *Bjarbi* for *Barri* (*Hist.,* p. 250). In accordance witi this the Latin form *Fjallerus* must correspond to the Norse *Falr,* and there is, in fact, in the whole Old Norse literature, not a single name to be found corresponding to this excepting Falr, for the name *Fjalarr,* the only other one to be thought of in this connection should, according to tie rules followed by Saxo, be Latinised into *Fjallarus* or *Fjalarus,* but not into *Fjallerus.*

Of this *Fjallerus* Saxo relates that he was banished by an enemy, and the report says that *Fjallerus* betook himself to the place which is unknown to our populations, and which is called *Odáins-akr* (*quem ad locum, cui Undensakre nomen est, nostris ignotum populis concess-isse est fama*—p. 160.)

The mythology mentions only a single person who by an enemy was transferred to *Odáinsakr,* and that is Balder. (Of *Odáinsakr* and Balder's abode there, see Nos. 44-53).

The enemy who transfers *Falr* to the realm of immortality is, according to Saxo, a son of *Horvendillus,* that is to say, a son of the mythological *Örvandill,* Groa's husband and Svipdag's father (see Nos. 108, 109). Svipdag has already once before been mistaken by Saxo for *Hotherus* (see No. 101). *Hotherus* is, again, the Latin form for *Hödr*. Hence it is Balder's banishment by *Hödr* to the subterranean realms of immortality of which we here read in Saxo where the latter speaks of Fal's banishment to *Odáinsakr* by a son of Orvandel.

When Balder dies by a *flaug* hurled by *Hödr* he stands in the midst of a rain of javelins. He is the centre of a *mannhringr,* where all throw or shoot at him: *sumir skjóta á hann, sumir höggva til, sumir berja grjóti* (Gylfaginning). In this lies the mythical explanation of the paraphrase *Fal's rain,* which occurs in the last strophe of a poem attributed to the skald Gisle Surson. In Gisle's saga we read that he was banished on account of manslaughter, but by the aid of his faithful wife he was able for thirteen years to endure a life of persecutions and conflicts, until he finally was surprised and fell by the weapons of his foes. Surrounded by his assailants, he is said to have sung the strophe in question, in which he says that "the beloved, beautiful, brave Fulla of his hall," that is to say, his wife, "is to enquire for him, her friend," for whose sake "Fal's rain" now "falls thick and fast," while "keen edges bite him." In a foregoing strophe Gisle has been compared with a "Balder of the shield," and this shield-Balder now, as in the Balder of the myth, is the focus of javelins and swords, while he like Balder, has a beautiful and faithful wife, who, like Nanna, is to take his death to heart. If the name Nanna, as has been assumed by Vigfusson and others, is connected with the verb *nenna,* and means "the brave one," then *rekkilát* Fulla, "the brave Fulla of Gisle's hall," is an all the more appropriate reference to Nanna, since Fulla and she are intimately connected in the mythology, and are described as the warmest of friends (Gylfaginning). Briefly stated: in the poem Gisle is compared with Balder, his wife with Nanna, his death with Balder's death, and the rain of weapons by which he falls with *Fal's rain*.

In a strophe composed by *Refr* (Younger Edda, i. 240) the skald offers thanks to Odin, the giver of the skaldic art. The Asa-father is here called *Fals hrannvala brautar fannar salar valdi* ("The ruler of the hall of the drift of the way of the billow-falcons of Fal"). This long paraphrase means, as has also been assumed by others, the ruler of heaven. Thus heaven is designated as "the hall of the drift of the way of the billow-falcons of Fal." The "drift" which belongs to heaven, and not to the earth, is the cloud. The heavens are "the hall of the cloud." But in order that the word "drift" might be applied in this manner it had to be united with an appropriate word, showing that the heavens were meant. This is done by the adjective phrase "of the way of the billow-falcons of Fal." Standing alone, "the drift of the way of the billow-falcons" could not possibly mean anything else than the billow white with foam, since "billow-falcons" is a paraphrase for ships, and the "way of the billow-falcons" is a paraphrase for the sea. By adding the name *Falr* the meaning is changed from "sea" to "sky." By Fal's "billow-falcons" must therefore be meant objects whose course is through the air, just as the course of the ships is on the sea, and which traverse the drift of the sky, the cloud, just as the ships plough through the drift of the sea, the white-crested billow. Such a paraphrase could not possibly avoid drawing the fancy of the hearers and readers to the atmosphere strewn with clouds and penetrated by sunbeams, that is, to Odin's hall. Balder is a sun-god, as his myth, taken as a whole, plainly shows, and as is manifested by his epithet: *raudbrikar rikr rækir* (see No. 53). Thus Fal, like Balder, is a divinity of the sun, a being which sends the sunbeams down through the drifts of the clouds. As he, furthermore, like Balder, stood in a rain of weapons under circumstances sufficiently familiar for such a rain to be recognised when designated as Fal's, and as he, finally, like Balder, was sent by an opponent to the realm of immortality in the lower world, then *Falr* and Balder must be identical.

Their identity is furthermore confirmed by the fact that Balder in early Christian times was made a historical king of Westphalia. The statement concerning this, taken from Anglo-Saxon or German sources, has entered into the foreword to Gylfaginning. Nearly all lands and peoples have, according to the belief of that time, received their names from ancient chiefs. The Franks were said to be named after one Francio, the East Goth after Ostrogotha, the Angles after Angul, Denmark after Dan, &c. The name Phalia, Westphalia, was explained in the same manner, and as Balder's name was Phol, Fal, this name of his gave rise to the name of the country in question. For the same reason the German poem Biterolf makes Balder (Paltram) into king *ze Pülle*. (Compare the local name Pölde, which, according to J. Grimm, is found in old manuscripts written *Polidi* and *Pholidi*.) In the one source Balder is made a king in Pholidi, since Phol is a name of Balder, and in the other source he is for the same reason made a king in Westphalia, since Phal is a variation of Phol, and likewise designated Balder. "Biterolf" has preserved the record of the fact that Balder was not only the stateliest hero to be found, but also the most pure in morals, and a man much praised. Along with Balder, Gylfaginning speaks of another son of Odin, *Siggi,* who is said to have become a king in Frankland. The same reason for which Fal-Balder was made a king in Westphalia also made the apocryphal *Siggi* in question the progenitor of Frankian kings. The Frankian branch to which the Merovingian kings belonged bore the name *Sigambrians,* and to explain this name the son *Siggi* was given to Odin, and he was made the progenitor and eponym of the Sigambrians.

After this investigation which is to be continued more elaborately in another volume, I now return to the Merseburg formula:

> "Fall and Odin
> Went to the wood,
> Then the foot was sprained
> Of Balder's foal."

With what here is said about Balder's steed, we must compare what Saxo relates about Balder himself: *Adeo in adversam corporis valetudinem incidit, ut ni pedibus quidem incedere posset (Hist., 120).*

The misfortune which happened first to Balder and then

to Balder's horse must be counted among the warnings which foreboded the death of the son of Odin. There a:e also other passages which indicate that Balder's horse must have had a conspicuous signification in the mythology, and the tradition concerning Balder as rider is preserved not only in northern sources (Lokasenna, Gylfaginning), and in the Merseburg formula, but also in the German poetry of the middle ages. That there was some witchcraft connected with this misfortune which happened to Balder's horse is evident from the fact that the magic songs sung by the goddesses accompanying him availed nothing. According to the Norse ancient records, the women particularly exercise the healing art of witchcraft (compare Groa and Sigrdrifva), but still Odin has the profoundest knowledge of the secrets of this art; he is *galdrs fadir* (Veg., 3). And so Odin comes in this instance, and is successful after the goddesses have tried in vain. We must fancy that the goddesses make haste 'to render assistance in the order in which they ride in relation to Balder, for the event would lose its seriousness if we should conceive Odin as being very near to Balder from the beginning, but postponing his activity in order to shine afterwards with all the greater magic power, which nobody disputed.

The goddesses constitute two pairs of sisters: Sinhtgunt and her sister Sunna, and Frigg and her sister Fulla. According to the Norse sources, Frigg is Balder's mother. According to the same records, Fulla is always near Frigg, enjoys her whole confidence, and wears a diadem as a token of her high rank among the goddesses. An explanation of this is furnished by the Merseburg formula, which informs us that Fulla is Frigg's sister, and so a sister of Balder's mother. And as Odin is Balder's father, we find in the Merseburg formula the Balder of the Norse records, surrounded by the kindred assigned to him in these records.

Under such circumstances it would be strange, indeed, if Sinhtgunt and the sun-dis, Sunna, did not also belong to the kin of the sun-god, Balder, as they not only take part in this excursion of the Balder family, but are also described as those nearest to him, and as the first who give him assistance.

The Norse records have given to Balder as wife Nanna, daughter of that divinity which under Odin's supremacy is the ward of the atmosphere and the owner of the moon-ship. If the continental Teutons in their mythological conceptions also gave Balder a wife devoted and faithful as Nanna, then it would be in the highest degree improbable that the Merseburg formula should not let her be one of those who, as a body-guard, attend Balder on his expedition to the forest. Besides Frigg and Fulla, there are two goddesses who accompany Balder. One of them is a sun-dis, as is evident from the name Sunna; the other, Sinhtgunt, is, according to Bugge's discriminating interpretation of this epithet, the dis "who night after night has to battle her way." A goddess who is the sister of the sun-dis, but who not in the daytime but in the night has to battle on her journey across the sky, must be a goddess of the moon, a moon-dis. This moon-goddess is the one who is nearest at hand to bring assistance to Balder. Hence she can be none else than Nanna, who we know is the daughter of the owner of the moon-ship. The fact that she has to battle her way across the sky is explained by the Norse mythic statement, according to which the wolf-giant Hate is greedy to capture the moon, and finally secures it as his prey (Völuspa, Gylfaginning). In the poem about Helge Hjorvardson, which is merely a free reproduction of the materials in the Balder-myth (which shall be demonstrated in the second part of this work), the giant Hate is conquered by the hero of the poem, a Balder figure, whose wife is a dis, who, "white" herself, has a shining horse (str. 25, 28), controls weather and harvests (str. 28), and makes *nightly* journeys on her steed, and "inspects the harbours" (str. 25).

The name Nanna (from the verb *nenna;* cp. Vigfusson, *Lex.*) means "the brave one." With her husband she has fought the battles of light, and in the Norse, as in the Teutonic, mythology, she was with all her tenderness a heroine.

The Merseburg formula makes the sun-dis and the moon-dis sisters. The Norse variation of the Teutonic myth has done the same. Vafthrudnersmal and Gylfaginning (ch. 11) inform us that the divinities which govern the chariots of the sun and moon were brother and sister, but from the masculine form *Máni* Gylfaginning has drawn the false conclusion that the one who governed the car of the moon was not a sister but a brother of the sun. In the mythology a masculine divinity *Máni* was certainly known, but he was the father of the sun-dis and moon-dis, and identical with *Gevarr-Nökkvi-Nefr,* the owner of the moon-ship. The god *Máni* is the father of the sun-dis for the same reason as Nat is the mother of Dag.

Vafthrudnersmal informs us that the father of the managers of the sun- and moon-cars was called *Mundilföri.* We are already familiar with this mythic personality (see Nos. 81-83) as the one who is appointed to superintend the mechanism of the world, by whose *Möndull* the starry firmament is revolved. It is not probable that the power governing the motion of the stars is any other than the one who under Odin's supremacy is ruler of the sun and moon, and ward of all the visible phenomena in space, among which are also the stars. As, by comparison of the old records, we have thus reached the conclusion that the managers of the sun and moon are daughters of the ward of the atmosphere, and as we have also learned that they are daughters of him who superintends the motion of the constellations, we are unable to see anything but harmony in these statements. *Mundilföri* and *Gevarr-Nökkvi-Nefr* are the same person.

It should be added that the moon-goddess, like her father, could be called *Máni* without there being any obstacle in the masculine form of the word. The name of the goddess *Skadi* is also masculine in form, and is inflected as a masculine noun (oblique case, *Skada*— Younger Edda, 212, 268).

93.

COSMOGRAPHIC REVIEW.

In the preceding pages various scattered contributions have been made to Teutonic cosmography, and particularly to the topography of the lower world. It may not be out of the way to gather and complete these fragments.

The world-tree's three roots, which divide themselves in the lower world and penetrate through the three lower-world fountains into the foundations of the world-structure and hold it together, stand in a direction from north to south—the northernmost over the Hvergelmer fountain, with its cold waters; the middle one over Mimer's well, which is the fountain of spiritual forces; and the third over Urd's well, whose liquids give warmth to Ygdrasil (see No. 63).

In a north and south direction stands likewise the bridge *Bifröst,* also called *Bilröst, Ásbru* (Grimnersmal, 29), and in a bold paraphrase, hitherto not understood, *thiodvitnis fiscr,* "the fish of the folk-wolf." The paraphrase occurs in Grimnersmal (21) in its description of Valhal and other abodes of the gods:

> thytr thund,
> unir thiódvitnis
> fiscr fiódi i
> árstraumr thickir
> ofmicil
> valglaumi at vatha.

"Thund (the air-river) roars. The fish of the folk-wolf stands secure in the stream. To the noisy crowd of sword-fallen men the current seems too strong to wade through."

It has already been shown (No. 65) that those fallen by the sword ride with their psychopomps on Bifrost up to Valhal, and do not proceed thither through space, but have a solid foundation for the hoofs of their steeds. Here, as in Fafnersmal (15), the air is compared with a river, in which the horses are compelled to wade or swim if the bridge leading to Asgard is not used, and the current in this roaring stream is said to be very strong; while, on the other hand, "the fish" stands safe and inviting therein. That the author of Grimnersmal called the bridge a fish must seem strange, but has its natural explanation in Icelandic usage, which called every bridge-end or bridge-head a *spordr,* that is, a fish-tail. Compare Sigrdrifumal (16), which informs us that runes were risted on "the fish-tail" of the great mythic bridge (*á bruar spordi*), and the expression *brúarspordr* (bridge-head, bridge-"fish-tail") in Njala (246) and *Biskupa, s.* (1, 17). As a bridge-pier could be called a fish-tail, it was perfectly logical for the poem to make the bridge a fish. On the zenith of the bridge stands Valhal, that secures those fallen in battle, and whose entrance is decorated with images of the wolf and of the eagle (Grimnersmal, 10), animals that satisfy their hunger on the field of battle. This explains why the fish is called that of the folk-wolf or great wolf. The meaning of the paraphrase is simply "the Valhal bridge." That the bow of Bifrost stands north and south follows from the fact that the gods pass over one end of the bridge on their way to Urd's fountain, situated in the south of the lower world, while the other end is outside of Niefelhel, situated in the north. From the south the gods come to their judgment-seats in the realm of the dis of fate and death. From the north came, according to **Vegtams-kvida**, Odin when he rode through **Nifelhel** to that hall which awaited Balder. Why the Asa-father on that occasion chose that route Vegtamskvida does not inform us. But from Saxo (*Hist. Dan.*, 126), who knew an old heathen song about Odin's visit in the lower world on account of Balder's death, we get light on this point. According to this song* it was Rostiophus Phinnicus who told Odin that a son of the latter and Rind was to avenge Balder's death. Rostiophus is, as P. E. Müller has already remarked, the rimthurs *Hrossthiófr* mentioned in Hyndluljod as a son of *Hrimnir* and brother of the sorceress *Heidr,* the vala and witch well known from Völuspa and other sources. Nifelhel is, as shown above (No. 60), the abode of the rimthurses transferred to the lower world. Where his father *Hrimnir* (Bergelmer) and his progenitor *Hrimgrimnir* (Thrudgelmer) dwell in the thurs-hall mentioned in Skirnersmal, there we also find *Hrossthiófr,* and Odin must there seek him. Vegtamskvida makes Odin seek his sister.

It is Bifrost's north bridge-head which particularly

---

*Possibly the same as that of which a few strophes are preserved in *Baldrs draumar,* an old poetic fragment whose gaps have been filled in a very unsatisfactory manner in recent times with strophes which now are current as Vegtamskvida. That Odin, when he is about to proceed to the abode which in the subterranean realms of bliss is to receive Balder, chooses the route through Nifelhel is explained not by Vegtamskvida, where this fact is stated, but by the older poem mentioned by Saxo, which makes him seek the dweller in Nifelhel, the rimthurs *Hrossthiofr,* son of *Hrimnir.*

requires the vigilance of Heimdal, the ward of the gods, since the rimthurses and the damned are its neighbours. Heimdal is therefore "widely known" among the inhabitants of Nifelhel (Skirnersmal, 28), and Loke reproaches Heimdal that his vocation as watchman always compels him to expose his back to the torrents of an unfavourable sky (Lokas., 48). In the night which constantly broods over this northern zone shine the forms of the "white" god and of his gold-beaming horse *Gulltoppr,* when he makes spying expeditions there. His eye penetrates the darkness of a hundred "rasts," and his ear catches the faintest sound (Gylfag., 27). Near Bifrost, presumably at the very bridge-head, mythology has given him a fortified citadel, *Himinbjorg,* "the ward of heaven," with a comfortable hall well supplied with "the good mead" (Grimn., 13; Gylfag., 27).

The lower world is more extensive in all directions than the surface of the earth above it. Bifrost would not be able to pass outside and below the crust of the earth to rest with its bridge-heads on the domain of the three world-fountains if this were not the case. The lower world is therefore called *Jormungrund,* "the great ground or foundation" (Forspjallsljod, 25), and its uttermost zone, *jadarr Jormungrundar,* "the domain of the great ground," is open to the celestial canopy, and the under side of the earth is not its roof. From *Hlidskjalf,* the outlook of the gods in Asgard (Forspjallsljod, the prose texts in Skirnersmal and in Grimnersmal), the view is open to Midgard, to the sea, and to the giant-world situated beyond the Elivagar rivers (see the texts mentioned), and should accordingly also be so to the broad zone of Jormungrund, excepting its northernmost part, which always is shrouded in night. From *Hlidskjalf* the eye cannot discern what is done there. But Heimdal keeps watch there, and when anything unusual is perceived Odin sends the raven *Huginn* (*Hugr*) thither to spy it out (Forspjallsljod, 10, 3, which strophes belong together). But from Hlidskjalf as the point of observation the earth conceals all that part of Jormungrund below it; and as it is important to Odin that he should know all that happens there, *Huginn* and *Muninn* fly daily over these subterranean regions: *Huginn oc Muninn fljuga hverjan dag iormungrund yfir* (Grimnersmal, 20). The expeditions of the ravens over Nifelhel in the north and over Surt's "deep dales" in the south expose them to dangers: Odin expresses his fear that some misfortune may befall them on these excursions (Grimnersmal, 20).

In the western and eastern parts of *jadarr Jormungrundar* dwell the two divine clans the Vans and Elves, and the former rule over the whole zone ever since "the gods in time's morning," gave Frey, Njord's bounteous son, Alfheim as a tooth-gift (Grimners., 5). Delling is to be regarded as clan-chief of the Elves (light-Elves), since in the very theogony he is ranked with the most ancient powers. With Mimer's daughter Nat he becomes the father of Dag and the progenitor of *Dag's synir* (the light-Elves). It has already been emphasised (see No. 53) that he is the lord of the rosy-dawn, and that outside of his doors the song of awakening is sung every morning over the world: "Power to the Asas, success to the Elves, and wisdom to Hroptatyr" (Havamál, 100). The glow of dawn blazes up from his domain beyond the eastern horizon. Where this clan-chieftain of the Elves dwells, thither the mythology has referred the original home of his clan. *Alfheimr* occupies the eastern part of Jormungrund's zone. It is in the eastern part that Dag, Delling's son, and Sol, his kinswoman, mount their chariots to make their journey around the earth in the sky. Here is also the Hel-gate through which all the dead must pass in the lower world (No. 68).

There are many proofs that the giant settlement with the Ironwood or Myrkwood was conceived as extending from the north over large portions of the east (Völuspa, 39, 48, &c.). These regions of Alfheim constitute the southern coasts of the Elivagar, and are the scenes of important events in the epic of the mythology (see the treatise on the Ivalde race).

Vanaheimr is situated in the western half of the zone. At the banquet in *Ægir's* hall described in Lokasenna, Loke says to Njord:

> thu vast austr hedan
> gisl um sendr godum–

"From here you were sent out east as a hostage to the gods."

Ægir's hall is far out in the depths of the sea. The ocean known by the Teutons was the North Sea. The author has manifestly conceived Ægir's hall as situated in the same direction from Asgard as Vanaheim, and not far from the native home of the Vans. This lies in the word *hedan* (from here). According to Vafthrudnersmal (str. 39), Njord was "created in Vanaheim by wise *regin.*" When he was sent as a hostage to the gods to Asgard he had to journey eastward (*austr*). The western location of Vanaheim is tiereby demonstrated.

In the "western halls" of Vanaheim dwells Billing, Rind's father, the fatier of the Asa-god, Vale's mother (*Rindr berr Vala i væstrsölum*—Vegt., 11). His name has been preserved in both the German and the Anglo-Saxon mythic records. An Old German document mentions together Billunc and Nidunc, that is, Billing and Mimer (see No. 87). In the mythology Mimer's domain is bounded on the west by Billing's realm, and on tie east by Delling's. Delling is Mimer's son-in-law. According to Völuspa, 13 (Codex Hauk.), Billing is a being which in time's morning, on the resolve of the gods, was created by *Modsognir*-Mimer and *Durinn*. Mimer's neighbours in the east and in the west were therefore intimately connected with him. An Anglo-Saxon record (Codex Exoniensis, 320, 7) makes Billing the race-hero of the kinsmen and neighbours of the Angles, the Varnians (*Billing veold Vernum*). This too has a mythological foundation, as appears in Grimnersmal (39) and in the saga of Helge Hjorvardson, which, as before stated, is composed of mythic fragments. When Sol and Mane leave Delling's domain and begin their march across the heavens, their journey is not without danger. From the Ironwood (cp. Völuspa, 39) come the wolf-giants *Skoll* and *Hate* and pursue them. *Skoll* does not desist from the pursuit before the car of the bright-faced goddess has descended toward the western halls and reached *Varna vidr* (*Scaull hcitir ulfr, cr fylgir cno scirlcita godi til Varna vidar*—Grimnersmal, 39). *Varna vidr* is the forest of the mythic Varnians or Varinians. Varnians, Varinians, means "defenders," and the protection here referred to can be none other than that given to the journeying divinities of light when they have reached the western horizon. According to Helge Hjorvardson's saga, Hate, who pursues the moon, is slain near Varin's Bay. *Varinn,* the "defender," "protector," is the singular form of the same word as reappears in the genitive plural *Varna.* These expressions— *Billing veold Vernum, Varna vidr,* and *Varins vik*—are to be considered as belonging together. So also the local names borrowed from the mythology, *Varinsfjördr* and *Varinsey,* in Helge Hjorvardson's saga, where several names reappear, *e.g., Svarinn, Móinn, Álfr,* and *Yngvi.* which in connection with that of Billing occur in the list of the beings created by Mimer and *Durinn.* It is manifest that *Varna vidr,* where the wolf *Skoll* is obliged to turn back from his pursuit of Sol, and that *Varins vik,* where the moon's pursuer Hate is conquered, were conceived in the mythology as situated in the western horizon, since the sun and the moon making their journey from the east to west on the heavens are pursued and are not safe before they reach the western halls. And now as Billing dwells in the western halls and is remembered in the Anglo-Saxon mythic fragments as the prince of

23   699

the Varnians or Varinians, and as, furthermore, *Varins-fjördr* and *Varinsey* are connected with adventures in which there occur several names of mythic persons belonging to Billing's clan, then this proves absolutely an original mythic connection between Billing and his western halls and those western halls in whose regions *Varna vidr* and *Varinsvik* are situated, and where the divinities of light, their journey athwart the sky accomplished, find defenders and can take their rest. And when we add to this that Delling, Mimer's kinsman and eastern neighbour, is the lord of morning and the rosy dawn, and that Billing is Mimer's kinsman and western neighbour, then it follows that Billing, from the standpoint of a symbol of nature, represents the evening and the glow of twilight, and that in the epic he is ruler of those regions of the world where the divinities of light find rest and peace. The description which the Havamál strophes (97-101) give us of life in Billing's halls corresponds most perfectly with this view. Through the epic presentation there gleams, as it seems, a conscious symbolising of nature, which paints to the fancy the play of colours in the west when the sun is set. When eventide comes Billing's lass, "the sun-glittering one," sleeps on her bed (*Billing's mey ec fann bedjum á solhvita sofa—* str. 97). In his halls Billing has a body-guard of warriors, his *saldrótt, vigdrótt* (str. 100, 101), in whom we must recognise those Varnians who protect the divinities of light that come to his dwelling, and these warriors watch far into the night, "with burning lights and with torches in their hands," over the slumbering "sun-white" maiden. But when day breaks their services are no longer necessary. Then they in their turn go to sleep (*Oc nær morni . . .thá var saldrott um sofin*—str. 101).

When the Asas—all on horseback excepting Thor—on their daily journey to the thingstead near Urd's fountain, have reached the southern rune-risted bridge-head of Bifrost, they turn to the north and ride through a southern Hel-gate into the lower world proper. Here, in the south, and far below Jormungrund's southern zone, we must conceive those "deep dales" where the fire-giant Surt dwells with his race, Suttung's sons (not Muspel's sons). The idea presented in Gylfaginning's cosmogony, according to which there was a world of fire in the south and a world of cold in the north of that Ginungagap in which the world was formed, is certainly a genuine myth, resting on a view of nature which the very geographical position forced upon the Teutons. Both these border realms afterwards find their representatives in the organised world: the fire-world in *Surt's Sökkdalir,* and the frost-world in the Nifelhel incorporated with the eschatological places; and as the latter constitutes the northern part of the realm of death, we may in analogy herewith refer the dales of Surt and Suttung's sons to the south, and we may do this without fear of error, for Völuspa (50) states positively that Surt and his descendants come from the south to the Ragnarok conflict (*Surtr fer sunan med sviga læfi*). While the northern bridge-head of Bifrost is threatened by the rimthurses, the southern is exposed to attacks from Suttung's sons. In Ragnarok the gods have to meet storms from both quarters, and we must conceive the conflict as extending along Jormungrund's outer zone and especially near both ends of the Bifrost bridge. The plain around the south end of Bifrost where the gods are to "mix the liquor of the sword with Surt" is called *Oskópnir* in a part of a heathen poem incorporated with Fafnersmal. Here Frey with his hosts of einherjes meets Surt and Suttung's sons, and falls by the sword which once was his, after the arch of Bifrost on this side is already broken under the weight of the hosts of riders (Fafnersmal, 14, 15; Völuspa, 51). *Oskópnir's* plain must therefore be referred to the south end of Bifrost and outside of the southern Hel-gate of the lower world. The plain is also called *Vigridr* (Vafthrudnersmal, 18), and is said to be one hundred rasts long each way. As the gods who here appear in the conflict are called *in svaso god,* "the sweet," and as Frey falls in the battle, those who here go to meet Surt and his people seem to be particularly Vana-gods and Vans, while those who contend with the giants and with Loke's progeny are chiefly Asas.

When the gods have ridden through the southern Hel-gate, there lie before them magnificent regions over which Urd in particular rules, and which together with Mimer's domain constitute the realms of bliss in the lower world with abodes for departed children and women, and for men who were not chosen on the field of battle. Rivers flowing from Hvergelmer flow through Urd's domain after they have traversed Mimer's realm. The way leads the gods to the fountain of the norns, which waters the southern root of the world-tree, and over which Ygdrasil's lower branches spread their ever-green leaves, shading the gold-clad fountain, where swans swim and whose waters give the whitest colour to everything that comes in contact therewith. In the vicinity of this fountain are the thingstead with judgment-seats, a tribunal, and benches for the hosts of people who daily arrive to be blessed or damned.

These hosts enter through the Hel-gate of the east. They traverse deep and dark valleys, and come to a thorn-grown plain against whose pricks Hel-shoes protect those who were merciful in their life on earth, and thence to the river mixed with blood, which in its eddies whirls weapons and must be waded over by the wicked, but can be crossed by the good on the drift-wood which floats on the river. When this river is crossed the way of the dead leads southward to the thingstead of the gods.

Further up there is a golden bridge across the river to the glorious realm where *Mimer's holt* and the glittering halls are situated, in which Balder and the *ásmegir* await the regeneration. Many streams come from Hvergelmer, among them *Leiptr,* on whose waters holy oaths are taken, and cast their coils around these protected places, whence sorrow, aging, and death are banished. The halls are situated in the eastern part of Mimer's realm in the domain of the elf of the rosy dawn, for he is their watchman.

Further down in Mimer's land and under the middle root of the world-tree is the well of creative force and of inspiration, and near it are Mimer's own golden halls.

Through this middle part of the lower world goes from

west to east the road which Nat, Dag, Sol, and Mane travel from Billing's domain to Delling's. When the mother Nat whose car is drawn by *Hrimfaxi* makes her entrance through the western Hel-gate, darkness is diffused along her course over the regions of bliss and accompanies her chariot to the north, where the hall of Sindre, the great artist, is located, and toward the Nida mountains, at whose southern foot Nat takes her rest in her own home. Then those who dwell in the northern regions of Jormungrund retire to rest (Forspjallsljod, 25); but on the outer rim of Midgard there is life and activity, for there Dag's and Sol's cars then diffuse light and splendour on land and sea. The hall of Sindre's race has a special peculiarity. It is, as shall be shown below, the prototype of "the sleeping castle" mentioned in the sagas of the middle ages.

Over the Nida mountains and the lands beyond them we find Ygdrasil's third root, watered by the Hvergelmer fountain, the mother of all waters. The Nida mountains constitute Jormungrund's great watershed, from which rivers rush down to the south and to the north. In Hvergelmer's fountain and above it the world-mill is built through whose mill-stone eye water rushes up and down, causing the maelstrom and ebb and flood tide, and scattering the meal of the mill over the bottom of the sea. Nine giantesses march along the outer edge of the world pushing the mill-handle before them, while the mill and the starry heavens at the same time are revolved.

Where the Elivagar rivers rise out of Hvergelmer,

and on the southern strand of the mythic Gandvik, is found a region which, after one of its inhabitants, is called *Ide's* pasture (*sctr*—Younger Edda, i. 292). Here dwells warriors of mixed elf and giant blood (see the treatise on the Ivalde race), who received from the gods the task of being a guard of protection against the neighbouring giant-world.

Farther toward the north rise the Nida mountains and form the steep wall which constitutes Nifelhel's southern boundary. In this wall are the Na-gates, through which the damned when they have died their second death are brought into the realm of torture, whose ruler is *Leikinn*. Nifelheim is inhabited by the spirits of the primeval giants, by the spirits of disease, and by giants who have fallen in conflict with the gods. Under Nifelhel extend the enormous caves in which the various kinds of criminals are tortured. In one of these caves is the torture hall of the Nastrands. Outside of its northern door is a grotto guarded by swarthy elves. The door opens to Armsvartner's sea, over which eternal darkness broods. In this sea lies the Lyngve-holm, within whose jurisdiction Loke, Fenrer, and "Muspel's sons" are fettered. Somewhere in the same region Bifrost descends to its well fortified northern bridge-head. The citadel is called *Himinbjörg,* "the defence or rampart of heaven." Its chieftain is Heimdal.

While Bifrost's arch stands in a direction from north to south, the way on which Mane and Sol travel across the heavens goes from east to west. Mane's way is below Asgard.

The movable starry heaven is not the only, nor is it the highest, canopy stretched over all that has been mentioned above. One can go so far to the north that even the horizon of the starry heavens is left in the rear. Outside, the heavens *Andlánger* and *Vidblainn* support their edges against Jormungrund (Gylfag., 17). All this creation is supported by the world-tree, on whose topmost bough the cock Vidofner glitters.

(Continuation of Part IV in Volume III.)

WS - #0037 - 170321 - C0 - 229/152/21 - PB - 9781330282373